Lecture Notes in Computer Science 11615

Commenced Publication in 1973
Founding and Former Series Editors:
Gerhard Goos, Juris Hartmanis, and Jan van Leeuwen

More information about this series at http://www.springer.com/series/7409

Roger Chamberlain · Walid Taha ·
Martin Törngren (Eds.)

Cyber Physical Systems

Model-Based Design

8th International Workshop, CyPhy 2018
and 14th International Workshop, WESE 2018
Turin, Italy, October 4–5, 2018
Revised Selected Papers

Springer

Editors
Roger Chamberlain (iD)
Computer Science and Engineering
Washington University
St. Louis, MO, USA

Walid Taha (iD)
School of Information Technology
Halmstad University
Halmstad, Sweden

Martin Törngren (iD)
Department of Machine Design
KTH Royal Institute of Technology
Stockholm, Sweden

ISSN 0302-9743   ISSN 1611-3349   (electronic)
Lecture Notes in Computer Science
ISBN 978-3-030-23702-8   ISBN 978-3-030-23703-5   (eBook)
https://doi.org/10.1007/978-3-030-23703-5

LNCS Sublibrary: SL3 – Information Systems and Applications, incl. Internet/Web, and HCI

This Springer imprint is published by the registered company Springer Nature Switzerland AG
The registered company address is: Gewerbestrasse 11, 6330 Cham, Switzerland

Preface

This volume contains the joint proceedings of the Workshop on Model-Based Design of Cyber Physical Systems (CyPhy 2018) and the Workshop on Embedded and Cyber-Physical Systems Education (WESE 2018). The two events were co-located and coordinated for the second time in a row with the goal of exploring opportunities for closer collaboration.

This year, CyPhy planned from the outset to have post-workshop proceedings to allow authors to incorporate feedback and insights from discussions at the workshop. The workshop received 13 submissions. The Program Committee decided to accept nine of these papers. Each paper received at least three reviews, and the vast majority received four or more. The Program Committee was large and diverse, consisting of 40 members from 14 different countries.

The WESE workshop contributed five papers to the proceedings.

We would like to acknowledge several individuals who were key to the success of the event, including the WESE co-chairs: Martin Edin Grimheden and Falk Salewski, the Program Committees, the external reviewers, the publicity chair, Abdelhamid Taha, and the organizers of ESWEEK 2018.

May 2019

Roger Chamberlain
Walid Taha
Martin Törngren

Organization

General Chair (CyPhy)

Walid Taha   Halmstad University, Sweden

Program Committee Chairs (CyPhy)

Walid Taha   Halmstad University, Sweden
Martin Törngren   KTH Royal Institute of Technology, Sweden

Program Committee Chairs (WESE)

Martin Törngren   KTH Royal Institute of Technology, Sweden
Martin Edin Grimheden   KTH Royal Institute of Technology, Sweden
Falk Salewski   Muenster University of Applied Sciences, Germany

Program Committee (CyPhy + WESE)

Houssam Abbas   University of Pennsylvania, USA
Erika Abraham   RWTH Aachen University, Germany
Julien Alexandre dit   ENSTA ParisTech, France
  Sandretto
Henric Andersson   Environment & Innovation, Sweden
Hugo Andrade   National Instruments, USA
Stanley Bak   Air Force Rome Labs, USA
Saddek Bensalem   University of Grenoble, France
Christian Berger   Chalmers and University of Gothenburg, Sweden
Sergiy Bogomolov   Australian National University, Australia
David Broman   UC Berkeley, USA, and KTH Royal Institute
                                of Technology, Sweden
Manuela Bujorianu   University of Strathclyde, UK
Daniela Cancila   Commissariat à l'Énergie Atomique (CEA), France
Janette Cardoso   Institut Supérieur de l'Aéronautique et de l'Espace
                                (ISAE), France
De-Jiu Chen   KTH Royal Institute of Technology, Sweden
Thao Dang   Verimag, France
Alex Dean   North Carolina State University, USA
Sinem Coleri Ergen   Koc University, Turkey
Martin Fränzle   University of Oldenburg, Germany
Goran Frehse   Université Grenoble Alpes, France

Laurent Fribourg	CNRS, France
Ichiro Hasuo	University of Tokyo, Japan
Daisuke Ishii	Tokyo Institute of Technology, Japan
Taylor T. Johnson	Vanderbilt University, USA
Mehdi Kargahi	University of Tehran, Iran
Ueda Kazunori	Waseda University, Japan
Michal Konečný	Aston University, UK
Tei-Wei Kuo	National Taiwan University, Taiwan
Lucia Lo Bello	University of Catania, Italy
Peter Marwedel	TU Dortmund, Germany
Karl Meinke	KTH Royal Institute of Technology, Sweden
Nacim Meslem	Grenoble INP, France
Stefan Mitsch	Carnegie Mellon University, USA
Eugenio Moggi	Università degli studi di Genova, Italy
Wojciech Mostowski	Halmstad University, Sweden
Mohammad Reza Mousavi	University of Leicester, UK
Jogesh Muppala	Hong Kong University of Science and Technology, SAR China
Marc Pouzet	ENS, France
Maria Prandini	Politecnico di Milano, Italy
Nacim Ramdani	University of Orleans, France
Andreas Rauh	University of Rostock, Germany
Michel Reniers	Eindhoven University of Technology, The Netherlands
Bernhard Rumpe	RWTH University Aachen, Germany
Erwin Schoitsch	Austrian Institute of Technology, Austria
Christoph Seidl	TU Braunschweig, Germany
Jack Stankovic	University of Virginia, USA
Martin Steffen	Oslo University, Norway
Shiao-Li Tsao	National Chiao Tung University, Taiwan
Zain Ul-Abdin	Halmstad University, Sweden
Jon Wade	Stevens Institute of Technology, USA

Additional Reviewers

Imke Helene Drave	Ingo Stierand
Martijn Goorden	Bert van Beek
Dongxu Li	Alexey Vinel
Judith Michael	

Advisory Committee (CyPhy)

Manfred Broy	Technische Universität München, Germany
Karl Iagnemma	Massachusetts Institute of Technology, USA
Karl Henrik Johansson	KTH Royal Institute of Technology, Sweden
Insup Lee	University of Pennsylvania, USA
Pieter Mosterman	McGill University, Canada
Janos Sztipanovits	Vanderbilt University, USA
Walid Taha	Halmstad University, Sweden

Contents

Design

Hybrid Rebeca: Modeling and Analyzing of Cyber-Physical Systems   3
  Iman Jahandideh, Fatemeh Ghassemi, and Marjan Sirjani

Challenges in Digital Twin Development for Cyber-Physical
Production Systems.   28
  Heejong Park, Arvind Easwaran, and Sidharta Andalam

Simulation and Tools

Subjecting Legacy Simulink Models to Timing Specifications.   51
  Andreas Naderlinger

Model-Implemented Hybrid Fault Injection for Simulink
(Tool Demonstrations).   71
  Mehrdad Moradi, Bert Van Acker, Ken Vanherpen, and Joachim Denil

A Component-Based Hybrid Systems Verification and Implementation
Tool in KeYmaera X (Tool Demonstration)   91
  Andreas Müller, Stefan Mitsch, Wieland Schwinger, and André Platzer

Formal Methods

Guaranteed Control Synthesis for Continuous Systems in UPPAAL TIGA 113
  Kim Guldstrand Larsen, Adrien Le Coënt, Marius Mikučionis,
  and Jakob Haahr Taankvist

CPS Dependability Framework Based on Inhomogeneous Stochastic
Hybrid Systems 134
  Manuela L. Bujorianu

Controlled Recurrence of a Biped with Torso. 154
  Adrien Le Coënt and Laurent Fribourg

A Quantitative Metric Temporal Logic for Execution-Time
Constrained Verification. 170
  Sascha Lehmann, Sven-Thomas Antoni, Alexander Schlaefer,
  and Sibylle Schupp

Workshop on Embedded and Cyber-Physical Systems Education

Introducing IoT Subjects to an Existing Curriculum. An Ongoing
Experience at the Faculty of the Technology Management - HIT   193
   Sofia Amador Nelke and Michael Winokur

Computers Interacting with the Physical World: A First-Year Course   197
   Roger D. Chamberlain, Ron K. Cytron, Doug Shook, and Bill Siever

CPS/IoT Ecosystem: A Platform for Research and Education   206
   Haris Isakovic, Denise Ratasich, Christian Hirsch, Michael Platzer,
   Bernhard Wally, Thomas Rausch, Dejan Nickovic, Willibald Krenn,
   Gerti Kappel, Schahram Dustdar, and Radu Grosu

MicroITS: A Scaled-Down ITS Platform   214
   Judicaël Marchand, Gaël Puissochet, Thomas Lithén, and Walid Taha

Further Experiences Teaching an FPGA-Based Embedded Systems Class. . . .   222
   Stephen A. Edwards

Author Index   231

Design

Hybrid Rebeca: Modeling and Analyzing of Cyber-Physical Systems

Iman Jahandideh[1], Fatemeh Ghassemi[1(✉)], and Marjan Sirjani[2,3]

[1] School of Electrical and Computer Engineering, University of Tehran, Tehran, Iran
{jahandideh.iman,fghassemi}@ut.ac.ir
[2] School of Innovation, Design and Engineering, Mälardalen University,
Västerås, Sweden
marjan.sirjani@mdh.se
[3] School of Computer Science, Reykjavik University, Reykjavik, Iceland

Abstract. In cyber-physical systems like automotive systems, there are components like sensors, actuators, and controllers that communicate asynchronously with each other. The computational model of actor supports modeling distributed asynchronously communicating systems. We propose Hybrid Rebeca language to support modeling of cyber-physical systems. Hybrid Rebeca is an extension of actor-based language Rebeca. In this extension, physical actors are introduced as new computational entities to encapsulate physical behaviors. To support various means of communication among the entities, the network is explicitly modeled as a separate entity from actors. We derive hybrid automata as the basis for analysis of Hybrid Rebeca models. We demonstrate the applicability of our approach through a case study in the domain of automotive systems. We use SpaceEx framework for the analysis of the case study.

Keywords: Actor model · Cyber-physical systems · Hybrid automata

1 Introduction

Embedded systems consist of microprocessors which control a physical behavior. Ninety-eight percent of all microprocessors are manufactured as components of embedded systems [25]. In such *hybrid* systems, physical and cyber behaviors, characterized as continuous and discrete respectively, affect each other. Cyber-physical systems (CPSs) are heterogeneous systems with tight interactions between physical and software processes where components in the system usually communicate through network. These systems are used in wide variety of safety-critical applications, from automotive and avionic systems to robotic surgery and smart grids. This makes verifying and analyzing CPSs one of the main concerns while developing such systems.

Model-based design is an effective technique for developing correct CPSs [7]. It relies on models specifying the behavior of the system often in a formal way. Using models instead of physical realizations of the system, beside reducing the

© Springer Nature Switzerland AG 2019
R. Chamberlain et al. (Eds.): CyPhy 2018/WESE 2018, LNCS 11615, pp. 3–27, 2019.
https://doi.org/10.1007/978-3-030-23703-5_1

costs of the development, can provide new insights early in the design process and enable analyzing the system behavior in many complex situations that can not easily be reproduced in its real environment. Furthermore formal and extensive analysis of the model can provide more confidence in the correctness of the system. The heterogeneity of CPSs creates new modeling challenges that stem from interactions between different kinds of components. New theories and tools are needed to facilitate designing and analyzing CPSs. Furthermore, for dealing with such systems with complicated and heterogeneous components, besides expressiveness power, a level of *friendliness* is appealing in design tools. This friendliness can be as important as expressiveness [21]. Friendliness is evaluated by its *faithfulness* to the system it is modeling, and *usability* to the modeler.

Existing modeling frameworks for hybrid systems such as hybrid automata [3,10] and hybrid Petri nets [5] can be used to model CPSs. The former has higher analysis power while the latter can be more easily used for modeling event-based systems [5]. Due to the existence of network in CPSs, the provided modeling power in these frameworks is not satisfactory for systems composed of many interacting heterogeneous entities. In the domain of automotive, ECUs, sensors and actuators may be connected directly by wire or through a communication media such as a serial bus. Improving the level of abstraction is beneficial to reduce errors introduced during the design process and improve perception of the model.

The computation model of actors provides a suitable level of abstraction to faithfully model distributed asynchronously communicating systems [2,11]. Actors are units of computation which can only communicate by asynchronous message passing. Each actor is equipped by a mailbox in which the received messages are buffered. We extend the actor-based language Rebeca, with physical behavior to support hybrid systems. Additionally, we need to support various types of communication, namely wired connections with no delay, serial buses with deterministic behavior, and wireless communication among the actors. So, we decided not to model the behavior of the network as an actor within a model, and instead model it as a separate entity.

To implement the extended actor model, we propose *Hybrid Rebeca*, as an extension of (Timed) Rebeca [1,23]. Rebeca provides an operational interpretation of actor model through a Java-like syntax. Its timed extension supports modeling of the computation time, and network delay for message communication. Hybrid Rebeca, extends Timed Rebeca with continuous behaviors based on our extended actor model.

Hybrid Rebeca defines two types of classes, software and physical. Software classes are similar to reactive classes in Rebeca language where the computational behaviors are defined by message servers. Physical classes in addition to message servers, can also contain different modes, where the continuous behaviors are specified. A physical actor (which is instantiated from a physical class) must always have one active mode. This active mode defines the runtime continuous behavior of the actor. By changing the active mode of a physical actor, it's possible to change the continuous behavior of the actor. In this version, CAN network is defined as network model for communications of the actors. Actors can communicate with each other either through the CAN network or directly by wire. Since CAN is a priority-based network, a priority must be assigned for the messages that are sent through CAN. Real-valued variables are added on which continuous behaviors are defined. The modes of physical classes are similar to the concept of locations in hybrid automata, and to solve these behaviors, the semantics of Hybird Rebeca is defined as a hybrid automaton, for which many verification algorithms and tools are available.

The main contribution of the paper can be summarized as providing an actor-based formalism that supports "friendliness" with small number of primitive concepts. In particular it distinguishes between software and physical actors and supports two types of connections among actors (in principle one could have more types). A tool which automatically derives a hybrid automaton from a given model is implemented, which is suitable for formal reachability analysis. The rest of the paper is structured as follows. The next section defines hybrid automata, actor model and Rebeca language. Section 3 presents our extended actor model for modeling CPSs. In Sect. 4 the syntax and semantics of Hybrid Rebeca language is defined. Section 5 presents our case study and its results. In Sect. 6 we briefly mention some related works. In Sect. 7 we discuss one of our design decisions for our extend actor model. The conclusion is presented in Sect. 8.

2   Preliminaries

As we define the semantics of our framework based on hybrid automata, we first provide an overview on this model and then explain actor model and Timed Rebeca.

2.1   Hybrid Automata

Hybrid automata (HA) [3,10] is a formal model for systems with discrete and continuous behaviors. Informally a hybrid automaton is a finite state machine consisting of a set of real-valued variables, modes and transitions. Each mode, which we also call *location*, defines a continuous behavior on the variables of the model. The continuous behaviors or *flows* are usually described by ordinary differential equations which define how the values of the variables change with time. Transitions act as discrete actions between continuous behaviors of the system, where the variables can change instantaneously. In Fig. 1 a hybrid automaton for a simple heater model is presented. The variable t represents the temperature of the environment. The locations named *off* and *on* define the continuous behavior of the temperature when the heater is off and on, respectively. For each location, the flow of the temperature is defined accordingly. The transition with the guard $t == 22$ states that when the temperature is equal to 22 the heater *can* be turned off. In hybrid automaton, the choice between staying in one location and taking an enabled transition is nondeterministic. To make the turning off behavior deterministic, the invariant $t \leq 22$ is defined in the *on* location. This invariant states that the heater can only stay in this location as long as the temperature is less than 22. The turning on behavior of the heater is defined similarly. Initially the heater is off and the temperature is 20.

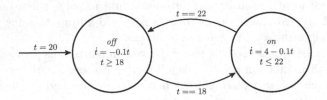

Fig. 1. A hybrid automaton for a heater which consists of two locations (modes) named *on* and *off*. Each location defines a flow and an invariant on the variable t which is the temperature. The mode of the heater changes by means of guarded transitions between the locations. The initial location is *off* and the initial value of t is 20.

Let a valuation $v : V \rightarrow Val$ be a function that assigns a value to each variable of V where Val is the set of values, defined by the context. We denote the set of valuations on the set of variables V as $\mathcal{V}(V)$. Formally a hybrid automaton is defined by the tuple $(Loc, Var, Lab, \Rightarrow, Flws, Inv, Init)$ as follows:

- Loc is a finite set of locations,
- Var is a finite set of real-valued variables,
- Lab is a finite set of synchronization labels.
- $\Rightarrow$ is a finite set of transitions. A transition is a tuple $(l, a, \mu, l') \in \Rightarrow$ where $l \in Loc$ is the source location, $l' \in Loc$ is the destination location, $a \in Lab$ is a synchronization label and $\mu \in \mathcal{V}(Var)^2$ is a transition relation on variables. The elements of $\mu = (v, v')$ represents the valuation of the variables before and after taking the transition. In some models, like in our example, this transition relation is represented with a guard and a set of assignments on the variables. The guard defines the valuation v and the assignments define the valuation v'.
- $Flws$ is a labeling function that assigns a set of flows to each location $l \in Loc$. Each flow is a function from $\mathbb{R}^{\geq 0} \rightarrow \mathcal{V}(Var)$. Each flow specifies how the values of variables evolve over time. A flow is usually defined by a doted variable $\dot{v}$ which represents the first derivative.
- Inv is a labeling function that assigns an invariant $Inv(l) \subseteq \mathcal{V}(Var)$ to each location $l \in Loc$,
- $Init$ is a labeling function that assigns an initial condition $Init(l) \subseteq \mathcal{V}(Var)$ to each location $l \in Loc$.

In the example given in Fig. 1, the locations and the variables are defined as $Loc = \{on, off\}$ and $Var = \{t\}$ respectively. Since our example only consists of a single automaton, $Lab = \emptyset$ and the labels over the transitions are ϵ which is not shown for brevity. Also the transition relations only consist of guards and the assignments are empty. The flows and the invariant of each location is defined on the location itself. The initial condition for location *off* is $Init(off) = \{t = 20\}$ and for location *on* is $Init(off) = \emptyset$. Note that in our language, we do not use primed variables of the form v' to represent valuation after discrete transitions. We use v' instead of $\dot{v}$ to represent the first derivative of variable v.

2.2   Actor Model and Timed Rebeca

Actor model is used for modeling distributed systems. It was originally proposed by Hewitt [11]. In this model actors are self-contained and concurrent [2] and can be regarded as units of computation. Any communication is done through asynchronous message passing on a fair medium where message delivery is guaranteed but is not in-order. This model abstracts away the network effects like delays, message conflicts, node crashes, etc. In this model each actor has a an address and a mailbox which stores the received messages. The behavior of an actor is defined in its message handlers, called *methods*. The methods are executed by processing the messages.

To extend the actor model with hybrid concepts for specifying CPSs, we use Rebeca as our basis framework and hence, use the terms actor model and Rebeca interchangeably in this paper. Rebeca [23] is a formal actor-based modeling language and is supported by model checking tools to bridge the gap between formal methods and software engineering. Rebeca provides an operational interpretation of actor model through a Java-like syntax. It also offers a compositional verification approach to deal with the state-space explosion problem in model checking. Because of its design principle it is possible to extend the core language for a specific domain [22]. For example, different extensions have been introduced in various domains such as probabilistic systems [24], real-time systems [1], software product lines [20], and broadcasting environment [26].

In Rebeca, actors are called rebecs and are instances of *reactive classes* defined in the model. Rebecs communicate with each other through asynchronous message passing and a Rebec's mailbox is modeled by a message queue. A reactive class consists of *known rebecs* to specify the rebecs it can communicate with, *state variables* to maintain the internal state, and *message servers* to define the reaction of the rebec on the received messages. The computation in a rebec takes place by removing a message from the message queue and executing its corresponding message server.

Timed Rebeca [1] is an extension of Rebeca for distributed and asynchronous systems with timing constraints. It adds the timing concepts *computation time*, *message delivery time* and *message expiration*. These concepts are materialized by new constructs: *delay*, *after*, and *deadline*. In Timed Rebeca model, each rebec has it's own local clock which can be considered as synchronized distributed clocks. The *delay* statement models the passage of time during the execution of a message server. Statements *after* and *deadline* are used in conjunction with send statements and specify the network delay and the message deadline, respectively.

3   Actor Model for CPSs

Extending actor model for modeling cyber-physical systems can be divided to two parts, *offering more concrete models for network*, and *extending actors with physical behaviors*.

Rebeca offers a fair and nondeterministic network model. For many application of CPSs this network model is too abstract or completely invalid. For example Control Area Network (CAN) [18] protocol is a dominant networking protocol in automotive industry, which can not be faithfully modeled by Rebeca's network model as by this protocol, messages are deterministically delivered to their receivers. Modeling the network as an explicit actor, does not guarantee determinacy of message deliveries as the network actor is executed concurrently with other actors, therefore its determinacy is affected by the interleaving semantics. In other words, the massage delivery sequence by the network actor depends on the execution order of sending actors. So we modeled the network as a separate entity from the actors.

To extend the actor model with physical behaviors, we decided to separate physical actors from software actors. In this approach software actors will be similar to Timed Rebeca actors and the physical behaviors are defined in separate physical actors. Physical actors are similar to a hybrid automaton in syntax and semantics. Like a hybrid automaton, each physical actor consists of a set of modes. Each mode defines its flows, invariant, guard and actions where actions are a set of statements. The actions are the effect of the mode, when the continuous behavior is finished. A physical actor can only be in one mode (characterizing a specific continuous behavior) at any moment. In this approach the physical behavior of a system can easily be started, stopped or changed by changing the active modes of physical actors, either by the actor itself or by a request from another actor.

As we focus on automotive systems, to make the network specification more concrete, in the first step we consider the CAN protocol in our language. CAN is a serial bus network where nodes can send messages at any moment. When multiple nodes request to send a message at the same time, only the message with the highest priority is accepted and sent through the network. After a message is sent, the network chooses another message from the requested messages. The messages are sent through the network one by one. As messages in this protocol must have unique priorities, messages are deterministically communicated. Furthermore, we assume that all CAN nodes implement a priority-based buffer. This simplifies the network model which can be represented by a single global priority-based queue [6]. To implement this protocol, a unique priority must be assigned to each message and the communication delay between each two communicating actors must be specified. These specifications can be defined outside of the actors so that actors become agnostic about the underlying network of the model. This will also make the model more modular, since it is easier to change the network of the system without modifying the actors. Not all the actors communicate through CAN. Some of the actors may be connected by wire and have direct communication with each other. In our language, both types of communication are considered, and actors can communicate with each other either via wire or CAN. All messages, irrespective of the communication medium, are eventually inserted to their receiver's message queue. If two or more simultaneous messages (from wire or CAN) got inserted into a message queue, the resulting ordering will be nondeterministic. Note that there can not be two simultaneous messages from CAN, since CAN is a serial bus. The resulting hybrid Rebeca model has been illustrated in Fig. 2.

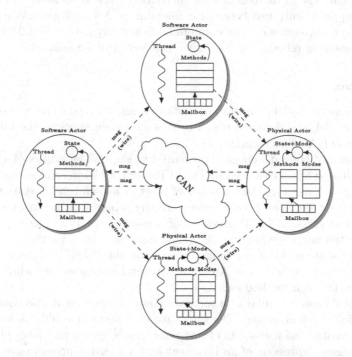

Fig. 2. Hybrid Rebeca model: each actor has its own thread of control, message queue, and ID. In addition to these, physical actors have modes that are defined by a guard, an invariant, and actions. Actors can communicate with each other either by sending messages through CAN or directly by wire.

4 Hybrid Rebeca

Hybrid Rebeca is an extension of Timed Rebeca to support physical behaviors. Timed Rebeca supports deadline specification for messages, but because of technical issues, Hybrid Rebeca does not support this feature. Other timing behaviors like network delay and computation time are supported.

In Hybrid Rebeca we have two types of rebecs: software and physical. These rebecs communicate through asynchronous message passing. Each rebec has a queue for messages, and services the message at the head of the queue by executing the corresponding message server for that message.

Software rebecs are for modeling software (discrete) behaviors. These rebecs are reactive and self-contained and they can have multiple message servers. Physical rebecs are for modeling physical (continuous) behaviors and the physical behaviors are defined by their modes. For physical rebecs a reserved message server is defined for changing the rebec's active mode.

Hybrid Rebeca has the concept of class for rebecs, and rebecs of the model are instantiated from these classes in the main block. In the instantiation phase the connection type of the rebecs with each other must be defined. For now our language supports only two types of connection: CAN and wire. When rebecs communicated through wire, the communication delay is considered to be zero. After instantiating rebecs, the CAN specification must be defined.

4.1 Syntax

A Hybrid Rebeca model definition consists of a set of *classes* and a *main* block, where classes define different types of rebecs and *main* specifies the initial configuration and CAN specification.

The syntax of Hybrid Rebeca is presented in Fig. 3. The syntax of a software class is similar to a reactive class in Timed Rebeca, which resembles a class definition in Java. A software class consists of a set of known rebecs, state variables and message servers. The known rebecs are the rebecs that an instance of this class can send message to. The syntax of message servers is like a method in object-oriented languages, expect that they have no return value.

The core statements of our language are variable/mode assignment, conditional, delay, and method calls. An actor can send a message asynchronously to other rebecs through method calls.

A physical class is similar to a software class except that it also contains the definition for physical modes. The structure of a mode resembles a location in hybrid automata, and it consists of invariant, flows, guard and a set of actions. The comparison expression of an invariant and a guard expression are specified by the reserved words inv and guard, respectively. The actions following the guard expression, which are expressed as a statement block, define the behavior of the rebec upon leaving the corresponding mode. We remark that the next entering mode is either explicitly defined by the user through the statement *setmode* in the statement block or the default mode none if it was not specified. Mode none is a special mode defined in all physical rebecs. This mode represents an idle behavior and its flows are defined as zero. Activating this mode can be interpreted as stopping the physical behavior of a physical rebec. Other rebecs can change the mode of a physical rebecs by sending the message *setMode*.

Three primitive data types are available in Hybrid Rebeca: *int*, *real*, and *float*. Variables of types *int* and *real* are only allowed in software and physical classes, respectively. Message parameters and state variables can be only defined of primitive type with some restrictions. Variables of type *float* can be used in both types of classes. Mathematically the float and real values are the same. However to each real variable, a flow is assigned which determines how its value evolve with time. A float variable can be used to capture the value of a real variable in different snapshots. This can be used in communication with software rebecs. The value of a float variable can be changed only by assignment, but the value of a real variable can be changed by both assignment and the flow defined on the variable. The assignment of a real value to float is managed implicitly in the semantics and no explicit casting is needed.

Every class definition must have at least one message server, named *initial*. In the initial state of the model, an *initial* message is put in all rebecs's message queue. The state variables and behavior of rebecs are initialized by executing this message server. The keyword self is used for sending a message to the rebec itself.

Rebecs are instantiated in the *main* block of the model. To instantiate a rebec, its known rebecs must be specified to be binded to the appropriate instances. Furthermore for each known rebec, the connection type must also be specified, which can either be *CAN* or *Wire*. For example, by the statement *A a* (@*Wire b*, @*CAN c*) : (), a rebec named *a* is instantiated from the class *A* that its known rebecs are *b* and *c* while the communication from *a* to *b* is through wire and *a* to *c* through CAN. We remark that the connection type between two rebecs can be different for each communication direction. The pair of parenthesizes () after the colon represents the parameters of the *initial* message server (which is empty in this case). After instantiation, the *CAN* specification is defined on the messages that may be transmitted through CAN. This specification consists of two parts. First the *priorities* of these messages must be specified. To this aim, a unique priority is assigned to a message. For example the statement *a b.m* 1; means that a message sent from rebec *a* to rebec *b* containing the message server name *m* has a priority of 1. A lesser number indicates a higher priority. After the priorities, the network *delays* of CAN communications are specified. For instance the statement *a b.m* 0.01; expresses that the communication delay of sending a message from *a* to *b* containing the message server name *m* is 0.01.

Example. Here we use a part of our case study to show the basics of our language. The model of the case study is presented in Fig. 5. Our case study is a Brake-By-Wire (BBW) with an Anti-lock Braking System (ABS). Here we only describe two classes *Wheel* and *WCtlr* which define the behavior of wheels and wheel controllers, respectively. The physical class *Wheel* has one known rebec *ctlr*, which is the wheel controller of the wheel. It also has three variables *trq*, *spd* and *t* which are respectively the amount of torque that must be applied during brake, the speed of the wheel and an auxiliary timer for periodic behavior of the wheel's sensor. In its *initial* message server, the *spd* is initialized to the given value and the active mode of the rebec is set to *Rolling* mode by using the *setmode* statement. *Wheel* defines a setter message server *setTrq* for updating the value of *trq*. This class has one mode named *Rolling*. This mode has a periodic behavior that every 50 ms, sends the value of *spd* to its wheel controller defined by *ctlr*. For the periodic behavior the invariant $t \leq 0.05$, the flow $t' = 1$ and the guard $t == 0.05$ are defined. The flow equation for *spd* variable is defined simply

$$
\begin{aligned}
\text{Model} &::= (\text{SClass} \mid \text{PClass})^+ \text{ Main} \\
\text{Main} &::= \text{main } \{\text{InstanceDcl}^* \text{ CANSpec}\} \\
\text{InstanceDcl} &::= \text{C r } (\langle \text{ @CAN} \mid \text{@Wire r}\rangle^*) : (\langle c\rangle^*) \\
\text{CANSpec} &::= \text{CAN } \{\text{Priorities Delays}\} \\
\text{Priorities} &::= \text{priorities } \{\langle r \text{ r.m c;}\rangle^*\} \\
\text{Delays} &::= \text{delays } \{\langle r \text{ r.m c;}\rangle^*\} \\
\text{SClass} &::= \text{softwareclass C } \{\text{KnownRebecs Vars MsgSrv}^*\} \\
\text{PClass} &::= \text{physicalclass C } \{\text{KnownRebecs Vars MsgSrv}^* \text{ Mode}^*\} \\
\text{KnowRebecs} &::= \text{knownrebecs } \{\text{VarDcl}^*\} \\
\text{Vars} &::= \text{statevars } \{\text{VarDcl}^*\} \\
\text{VarDcl} &::= \text{T } \langle v\rangle^+; \\
\text{MesgSrv} &::= \text{msgsrv m } (\langle T \text{ v}\rangle^*) \{\text{Stmt}^*\} \\
\text{Mode} &::= \text{mode m } \{\text{inv(e) } (v' = e)^+ \text{ guard(e) MSt}\} \\
\text{Stmt} &::= \text{v} = \text{e; } \mid \text{Call; } \mid \text{if(e) MSt [else MSt] } \mid \text{delay(t); } \mid \text{setmode(m);} \\
\text{Call} &::= \text{r.m}(\langle e\rangle^*) \mid \text{r.}setMode\text{(m)} \\
\text{MSt} &::= \{\text{Stmt}^*\} \mid \text{Stmt}
\end{aligned}
$$

Fig. 3. Abstract syntax of Hybrid Rebeca. The main differences in syntax compared to Timed Rebeca, are highlighted with color green. Angle brackets $\langle\ \rangle$ denotes meta parenthesis, superscripts + and * respectively are used for repetition of one or more and repetition of zero or more times. Combination of $\langle\ \rangle$ with repetition is used for comma separated list. Brackets [ ] are used for optional syntax. Identifiers C, T, m, m, v, c, r and e respectively denote class, primitive type, method name, mode name, variable, constant, and rebec name, respectively; and e denotes an expression. (Color figure online)

as $spd' = -0.1 - trq$. The constant -0.1 models the friction of the wheel with the road. In the actions of this mode, after reseting the timer value and sending the wheel's speed to its controller, the rebec's mode is again set to the *Rolling* mode if the wheel's speed is greater than zero.

The ABS behavior is defined by the software class *WCtlr*. It has two known rebecs w and *bctrl*, which are the controlled wheel of the controller and the global brake controller of the system, respectively. It also has three state variables *id*, *wspd* and *slprt*. The variable *id* is the identifier of the wheel controller and is used to differentiate between multiple wheel controllers in the model, *wspd* is the speed of the controlled wheel, and *slprt* is an auxiliary variable for calculating the slip rate. The variable *slprt* is used to determine whether the brake must be applied or not (this will be explained more in Sect. 5). The *wspd* variable gets updated by *setWspd* message server. This message server also sends the wheel's speed along side the controller's identifier, to the *bctrl*. To calculate the brake torque for wheels, the global brake controller sends an *applyTrq* message to each *WCtlr* in the system. The corresponding message server has two parameters named *reqTrq* and *vspd* which are the requested braking torque and the estimated vehicle speed, respectively. In this message server first the slip rate, denoted by the variable *slprt*, is calculated. Here the constant *WRAD* denotes the radius of the wheel. After calculating the slip rate, if the value of *slprt* is greater than 0.2, it sets its wheel's brake torque to zero by using the *setTrq* message. Otherwise it sets the wheels brake torque to the requested torque.

In the main block, two rebecs of type *Wheel* and two rebecs of type *WCtlr* are instantiated. Here we explain one instantiation of each class. The term *Wheel wR* (*@Wire wctlrR*) : (1); is used to instantiate a rebec named *wR* of type *Wheel*. The known rebec of *wR* is assigned to *wctlrR*. The tag *@Wire* is used to indicate that the communications of this rebec to *wctlrR* are via wire. The parameter (1) is the parameter of the *initial* message server of the rebec, which is the initial speed of the wheel. The term *WCtlr wctlrR* (*@Wire wR*, *@CAN bctlr*) : (0); is used to instantiate a rebec named *wctlrR* of type *WCtlr*. The known rebecs of *wctlrR* are assigned to *wR* and *bctlr*. For the second known rebec, the tag *@CAN* is used to indicate that the communications of this rebec to *bctlr* are via CAN. The parameter (0) is the identifier of the wheel controller. In the priorities of CAN specification, the term *wctlrR bctlr.setWspd* 3, specifies that the priority of a message sent from *wctlrR* to *bctlr* containing the message server name *setWspd* is 3. The term *wctlrR bctlr.setWspd* −> 0.01 in the delays of CAN specification, specifies that the delay of the same message is 0.01.

4.2 Operational Semantics

Rebecs are executed concurrently in response to a physical mode being finished or by taking a message from their message queues. The actions of a physical mode are executed when its behavior is finished, and each message is processed by executing its corresponding message server. The execution of all the statements except the delay statement is instantaneous. To model communication via CAN, a network entity is considered in the semantics which buffers the messages from the rebecs and delivers them one-by-one to the respective receivers based on the messages' priorities and delays specified in the model. The message selection mechanism of CAN protocol is time consuming. We assume that this time is negligible. We abstract away from this time by considering the effect of the network entity when no actor can progress instantaneously. For communication via wire, the message is directly inserted into the receiver's message queue instantaneously.

A Hybrid Rebeca model consists of the rebecs of the model and the network specification. A software rebec consists of the definitions of its variables, message servers and known rebecs. A physical rebec is defined like a software rebec plus the definitions of its modes. The network specification consists of the communication types of rebecs, which can either be CAN or wire, the message priorities and message delivery delays.

Definition 1 (Hybrid Rebeca model). *A Hybrid Rebeca model is defined as a tuple* (R_s, R_p, N) *where* R_s *and* R_p *are the set of software and physical rebecs in the model, respectively, and* N *is the network specification. The set* $R = R_s \cup R_p$ *denotes the set of all rebecs in the model.*

A software rebec $r_{s_i} \in R_s$ and physical rebec $r_{p_i} \in R_p$ with a unique identifier i, are defined by tuples $(i, V_i, msgsrvs_i, K_i)$ and $(i, V_i, msgsrvs_i, modes_i, K_i)$, respectively, where V_i is the set of its variables, $msgsrvs_i$ is the set of its message servers, K_i is the set of its known rebecs, and $modes_i$ is the set of modes.

A network specification is defined as a tuple $N = (conn, netPriority, netDelay)$ where $conn$ is a partial function $R \times R \rightarrow \{Wire, CAN\}$ which defines the one way connection type from a rebec to another rebec, $netPriority : Msg \rightarrow \mathbb{N}$ and $netDelay : Msg \rightarrow \mathbb{R}$ define the priority and the network delivery delay for a message, respectively. Msg denotes the set of all messages in the model.

Definition 2 (Message). *A message is defined as a tuple* $(sender, m, receiver) \in R \times Name \times R$ *where sender is the sending rebec, m is the name of the message server in the receiver, and receiver is the receiving rebec.*

The operational semantics of a Hybrid Rebeca model is defined as a monolithic hybrid automaton. The semantics could be defined in a compositional way by providing a translation for constitutive elements of a hybrid rebeca model. By composing the translations with the operational semantics of hybrid automata, the final model can be derived. However, this approach will lead to many real-valued variables which reduces analyzability of the resulting model.

Definition 3 (Hybrid automaton for Hybrid Rebeca model). *Given a Hybrid Rebeca model $\mathfrak{H} = (R_s, R_p, N)$, its formal semantics based on hybrid automata is defined by $H_{\mathfrak{H}} = (Loc, Var, Lab, \Rightarrow, Flws, Inv, Init)$, where Var is the set of all continuous variables in the model (variables of types float or real), Lab is the set of labels which is empty as we generate a monolithic hybrid automaton. The set of locations Loc, transitions $\Rightarrow$, flows Flws, invariants Inv, and initial conditions Init are defined in the following.*

Locations. Each location has four entities: the states of software rebecs, physical rebecs, network, and pending event list. The state of a software rebec consists of the valuation of its discrete variables, the state of its message queue and a program counter. The program counter points to a statement that the rebec must execute. The state of a physical rebec consists of its active mode, the state of its message queue and a program counter. The state of a physical rebec does not contain any valuation since discrete variables are not defined for physical rebecs and the continuous variables are handled in the hybrid automaton. A software rebec has the notion of being suspended (due to the execution of a delay statement). The suspension status is maintained by a reserved variable in the valuation of the rebec. Delay statements are not allowed in physical rebecs.

Definition 4 (State of a rebec). *The state of a software rebec is denoted by the tuple (v, q, c) where v is the valuation of its variables, q is the message queue of the rebec, and c denotes the program counter. The state of a physical rebec is a tuple of the form $(\mathfrak{M}, q, c)$ where $\mathfrak{M}$ is the active mode and q and c are defined as in the software rebec's state.*

The network state, which is the state of the CAN network, consists of the buffered messages in the network and the status of the network which indicates that the network is busy sending a message or is ready to send one.

Definition 5 (State of network). *The network state is defined by the pair* (B, r)*, where B is the network buffer and the boolean flag r indicates the status of the network, which can be ready or busy.*

The forth entity, pending event list, represents the sequence of pending events. Events are used for time consuming actions. For a time consuming action an event is stored, to be triggered at the time that the action is over. Two types of events are defined in the semantics of Hybrid Rebca: *Resume* and *Transfer*. A pending event with event *Resume* is generated and inserted into the pending event list when a delay statement is seen in Rebeca model, and the corresponding rebec is suspended. To model the passage of time for the delay statement, a timer variable is used by the pending event. After the specified delay has passed, the event is triggered, and consequently the behavior of the given rebec is resumed by updating the suspension status of the rebec. A pending event with event *Transfer* is generated when a message from the network buffer is chosen to be sent to its receiver. A timer is assigned to model the message delivery delay, and the pending event is inserted into the pending event list. Upon triggering of a *Transfer* event, the specified message is enqueued in the receiver's message queue, and the network status is set to ready which means the network is ready to send another message.

Definition 6 (Pending event). *A pending event is a tuple* (d, e, t) *where d is the delay of the event e and t is a timer variable that is assigned to this event. The event e can either be a Resume or Transfer event. The timer variable is used for defining the timing behavior for the delay of the pending event. The event is triggered (and executed) after d units of time after the pending event is created.*

Transitions. We define two general types of transitions: urgent and nonurgent transitions. The urgent transitions are further divided to message, statement and network transitions which are respectively shown as $\Rightarrow_m$, $\Rightarrow_s$ and $\Rightarrow_n$. The nonurgent transitions are shown as $\Rightarrow_N$. We use these transitions to differentiate between different types of actions. Message transitions are only for taking a message. Statement transitions are for executing the statements. A network transition chooses a message from the buffer of the network to be sent. This transition is only about choosing the message and not the act of sending. Non-urgent transitions are used to model the passage of time. These transitions include the behaviors of physical actors' active modes and pending time of events since they are time consuming.

An ordering is defined among these transitions. The ordering is $\Rightarrow_m = \Rightarrow_s > \Rightarrow_n > \Rightarrow_N$. Whenever a higher order transition is enabled in a location, no lower order transition can be taken in that location. The semantics of the actions in Hybrid Rebeca are defined using these transitions on the locations. In the following we define these transitions.

Message Transitions: Message transitions define the act of taking a message. A message transition can take place whenever a rebec is not suspended. A rebec is suspended when it executes a delay statement. Let the tuples (v, q, c) and $(\mathfrak{M}, q, c)$ denote the state of a software rebec and a physical rebec respectively. The message transition is defined as follows:

– *Taking a Message:* A rebec takes a message from the head of its message queue q, whenever the rebec has no statement to execute. When a message is taken, the program counter c is updated to point to the beginning of the corresponding message server, and the message is removed from the message queue q.

Statement Transitions: Statement transitions define the act of executing the statements. Like message transitions, a statement transition can take place whenever a rebec is not suspended. Consider the tuples (v, q, c) and $(\mathfrak{M}, q, c)$ as the states of a software rebec and a physical rebec respectively. The statement transitions include the followings:

– *Assignment Statement:* This statement has two cases. When assigning to a discrete variable, the value of the variable is update in the valuation v of the rebec. When assigning to a continuous variable, since its value is not determined (it may depend on the continuous behaviors), the assignment is transfered over to the transition to be handled by the resulting hybrid automaton.
– *Conditional Statement:* This statement has two cases. If the value of the condition is determined, the program counter c is updated to point to the appropriate statement block. If the value of the condition is not determined (because of continuous variables used in the condition), both possible paths are considered by creating two separate transitions. The condition and its negation act as the guards for these transitions.
– *Send Statement:* This statement, depending on the communication type, has two behaviors. When the communication is via wire, the message is directly added to the receiver's message queue. When the communication is via CAN, the message is added to the CAN buffer to be handled by the CAN behavior.
– *Delay Statement:* This statement suspends the software rebec by updating the corresponding variable (suspension status) in the valuation v and creates a pending event $(d, Resume, t)$ for resuming the rebec after d units of time. d is the delay specified in the delay statement and t is a timer variable.
– *Set Mode Statement:* This statement changes the active mode $\mathfrak{M}$ of the physical rebec to the specified mode.

Network Transitions: These transitions define the behavior of the CAN network which only includes the behavior of choosing a message from the network buffer to be sent. Since network transitions have a lower priority than message and statement transitions, this makes the choosing behavior to happen only when no rebec can progress instantaneously. Let (B, r) be the network state. The choosing transition is as follows:

– *Choosing a Message:* For this behavior, the message with the highest priority is removed from the network buffer B, a pending event $(d, \textit{Transfer}, t)$ for sending the message is created, and the flag r of the network is updated to indicate that the network is busy. The delay d for the created pending event is the network delay of the message.

Nonurgent Transitions: Nonurgent transitions are used to define the end of active physical modes and triggering pending events. These transitions are defined only when no urgent transition is possible. These transitions are as follows:

– *End of an Active Mode:* For a physical rebec $(\mathfrak{M}, q, c)$ if $\mathfrak{M}$ is not none, the guard of the active mode $\mathfrak{M}$ is transfered to the transition, and the program counter c of the rebec is updated to point to the actions of this active mode, and the active mode is set to none.
– *Triggering of an Event:* For a pending event (d, e, t), the guard $t == d$ is defined on the transition where t and d are the timer and the delay of the pending event respectively. The event e is executed as a result of this transition and the pending event is removed from the pending event list.

Flows and Invariants. To define flows and invariants for each location we need to consider continuous and instantaneous behaviors separately. There are two kinds of continuous behaviors in the model, behaviors regarding physical rebecs' modes and behaviors regarding pending events. Physical modes have all the necessary information in themselves and the pending events have simple timing behaviors. The functions $flows(r_p, \mathfrak{M})$ and $invariant(r_p, \mathfrak{M})$ return the flow and invariant of a mode $\mathfrak{M}$ in a physical rebec r_p respectively. Instantaneous behaviors should be executed without allowing the time passage. So time should not be passed when the system resides in the source locations of such transitions, called *urgent* locations.

Definition 7 (Urgent location flow and invariant). *A possible implementation for an urgent location is $urg' = 1$ as flow and $urg \leq 0$ as invariant, where urg is a specific variable. Note that in this method, this new variable must be added to the set Var of the hybrid automaton. Also the assignment $urg = 0$ must be added to all incoming transitions to an urgent location. The defined invariant prevents the model from staying in the location as the value of urg will be increased by the defined flow.*

If a location is urgent, the urgency flow, as defined above, should be set as its flows. In case a location is not urgent, it inherits the flows of all physical rebecs' active modes, the flows for timers of pending events, and a flow of zero for each float variable to freeze its value. The flow of a pending event is simply defined as $t' = 1$ where t is the timer variable of the pending event.

Similarly, if a location is urgent, its invariant is set to urgency invariant, otherwise it inherits the invariants of all physical rebecs' active modes, and the invariants for corresponding pending events' timers. The invariant of a pending event is defined as $t \leq d$ where t and d are the timer variable and the delay of the pending event, respectively.

Initial Location and Initial Condition. For the initial location l_0, we initialize all discrete variables of rebecs to the value zero. Furthermore, the initial message for each instantiated rebec, is put into its message queue. We also set the value of all continuous variable to zero in the initial condition of the initial location.

4.3   Technical Details

For simplicity some details were omitted from our semantics. Here we describe these details informally.

Limited Size for Message Queues: In the semantics of Hybrid Rebeca, the message queues of rebecs are considered unbounded. But in practice a specific size must be specified for message queues of rebecs.

Message Arguments: To incorporate message arguments, we must consider discrete and continuous arguments separately. For discrete arguments, since their values are known in the state, that value is included in the message and when the message is taken, its arguments are added to the rebec's valuation. When the execution of the message is finished, the arguments are removed from the valuation. For continuous arguments, the values are not generally determined during the translation to hybrid automata, so it's not possible to send the value within the message. To this aim, a non-evolving auxiliary variable is used. Before sending a message, each continuous argument is assigned to an auxiliary variable (by using continuous variable assignment). Then, a reference to the auxiliary variable is included in the message. When the message is taken, for each continuous argument, an assignment from the auxiliary variable to its respective parameter variable is implicitly executed.

Continuous Variable Pools: When creating a new event (for a delay statement or for sending a message from CAN), a new timer is assigned to each event. But in hybrid automata all continuous variables must be defined statically. To handle this, variable pools with fixed sizes are used. There are two variable pools in our semantics, one for timer variables and one for the auxiliary variables of message arguments (as mentioned above). The size of the variable pools affects the behavior of the model. A small size will lead to an incomplete model, and a large size will lead to a huge model which can not be easily analyzed.

5   Case Study

We demonstrate the applicability of our language on a simplified Brake-by-Wire (BBW) system with Anti-lock Braking System (ABS) [8,12,16]. In a BBW system instead of using mechanical parts, braking is managed by electronic sensors and actuators. In ABS, the safety is increased by releasing the brake based on the slip rate to prevent uncontrolled skidding.

In this system, the brake pedal sensor calculates the brake percentage based on the position of the brake pedal. A global brake controller computes the brake torque and sends this value to each wheel controllers in the vehicle. Each wheel controller monitors the slip rate of its controlled wheel and releases the brake if the slip rate is greater than 0.2. There is a nonlinear relationship between the friction coefficient of the wheel and the slip rate. When the slip rate is between zero and around 0.2, any increase in the slip rate increases the friction coefficient, but after 0.2, further increase in the slip rate, leads to a reduction in the friction coefficient. For this reason when the slip rate is greater than 0.2, no brake will be applied to the wheel. In this system, each pair of wheel and its wheel controller are connected directly by wire. Furthermore, the brake pedal sensor sends the brake percentage value to the global brake controller through wire. All other communications are done through a shared CAN network. A representation of the system is shown in Fig. 4.

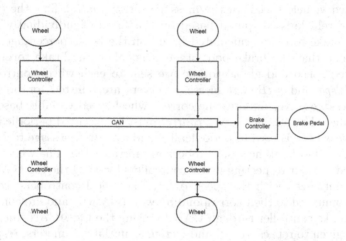

Fig. 4. The schematic of the BBW system. The physical components are shown as ellipses and computational components are shown as rectangles.

5.1   Model Definition

The model is defined in Fig. 5. Note that For simplicity, we have considered two wheels in our model. The model consists of 5 classes. *Wheel* and *WCtlr* classes were defined previously in Sect. 4.1. *Wheel* class models the sensors and actuators of the wheel. It periodically sends the speed of the wheel to the controller and defines the effect of braking on the wheel speed. *WCtlr* class defines the behavior of the wheel controller. It monitors the slip rate of the wheel and decides to apply the brake based on its value.

Brake class defines the behavior for the brake pedal. Here we assume a simple behavior where the brake percentage is increased by a constant rate until it reaches a predefined max percentage. The class have one known rebec *bctrl* which is the global brake controller. It defines four state variables *bprcnt, mxprcnt, t* and *r* which are the brake percentage, maximum brake percentage, an auxiliary timer variable and a variable that defines the rate for the brake percentage. In the *initial* message server, the values of the initial and maximum brake percentage are initialized with the given values and the rate variable is set to 1 and the active mode of the rebec is set to *Braking*. *Braking* mode defines a periodic behavior where the value of *bprcnt* is sent to *bctrl* and the brake percentage is increased by the rate defined by *r*. In the actions of this behavior, if the brake percentage is equal or greater than *mxprcnt*, the rate variable *r* is set to zero to stop the brake percentage from changing by time.

BrakeCtrl class is the global brake controller and has the responsibility of delegating the brake torque to wheel controllers. It defines two known rebecs for each wheel controller named *wctlrR* and *wctlrL*. *BrakeCtrl* class has five state variables for the speed of the right and left wheels, the brake percentage from the brake pedal, the global torque calculated from the brake percentage and the estimated vehicle speed. In the message server *control*, first the estimated speed of the vehicle is computed based on the speed of individual wheels and the desired brake torque is calculated based on the brake percentage. Here we simply assume that the brake percentage is equal to the brake torque. Then, the estimated speed and global torque are sent to each wheel controller. The *initial*, *setWspd* and *setBprcnt* message servers are omitted for brevity. The *setWspd* message server updates the correct wheel speed variable based on the input identifier. The message server *control* must be executed periodically, so an auxiliary *Clock* class is used to periodically send a *control* message to *BrakeCtrl*.

In the main block, all necessary rebecs are instantiated. The wheels *wR* and *wL* are wired to their respecting wheel controllers by using the tag @Wire. Both wheels are initialized with the speed of 1^1. The wheel controllers *wctlrR* and *wctlrL* are connected to their corresponding wheels by wire and are connected to the global brake controller through CAN by using the tag @CAN. Identifiers of 0 and 1 are given to rebecs *wctlrR* and *wctlrL* as initial parameters, respectively. The brake controller *bctlr* is connected to both wheel controllers through the CAN network and the brake *brake* is initialized with the brake percent 60 and maximum brake percent of 65. Both brake *brake* and clock *clock* are connected to *bctlr* by wire. There are four CAN messages in the model. The brake controller *bctlr* sends *applyTrq* message to the wheel controllers *wctlrR* and *wctlrL*. The wheels *wR* and *wL* send *setWspd* message to *bctlr* respectively. A higher priority is defined for *applyTrq* messages. Note that a lower number indicates a higher priority. The network delay of all four CAN messages is specified as 10 ms.

5.2   Analysis and Verification

For the analysis of this model the queue size of *bctlr* is set to 4, the queue sizes of both *wctlrR* and *wctlrL* is set to 2, and for other rebecs the queue size is set to 1. The size of timer variable pool is set to 1 and the size of arguments variable pool is set to 11. The hybrid automaton derived from the model consists of 10097 locations and 25476 transitions. We use SpaceEx [9] tool to verify our

---

[1] As the properties to be verified do not depend on the value of the speed, to minimize the analysis time, this value has been chosen.

model. Note that the slip rate equation used in the model is not supported by SpaceEx, since it's a nonlinear equation. We simplified this equation for analysis. By specifying a set of forbidden states, safety properties can be verified by SpaceEx. We developed an initial tool[2] for our language that automatically translates a Hybrid Rebeca model to a SpaceEx model based on the semantics of our language. We verified three properties for our case study. The first property is "design-fault freedom". Here by design-fault we mean a fault caused by following situations: exceeding the capacity of a message queue, running out of pooled variables, and having messages with same priority in CAN buffer. We assume the message with the highest priority must always be unique in CAN buffer. Note that in practice, this property must be implicitly checked for all models in Hybrid Rebeca, but for now it must be manually verified by SpaceEx. The second property is a timing constraint. This property states that the time between the transmission of the brake percentage from the brake pedal, and its reaction by wheel actuators, must not exceed 0.2 s. The third property states that whenever the slip rate of a wheel exceeds 0.2, the brake actuator of that wheel must immediately be released.

For the first property, a specific location, called *Fault*, is created for the mentioned situations, and during the semantic derivation, occurrences of such design-faults are handled by generating a transition to the specified location *Fault*. The verified forbidden condition in SpaceEx for this property is $loc() ==$ *Fault*, where the term $loc()$ specifies the current location in SpaceEx.

The second property can not directly be specified with a set of forbidden states, since there is no direct concept of time in hybrid automata. To this aim, a monitor class is added to the model to measure the time between two events. Here the events are sending the brake percentage from the brake pedal to the global brake controller and processing the received brake torque in the wheels. The monitor class is a simple physical class with one physical mode and two stop and start message servers. The physical mode tracks the time and the message servers are used to stop and start the tracking. Note that in the start message server the tracked time is reset.

For the second property, one monitor rebec is instantiated and is wired to the brake pedal and one of the wheels. A start message is sent in the actions of the *Braking* mode of the brake pedal after the brake percentage is sent to the brake controller and a stop message is sent by *setTrq* message server of the wired wheel. In SpaceEx the forbidden condition $monitor\_time > 0.2$ is verified where $monitor\_time$ is the name of the monitor's timer in the resulted hybrid automaton.

The third property may seem to be straightforward, but because the semantics of our language is fine-grained, the request of releasing the brake and the actual act, take place in different locations, even though the time does not advance between these locations because they are urgent locations. For this property, the monitor class is used again. This time, a monitor rebec is wired

[2] The implementation can be found in https://github.com/jahandideh-iman/HybridRebeca.

```
 1 | physicalclass Wheel{
 2 | knownrebecs {WCtlr ctlr;}
 3 | statevars {float trq; real
   |     spd; real t;}
 4 | msgsrv initial (float spd_){
 5 | spd = spd_;
 6 | setmode(Rolling);
 7 | }
 8 | msgsrv setTrq(float trq_){
 9 | trq = trq_;
10 | }
11 | mode Rolling{
12 | inv(t <= 0.05){
13 | t' = 1;
14 | spd' = −0.1−trq;
15 | }
16 | guard(t == 0.05){
17 | t = 0;
18 | ctlr .setWspd(spd);
19 | if (spd > 0)
20 | setmode(Rolling);
21 | }}}
23 | softwareclass WCtlr{
24 | knownrebecs {Wheel w;
   |     BrakeCtlr bctlr;}
25 | statevars {int id; float
   |     wspd; float slprt ;}
26 | msgsrv initial (int id_){
27 | id = id_;
28 | }
29 | msgsrv setWspd(float
   |     wspd_){
30 | wspd = wspd_;
31 | bctlr .setWspd(id,wspd);
32 | }
33 | msgsrv applyTrq(float
   |     reqTrq, float vspd){
34 | if (vspd == 0)
35 | slprt = 0;
36 | else
37 | slprt = (vspd − wspd *
   |     WRAD)/vspd;
38 | if (slprt > 0.2)
39 | wheel.setTrq(0);
40 | else
41 | wheel.setTrq(reqTrq);
42 | }}

44 | physicalclass Brake{
45 | knownrebecs {BrakeCtlr
   |     bctlr;}
46 | statevars {real bprcnt; real
   |     t; float mxprcnt;
   |     float r}
47 | msgsrv initial (float
   |     bprcnt_, float
   |     mxprcnt_){
48 | bprcnt = bprcnt_;
49 | mxprcnt = mxprcnt_;
50 | r = 1;
51 | setmode(Braking);
52 | }
53 | mode Braking{
54 | inv(t <= 0.05){
55 | t' = 1;
56 | bprcnt' = r;
57 | }
58 | guard(t == 0.05){
59 | t = 0;
60 | bctrl .setBprcnt(bprcnt);
61 | if (bprcnt>=mxprcnt)
62 | r = 0;
63 | setmode(Braking);
64 | }}}
66 | softwareclass BrakeCtlr{
67 | knownrebecs{
68 | WCtlr wctlrR;WCtlr
   |     wctlrL;}
69 | statevars {float
   |     wspdR;float
   |     wspdL;float
   |     bprcnt;float gtrq; float
   |     espd;}
70 | msgsrv control(){
71 | espd = (wspdR +
   |     wspdL)/2;
72 | gtrq = bprcnt;
73 | wctlrR.applyTrq(gtrq, espd);
74 | wctlrL.applyTrq(gtrq, espd);
75 | }
76 | // Setters for wspdR,
   |     wspdL and bprcnt
77 | ...
78 | }
80 | physicalclass Clock{

 81 | knownrebecs {BrakeCtlr
    |     bctlr;}
 82 | statevars {real t;}
 83 | msgsrv initial (){
 84 | setmode(Running)
 85 | }
 86 | mode Running(){
 87 | inv(t <= 0.05){
 88 | t' = 1;
 89 | }
 90 | guard(t == 0.05){
 91 | t = 0;
 92 | bctlr .control();
 93 | setmode(Running);
 94 | }}}
 96 | main {
 97 | Wheel wR (@Wire
    |     wctlrR):(1);
 98 | Wheel wL (@Wire
    |     wctlrL):(1);
 99 | WCtlr wctlrR (@Wire wR,
    |     @CAN bctlr):(0);
100 | WCtlr wctlrL (@Wire wL,
    |     @CAN bctlr):(1);
101 | BrakeCtlr bctlr (@CAN
    |     wctlrR, @CAN
    |     wctlrL):();
102 | Brake brake(@Wire
    |     bctlr):(60,65);
103 | Clock clock(@Wire bctlr):();
105 | CAN{
106 | priorities {
107 | bctlr wctlrR.applyTrq  1;
108 | bctlr wctlrL.applyTrq  2;
109 | wctlrR bctlr.setWspd  3;
110 | wctlrL bctlr.setWspd  4;
111 | }
112 | delays{
113 | bctlr wctlrR.applyTrq
    |     0.01;
114 | bctlr wctlrL.applyTrq
    |     0.01;
115 | wctlrR bctlr.setWspd
    |     0.01;
116 | wctlrL bctlr.setWspd
    |     0.01;
117 | }}}
```

Fig. 5. The model definition of the BBW model.

to one of the wheels and its wheel controller. A start message is sent from the wheel controller when the slip rate is greater than 0.2 and a stop message is sent like the second property. By using the monitor rebec, the states which the brake is not released and time has not progressed while the slip rate is greater than 0.2 can be considered safe. The verified forbidden condition in SpaceEx is

$$wctlr\_slprate > 0.2 \wedge wheel\_torque > 0 \wedge monitor\_time > 0$$

where $wctlr\_slprate$, $wheel\_torque$ and $monitor\_time$ are the names of the slip rate of the wheel, the brake torque of the wheel and the timer of the monitor, respectively, in the resulted hybrid automaton.

The resulted hybrid automaton for the first property has 10097 locations and 25476 transitions, which is huge for verification purposes. This huge size stems from the fine-grained semantics of our language. But most of these locations are urgent locations where time does not advance and can be aggregated for the properties mentioned here. After aggregating these urgent locations, the size of the resulting hybrid automaton is reduced to 21 locations and 1148 transitions. The aggregation process is implemented in our tool. The three properties are verified on their respective reduced hybrid automaton. The verification result of these properties are provided in the Table 1.

Table 1. The verification result of the case study. Legends: **Property:** verified property, **Derived HA:** derived hybrid automaton size where the first and second columns are the number of locations and transitions, respectively, **Gen Time:** duration of hybrid automaton generation in seconds, **Red HA:** reduced hybrid automaton size, **Verif Result:** result of verified property, **Verif Duration:** duration of verification in seconds.

Property	Derived HA		Gen Time (s)	Red HA		Verif Result	Verif Duration (s)
Design-fault freedom	10097	25476	12	21	1148	Passed	3705
Reaction time	16317	42976	20	21	1168	Passed	7521
Brake release	54097	175036	64	21	1168	Passed	3541

6 Related Work

There are some frameworks for modeling and analyzing cyber-physical systems. Some of these frameworks rely on simulation for analysis and others offer formal verification.

Ptolemy II [19] relies on simulation for analysis and is a framework that uses the concept of *model of computation* (MoC) which defines the rules for concurrent execution of components and their communications. Ptolemy supports many models of computation like process networks, discrete events, dataflow and continuous time. Heterogeneous model can be made by nesting these models of computations in a hierarchical structure. As far as we know there is no formal semantics for the hybrid models of Ptolemy framework to enable formal verification. In [4] an agent-based and control centric methodology is presented for development of CPSs. This approach includes all development stages of a system from analysis by simulation to the execution of the final system. For the modeling phase concepts like actors, message, actions, processing units and environmental gateway are presented in this methodology. The message passing among actors is asynchronous and the computations of the model take place in the actions that are submitted to the processing units by the actor for execution. The environmental gateway is used for abstracting the physical processes where in later stages is replaced by the real entities. This approach relies on simulation to analyze a system, and no formal analysis is supported. In [17] a modular approach for specifying and validating CPSs using rewriting logic-based technique is purposed. In this work a CPS is described as a linear hybrid automata in rewriting logic where the components of the system communicate asynchronously. Timed hybrid Petri nets [5] can also be used to model hybrid systems and CPSs. For analysis of these hybrid Petri nets in [5] a translation to hybrid automata is presented. However, Petri-net based approaches prohibit modular specification of systems. The framework of [13] provides a hybrid process calculus tailored for modeling CPSs and analyzing their security properties [14,15]. In this approach network governing the interactions between physical and cyber entities is not addressed.

7   Discussions

In Sect. 3 we presented our extended actor model for cyber-physical systems. In our model, the software and physical actors are separated and modes are added to physical actors for specifying the continuous behaviors. The separation of software and physical rebecs prevents the interference of continuous behaviors with software behaviors. In Rebeca, each actor has only one thread of execution and its local state is encapsulated from other actors. This greatly simplifies the interactions between actors. But having both continuous and discrete behaviors in one actor, can be considered as having multiple threads of execution in the actor. Since these threads share the same variables, this approach is inconsistent with Rebeca and can surprise the modeler. A simple example to highlight this issue is to consider the following code segment of a message server:

```
a = k;
delay(2);
b = a + c;
```

The constant k is assigned to the variable a. The delay statement is used to abstractly model the computation time of complex computations. After the specified delay, the value of variable a is used to update the variable b. Assume the rebec has a continuous behavior and during the execution of the delay statement, the continuous behavior is finished and changes the value of variable a in its actions. This affects the value of the variable b when the delay statement is over and can lead to a faulty behavior. The separation of software and physical actors, solves this issue. Note that the delay statement is not allowed in the physical actors.

8   Conclusion and Future Work

In this paper we presented an extended actor model for modeling hybrid systems and CPSs, where both continuous and discrete processes can be defined. In this actor model, two kinds of actors are defined: software actors and physical actors. The software actors contain the software behaviors of the model and similarly, physical actors contain the physical behaviors. We also introduced a network entity to the actor model, for modeling the behavior of the network of the model. We implemented this extended actor model in Hybrid Rebeca language. This language is an extension of Timed Rebeca language and allows defining classes to make models modular and reusable. The semantics of the language is defined based on hybrid automata, to allow for formal verification of the models. Since our focus was automotive domain, CAN network is modeled in this version of the language. To show the applicability of our language, we modeled and analyzed a Brake-by-Wire system. For the verification of the model, three safety properties were considered. We used SpaceEx framework to verify these properties. It was shown that for some properties new entities were needed to make the verification feasible.

Since we focused on the automotive domain, only CAN network was defined in our current version of the language. Other network models are needed for different applications of CPSs. Instead of defining multiple network models, it's also possible to allow for user-defined network models. To this aim, a set of basic functionalities must be defined to enable defining most network models. Also, defining multiple instances of a network model (e.g. multiple CAN networks) may be needed in some systems. Like network models, it's possible to allow for defining new internal message schedulers for the rebecs, since the FIFO scheduler can be inadequate for some systems.

Acknowledgments. We would like to thank Edward Lee for his supports and patient guidance on modeling and analyzing CPSs, Tom Henzinger for his fruitful discussion on the extended actor model, and MohammadReza Mousavi and Ehsan Khamespanah for their useful contributions.

References

1. Aceto, L., Cimini, M., Ingólfsdóttir, A., Reynisson, A.H., Sigurdarson, S.H., Sirjani, M.: Modelling and simulation of asynchronous real-time systems using timed rebeca. In: 10th International Workshop on the Foundations of Coordination Languages and Software Architectures, EPTCS, vol. 58, pp. 1–19 (2011)
2. Agha, G.A.: ACTORS - A Model of Concurrent Computation in Distributed Systems. MIT Press Series in Artificial Intelligence. MIT Press, Cambridge (1990)
3. Alur, R., et al.: The algorithmic analysis of hybrid systems. Theor. Comput. Sci. **138**(1), 3–34 (1995)
4. Cicirelli, F., Nigro, L., Sciammarella, P.F.: Model continuity in cyber-physical systems: a control-centered methodology based on agents. Simul. Model. Pract. Theory **83**, 93–107 (2018)
5. David, R., Alla, H.: On hybrid petri nets. Discrete Event Dyn. Syst. **11**(1–2), 9–40 (2001). https://doi.org/10.1023/A:1008330914786
6. Davis, R.I., Burns, A., Bril, R.J., Lukkien, J.J.: Controller area network (CAN) schedulability analysis: refuted, revisited and revised. Real-Time Syst. **35**(3), 239–272 (2007). https://doi.org/10.1007/s11241-007-9012-7
7. Derler, P., Lee, E.A., Sangiovanni-Vincentelli, A.L.: Modeling cyber-physical systems. Proc. IEEE **100**(1), 13–28 (2012)
8. Filipovikj, P., Mahmud, N., Marinescu, R., Seceleanu, C., Ljungkrantz, O., Lönn, H.: Simulink to UPPAAL statistical model checker: analyzing automotive industrial systems. In: Fitzgerald, J., Heitmeyer, C., Gnesi, S., Philippou, A. (eds.) FM 2016. LNCS, vol. 9995, pp. 748–756. Springer, Cham (2016). https://doi.org/10.1007/978-3-319-48989-6_46

9. Frehse, G., et al.: SpaceEx: scalable verification of hybrid systems. In: Gopalakrishnan, G., Qadeer, S. (eds.) CAV 2011. LNCS, vol. 6806, pp. 379–395. Springer, Heidelberg (2011). https://doi.org/10.1007/978-3-642-22110-1_30

10. Henzinger, T.A.: The theory of hybrid automata. In: Inan, M.K., Kurshan, R.P. (eds.) Verification of Digital and Hybrid Systems. NATO ASI Series (Series F: Computer and Systems Sciences), vol. 170, pp. 265–292. Springer, Heidelberg (2000). https://doi.org/10.1007/978-3-642-59615-5_13

11. Hewitt, C.: Description and theoretical analysis (using schemata) of planner: a language for proving theorems and manipulating models in a robot. Technical report, Massachusetts Institute of Technology, Artificial Intelligence Laboratory (1972)

12. Kang, E., Enoiu, E.P., Marinescu, R., Seceleanu, C.C., Schobbens, P., Pettersson, P.: A methodology for formal analysis and verification of EAST-ADL models. Reliab. Eng. Syst. Saf. **120**, 127–138 (2013)

13. Lanotte, R., Merro, M.: A calculus of cyber-physical systems. In: Drewes, F., Martín-Vide, C., Truthe, B. (eds.) LATA 2017. LNCS, vol. 10168, pp. 115–127. Springer, Cham (2017). https://doi.org/10.1007/978-3-319-53733-7_8

14. Lanotte, R., Merro, M., Muradore, R., Viganò, L.: A formal approach to cyber-physical attacks. In: 30th IEEE Computer Security Foundations Symposium, pp. 436–450. IEEE Computer Society (2017)

15. Lanotte, R., Merro, M., Tini, S.: Towards a formal notion of impact metric for cyber-physical attacks. In: 14th International Conference on Integrated Formal Methods (2018, to appear)

16. Marinescu, R., Mubeen, S., Seceleanu, C.: Pruning architectural models of automotive embedded systems via dependency analysis. In: 42th Euromicro Conference on Software Engineering and Advanced Applications, pp. 293–302. IEEE Computer Society (2016)

17. Metelo, A., Braga, C., Brandão, D.: Towards the modular specification and validation of cyber-physical systems. In: Gervasi, O., et al. (eds.) ICCSA 2018. LNCS, vol. 10960, pp. 80–95. Springer, Cham (2018). https://doi.org/10.1007/978-3-319-95162-1_6

18. Pfeiffer, O., Ayre, A., Keydel, C.: Embedded Networking with CAN and CANopen, 1st edn. Copperhill Media Corporation, Greenfield (2008)

19. Ptolemaeus, C. (ed.): System Design, Modeling, and Simulation Using Ptolemy II (2014). Ptolemy.org

20. Sabouri, H., Khosravi, R.: Delta modeling and model checking of product families. In: Arbab, F., Sirjani, M. (eds.) FSEN 2013. LNCS, vol. 8161, pp. 51–65. Springer, Heidelberg (2013). https://doi.org/10.1007/978-3-642-40213-5_4

21. Sirjani, M.: Power is overrated, go for friendliness! expressiveness, faithfulness, and usability in modeling: the actor experience. In: Lohstroh, M., Derler, P., Sirjani, M. (eds.) Principles of Modeling. LNCS, vol. 10760, pp. 423–448. Springer, Cham (2018). https://doi.org/10.1007/978-3-319-95246-8_25

22. Sirjani, M., Jaghoori, M.M.: Ten years of analyzing actors: rebeca experience. In: Agha, G., Danvy, O., Meseguer, J. (eds.) Formal Modeling: Actors, Open Systems, Biological Systems. LNCS, vol. 7000, pp. 20–56. Springer, Heidelberg (2011). https://doi.org/10.1007/978-3-642-24933-4_3

23. Sirjani, M., Movaghar, A., Shali, A., de Boer, F.S.: Modeling and verification of reactive systems using rebeca. Fundamenta Informaticae **63**(4), 385–410 (2004)

24. Varshosaz, M., Khosravi, R.: Modeling and verification of probabilistic actor systems using pRebeca. In: Aoki, T., Taguchi, K. (eds.) ICFEM 2012. LNCS, vol. 7635, pp. 135–150. Springer, Heidelberg (2012). https://doi.org/10.1007/978-3-642-34281-3_12
25. Wolf, W., Madsen, J.: Embedded systems education for the future. Proc. IEEE **88**(1), 23–30 (2000)
26. Yousefi, B., Ghassemi, F., Khosravi, R.: Modeling and efficient verification of broadcasting actors. In: Dastani, M., Sirjani, M. (eds.) FSEN 2015. LNCS, vol. 9392, pp. 69–83. Springer, Cham (2015). https://doi.org/10.1007/978-3-319-24644-4_5

Challenges in Digital Twin Development for Cyber-Physical Production Systems

Heejong Park[1], Arvind Easwaran[1]([⊠]), and Sidharta Andalam[2]

[1] Nanyang Technological University,
50 Nanyang Avenue, Singapore 639798, Singapore
{hj.park,arvinde}@ntu.edu.sg
[2] Delta Electronics, 50 Nanyang Avenue, Singapore 639798, Singapore
sidharta.andalam@deltaww.com

Abstract. The recent advancement of information and communication technology makes digitalisation of an entire manufacturing shop-floor possible where physical processes are tightly intertwined with their cyber counterparts. This led to an emergence of a concept of digital twin, which is a realistic virtual copy of a physical object. Digital twin will be the key technology in Cyber-Physical Production Systems (CPPS) and its market is expected to grow significantly in the coming years. Nevertheless, digital twin is still relatively a new concept that people have different perspectives on its requirements, capabilities, and limitations. To better understand an effect of digital twin's operations, mitigate complexity of capturing dynamics of physical phenomena, and improve analysis and predictability, it is important to have a development tool with a strong semantic foundation that can accurately model, simulate, and synthesise the digital twin. This paper reviews current state-of-art on tools and developments of digital twin in manufacturing and discusses potential design challenges.

Keywords: Digital twin · Cyber-physical system · Industry 4.0 ·
Smart manufacturing · Model of computation · Modelling tool

1 Introduction

The advancement of today's information and communication technologies (ICT) has enabled a collection and effective use of big data which give useful insights about various industrial assets and their operations. High availability of low-cost, low-powered sensors and Internet-of-Thing (IoT) devices together with their communication networks are the key enablers of cyber-physical systems. Cyber-physical system is the main technological concept of the fourth industrial revolution, so called Industry 4.0 [15], characterised by a tight integration of

This work was supported by Delta-NTU Corporate Lab for Cyber-Physical Systems with funding support from Delta Electronics Inc. and the National Research Foundation (NRF) Singapore under the Corp Lab@University Scheme.

© Springer Nature Switzerland AG 2019
R. Chamberlain et al. (Eds.): CyPhy 2018/WESE 2018, LNCS 11615, pp. 28–48, 2019.
https://doi.org/10.1007/978-3-030-23703-5_2

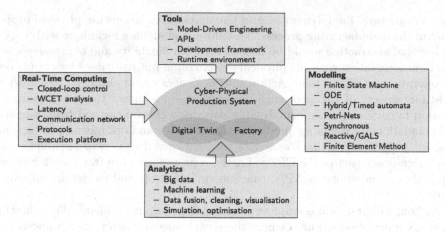

Fig. 1. Components of Cyber-Physical Production System

computations in a cyber world with physical processes in a real world. In cyber-physical system, changes in a physical process affect computations in a cyber world or vice-versa [17] where ICT enables a feedback between these two. A concept of digital twin, which is a ultra-realistic virtual counterpart of a real-world object, was introduced firstly by Grieves in 2003 [11]. Since the introduction of Industry 4.0 at the Hannover Fair in Germany in 2013, the capability the digital twin in cyber-physical system has been received a great attention along with the recent advancement information technologies. The digital twin market is likely to be worth USD 15.66 billion by 2023 at a compound annual growth rate of 37.87% [23].

Implementation of cyber-physical system in industrial manufacturing is called Cyber-Physical Production System (CPPS). In this domain, the use of digital twin has been mainly studied to improve time-to-market and MRO (Maintenance, Repair and Overhaul) costs, predict potential failures, and estimate remaining life of individual components, through high-fidelity simulation as well as real-time monitoring and control of manufacturing process. Since digital twins are built using the best available ICTs to mirror the physics of target objects in a virtual world, they can perform various simulations as if physical systems are tested in a real-life situation. Furthermore, digital twins can pause, resume, save, and restore their states to validate various corner-cases, which would rather be time-consuming and costly, if not impossible, to accomplish with physical systems. It is particularly valuable for the organisations who cannot afford very expensive resources to conduct exhaustive testing that may ruin their physical prototype or result in catastrophic events. For example, NASA and U.S. proposed digital twin concept to accelerate development of their future vehicles [10].

An overview of technologies that create digital twin in CPPS is shown in Fig. 1. CPPS is a combination of both logical and physical components that can be characterised by continuous and discrete dynamics. In addition, modelling and implementing a digital twin may require skills from multiple disciplines, such as electromagnetism, fluid dynamics, and kinematics etc., to capture physical properties of the manufacturing process. Therefore, a modelling technique with varying levels of abstraction would be needed for both flexibility and expressiveness. The tight integration with the physical system often put real-time constraints on the operations of digital twin. As a result, designers would also need to consider real-time aspects of the twin such as worst-case execution time and communication latency in the time-analysable networks. Data measured from sensors and simulation are useful for predictive maintenance and optimising production process. A platform for data analytics that enriches digital twin capabilities is also a significant part of the CPPS. Lastly, a proper software framework will be required that incorporates APIs, runtime environment, and model-driven engineering.

Although digital twin is employed for tackling various problems [25], it is still relatively a new research area where there exist several open research questions that have not yet been thoroughly explored such as:

1. How to build a highly-accurate, yet scalable, digital twin for both simulation and real-time closed-loop control.
2. How to mitigate issues related to *uncertainties* and *discrepancies* between the twin and the physical plant.
3. How digital twin merges with big data. Are big data related technologies such as machine learning and statistical approaches part of digital twin or separate services? What are use-case scenarios of digital twin with big data?
4. How to evaluate a digital twin that it faithfully mirrors its twinned system, how to quantitatively measure and compare two or more different digital twins of the same factory?
5. What are the requirements of a digital twin development tool that addresses the aforementioned questions.

The purpose of this paper is to review current state-of-art on tools and developments of digital twin in CPPS, discuss open research problems and suggest potential directions to address the aforementioned gaps.

The rest of this paper is organised as follows. Section 2 presents literature review on digital twin architectures and modelling strategies. Section 3 discusses an overview of digital twin in the context of smart manufacturing and CPPS. Section 4 introduces different models of computation. General-purpose as well as field-specific modelling tools are presented in Sect. 5. An industrial manufacturing case study with open research questions are presented in Sect. 6. Finally, conclusions are given in Sect. 7.

2   Literature Review

Digital twin is the cornerstone of the Industry 4.0 wave which has been an active research area in the past several years. Table 1 shows some of the recent literature where digital twin is introduced for addressing various problems in a number of

Table 1. Digital twin found in literature

Ref	Year	Domain	Purpose	Big data	Tools used
[16]	2016	General CPS	Model-based design tool for multidisciplinary, collaborating modelling of CPS	No	Modelio, Overture, Modelica, 20-sim, FMI
[34]	2017	Manufacturing	Predictive maintenance, simulation, resiliency	Yes	–
[1]	2017	Vehicle telematics	Optimising communication cost	No	Qfsm
[19]	2017	Manufacturing	Predictive maintenance, application development, simulation	Yes	–
[20]	2017	Process plants	Predictive maintenance, monitoring, 3D visualisation, simulation	Yes	ANSYS Simplorer, SCADE, PTC ThingWorx
[4]	2017	General CPS	CPS implementation	No	–
[18]	2017	Structural health monitoring	Predictive maintenance	No	–
[31]	2018	Manufacturing	Simulation-based systems engineering	No	SysML
[33]	2018	Manufacturing	Product lifecylcle management	Yes	–
[27]	2018	Manufacturing	Modelling, analysis, simulation	No	–
[30]	2018	Manufacturing	Modelling, simulation	No	Modelica, FEM

domains. The use of different modelling tools and whether the author highlights the use of big data analytics in their work are also indicated in the table.

An architecture of digital twin shop-floor (DTS) is presented in [34]. There are four main components in this architecture: physical shop-floor (PS), virtual shop-floor (VS), shop-floor service system (SSS), and shop-floor digital twin data (SDTD). VS is a digital twin of the PS and data generated from both PS and VS are merged into the SDTD database. SSS consists of many sub-services, which are transformed into composite services based on demands from PS and VS. VS is used to simulate, predict, and perform calibration using the real-time data generated from PS. While the work gives a good overview of digital twin based physical and virtual space interconnection, authors do not tackle modelling VS directly although they suggest a number of tools that can be used to model VS in different levels of hierarchy: geometry, physics, behaviour, and rule. The same research group also showed employing digital twin for product development and for managing entire product life-cycle [28,33]. In particular, [28] presented similarities and differences between digital twin and big data technologies and how they can be complementary with each other to enhance an overall manufacturing process.

A reference model for digital twin architecture for the cloud-based cyber-physical systems is presented in [1]. The architecture consists of three intermediary layers, namely cyber-things layer, peer-to-peer communication layer, and intelligent service layer. In this work, closely related physical and cyber *things* can create communication groups and peer-to-peer communication channels between those things are formed based on networking or communication criteria using a Bayesian belief network.

In [31], authors propose a concept of experimentable digital twin (EDT) that combines the ideas of digital twins with model-based systems engineering and simulation technology. In addition to digital twin itself, EDT also comprises of a model of external environment that interacts with the twin via simulated sensors and actuators. The authors showed modelling of automotive headlight housing assembly using the EDT approach.

A case study for modelling an industrial machine tool is presented in [30]. In this work, authors use Finite Element Method (FEM) based preprocessing approach for modelling structural flexibility of machine's components. The models of cutting process, kinematic chains, and control systems are developed using Modelica [8].

An integrated tool-chain for model-based design of cyber-physical systems is introduced in [16]. The tool enables co-simulation of multi-domain models by providing an integrated framework that combines multiple tools. They use Unifying Theories of Programming (UTP) [13] as a foundation to give semantics to their heterogeneous approach.

ANSYS and PTC worked together to demonstrate how a digital twin of a pump can help diagnose and solve operating problems faster. The pump model is developed using ANSYS's Simplorer and SCADE whereas PTC's ThingWorx platform, which provides data collection and analysis services, is used to create an IoT ecosystem for devices and sensors [20].

A concept of software-defined control (SDC) has emerged recently [19,27] which is inspired from the traditional software-defined networking (SDN), for programmatically configuring a communication network. A basic idea of SDC is to provide a central controller that has a global view of a system and separate decision making logic from the operations management solutions. In this framework, digital twin is suggested as a core simulation engine to improve decision making and detect faults in the manufacturing systems.

A concept of dynamic Bayesian network based digital twin is introduced in [18] for monitoring the health of an aircraft. The authors propose a modification to the traditional probabilistic network that significantly reduces the computational cost for Bayesian interference. The approach integrates physics models with sources of uncertainty to predict crack growth on the airframe.

Authors in [4] discuss modelling, discretisation, executability, simulation, and implementation of cyber-physical systems. The paper highlights the need of methods and tools with appropriate design languages underpinned by a solid semantic foundation which can model complex electromechanical systems. Various modelling techniques and respective challenges are discussed including detection of Zeno behaviours, difficulties in simulation of hybrid models in the presence of differential algebraic equations (DAE), physical systems modelling using linear and bond graphs. Although the authors do not particularly relate their work with digital twin development, the techniques and the design flow presented in the paper should definitely be considered in any digital twin development tools.

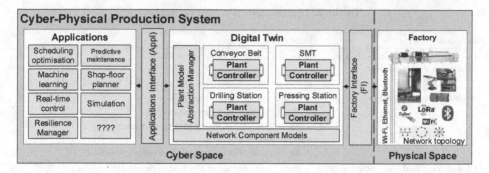

Fig. 2. An overview of the proposed Cyber-Physical Production System (CCPS) architecture

In literature, it is shown that digital twin is appeared the most in the manufacturing domain for predictive maintenance and simulation purposes. Several works [19,33,34] propose the digital twin based software architectures and foresee the importance of big data analysis and its linkage with the digital twin. The works in [4,16,18,27,30] focus more on the modelling aspects. Nevertheless, implementation details of the software architectures and their use case scenarios are somewhat abstracted. In addition, most of works lack a comprehensive modelling framework except [27], whose target is yet limited to discrete event systems, and [16], which focuses more on simulation of cyber-physical systems in general rather than digital twin itself. The next section discusses digital twin in the context of CPPS.

3   Digital Twin in Manufacturing

In literature and industries, the terms "Smart Manufacturing" and "Industry 4.0" are being used interchangeably and they are now almost synonymous with each other. The main objective is to leverage the recent advancement of information and communication technologies, such as cloud computing, IoT, and big data, to achieve autonomous, self-optimising, and self-diagnosing capabilities that can mitigate various problems in complex manufacturing scenarios. Digital twin is typically used in the context of cyber-physical systems to mirror the life of its real object via the best available physical models and sensor data. As a result, the digital twin enables simulation of real-world scenarios in a cyber world that otherwise would cost considerable amount of resource and time. Figure 2 shows our proposed digital twin architecture for CPPS.

CPPS is a mechanism used in smart manufacturing and Industry 4.0 design principles. It is comprised of five main components: (1) a factory, (2) a digital twin and its runtime environment, (3) a factory interface to extract sensor/actuator data from the physical space, (4) an application interface that provides Application Programming Interfaces (APIs) to applications that wish to utilise the digital twin, and (5) the application themselves.

Table 2. Digital twin use case scenarios

Features	References
Root-cause failure analysis and predictive maintenance	− Detection of a faulty valve [20]
	− Data-oriented analysis and prediction for wind turbines [9]
High-fidelity simulation	− Water pump simulation [20]
	− Financial and risk simulation [9]
	− Testing machineries for filling and packaging medications [32]
	− Simulation of a sheet metal punching machine [24]
Closed-loop real-time control	− Real-time control of the water pump [20]
	− Turbine control [9]
	− Human-robot collaborative assembly system [37]
3D visualisation	− 3D simulation model that shows cavitation inside a waterpump [20]
	− 3D visualisation of pharmaceutical machines [32]
	− 3D model of a brake pad wear [21]
	− 3D visualisation of the punching machine process [24]

Most often a factory, also called a *physical plant*, is a hybrid system, which is characterised with both continuous and discrete dynamics, modelled with a system of ODEs and DAEs, and state transitions, respectively. Examples of continuous dynamics of the plant are a movement of a workpiece on a conveyor belt and a movement of mechatronic arms during an assembly operation. On the other hand, discrete dynamics such as switching the operation mode from active to idle when no workpiece is detected for a certain amount of time.

The Plant Model Abstraction Manager and the Network Component Models are the parts of the digital twin runtime environment which manage lifecycles of individual twins and communication channels between them. Each twin consists of models of a plant and a controller that form a closed-loop control system via feedback and control signals. Interactions between these two models in the cyber space will also be accurately reflected in the physical space through the Factory Interface (FI).

The framework also provides a set of APIs that allow user applications to interact with the digital twin via the Application Interface (AppI). In this paper, we do not focus on the design of applications that utilise the digital twin, but rather on the digital twin development itself. However, it is worth to note here that technologies such as big data analysis can be employed in the application to deduce useful insights about the physical plant. The digital twin can communicate with this application to enhance its functionalities, for example, predicting potential failures and optimising throughput by adjusting its parameters. Similarly, the quality of data analysis can also be improved through data fusion of the physical plant and digital twin simulation.

Digital twin can be modelled using various levels of abstraction. Depending on requirements and resource availability, designers may choose a low-fidelity

✓: Supported □: Supported via extension ✗: Not supported

MoCs	Physical time	Hierarchy	Concurrency		Data	ODEs
			Sync	Async		
FSM	✗	✗	✗	✗	□	✗
PN	✗	✓	✗	✓	✗	✗
CPN	✗	✓	✗	✓	✓	✗
TPN	✓	✓	✗	✓	✗	✗
SR	□	✓	✓	✗	✓	✗
GALS	□	✓	✓	✓	✓	✗
TA	✓	✗	□	✗	□	✗
HA	✓	✗	✗	✗	□	✓

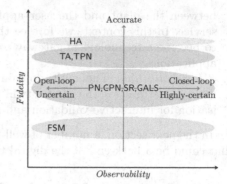

(a) A feature comparison among different MoCs

(b) Relationship between model fidelity and observability of a physical plant

Fig. 3. Models of computation and observability of a production system

model such as finite-state machine or a higher-fidelity hybrid automaton or finite element method (FEM). Specification of plant components at different levels fidelity allows generation of *mixed-fidelity digital twin*, which is a trade-off between accuracy and scalability. This trade-off makes implementing CPPS in bigger scale more practical since it would be computationally expensive to realise every aspect of physical plants using high-fidelity modelling approaches.

In manufacturing, employing a digital twin based cyber-physical system is favourable in a variety of scenarios. Table 2 shows examples of digital twin use case scenarios, which are grouped in four different categories. Since digital twins are often developed to handle multiple problems, most of the works overlap with each other in those categories:

1. *Root-cause failure analysis and predictive maintenance*: When there is a fault in the system, operators can utilise digital twin to pinpoint a root-cause thanks to its rich structural and behavioural information about the twinned system. In this case, choosing an appropriate formal *model of computation* (MoC) of the plant would play a pivotal role that facilitates semantic preservation between different design phases. From this, the digital twin will be able to back-trace the failure from an executable code all the way back to the modelling phase.

2. *High-fidelity simulation*: Data analytics, storage, and together with high-fidelity modelling techniques will enable the digital twin to assess different manufacturing as well as fault scenarios which provides highly accurate results that would be difficult to obtain via traditional simulation techniques.

3. *Closed-loop real-time control*: Digital twin augments the quality of the classical plant and controller closed-loop control where it can add additional values such as dynamicity, reconfigurability, connectivity, global intelligence, and predictability. This is possible because the digital twin can directly influence a behaviour of the physical plant and also acts as an intermediary entity

between the plant and the user applications which consume the twin as a service. In this context, we foresee that the digital twin has a great chance to become a technological gateway to a wide range of cyber-physical system applications.

4. *3D visualisation*: The multi-domain and multi-physics design approaches make it natural for the digital twin to be a good candidate for 3D visualisation for interactive validation and inspection.

In the next section, a number of well-known modelling strategies is presented that could be a back-end of the digital twin development framework.

4   An Overview of Models of Computation

Model of computation (MoC) deals with a set of theoretical choices that build an execution model of the design language. MoCs define how computations are carried out, for example sequentially or concurrently, interaction/synchronisation between computational units, and a notion of time, etc., without binding them to specific implementation details. Programming language equipped with formal MoC ensures that the resulting program follows the semantics of the corresponding MoC. On the other hand, a programming model for a certain MoC can also be built on a top of host programming language, for example through a library or a framework.

Many formal MoCs available for modelling a digital twin [6]. Some of them are shown in Fig. 3, which can be basis of the digital twin development framework. Each MoC supports different features: *Physical time* determines an ability for a MoC to relate its computations with a continuously evolving quantity, typically in real or integer domains. A simple example is when a Timed Automata (TA) [2] generate an output event after a clock value reaches 5. *Hierarchical composition* describes an ability to compose two or more basic design entities to achieve a more advanced and complex functionality. This can be easily found in many digital systems designs, for example an arithmetic logic unit composed of adders and subtractors, etc. *Concurrency* describes an ability of basic entities in a model that can be executed in overlapping time. Typically, it refers to either synchronous or asynchronous concurrency. *Data* indicates whether a MoC supports for variables, expressions, constructs, type systems, and etc., to perform data-oriented algorithmic computations. Lastly, *ODEs* refer to an ability to capture continuous dynamics of a system via a system of ordinary differential equations. There is no MoC that supports all the features. An FSM can be used to capture various control-dominated behaviours. However, it alone is not well suitable for accurately capturing a complex nature of physical systems that are inherently concurrent, time-dependent, and data-rich.

Petri-Nets [26] are good models for describing concurrent and distributed systems. However, it lacks expressiveness in data computations and timing properties. Coloured Petri-Nets (CPN) [14] and Timed Petri-Net (TPN) [29] are extensions of the PN with data and timing features, respectively. Nevertheless, they lack in capturing continuous dynamics of a system. Although the original formal definition of the PN do not include hierarchy, there is an extension of PN that supports hierarchical composition [7].

Synchronous Reactive (SR) MoC [3] provides a set of constructs for capturing reactive behaviours of a system. The execution semantics of SR constructs underpinned with rigorous mathematical foundation enables bug avoidance in the early design phase using correct-by-construction compilation and verification techniques [3], which increase confidence in the correctness of final designs. While SR MoC has a notion of time, they are only logical. Moreover, the SR MoC is not amenable to a large distributed systems since every design component is synchronised with a single global clock.

Globally Asynchronous Locally Synchronous (GALS) [22] is a superset of the SR MoC where a system is modelled using several synchronous subsystems, which run asynchronously and communicate with each other via a message passing mechanism. Still, the most of GALS-based modelling languages often lack an ability to model real-time behaviours and continuous dynamics of many physical systems.

Hybrid Automata (HA) [12] supports modelling of both discrete and continuous dynamics of a system. It uses a state machine with a finite set of real-valued variables whose values evolve according to a set of ODEs. A notion of reference time can also be defined in HA using a simple formula such as $\dot{t} = 1$. However, it is a flat structure similar to an FSM, and does not directly support concurrency and hierarchical composition.

Generating a highly accurate, time-synchronised, and scalable digital twin, therefore requires a technique that combines various MoCs to complement each other's weaknesses. Generally, fidelity of a model is based on how well it can capture dynamics of physical phenomena. On the other hand, effectiveness of a modelling technique varies depending on *observability* of the physical plant. As shown in Fig. 3b, the relationship between fidelity of a model and observability of a physical plant categorises the digital twin based CPPS into largely four groups:

1. *Accurate but uncertain model*: High-fidelity models can accurately capture a plant's behaviour according to the specification. However, since a less observable plant only provides feedback at certain discrete instants, there is a low confidence on dynamics of the plant between two feedback events. For example, a digital twin can only speculate the current position of an item that moves along a conveyor belt based on the motor speed. Any unexpected events that occur between two photoelectric sensors cannot be captured by the digital twin unless the item is enabled with RFID tracking.
2. *Less accurate and uncertain model*: In this case, a model does not capture the plant's behaviour accurately and the plant is also less observable. An example of this scenario is using an untimed model such as FSM for modelling a change of the temperature of the boiling water and the plant only provides feedback when the temperature reaches at T_{max} threshold.
3. *Less accurate and highly-certain model*: In this scenario, the plant is fully observable where it provides changes its states in a frequent manner. Low-

fidelity models, however may not fully utilise such information. For example, for a multi-axis arm movements, discrete event models may only react to events when the arm only reaches its final destination of the movement, ignoring how it reaches there.

4. *Accurate and highly-certain model*: This is when both the model and the plant fully synchronises and the model can accurately trace dynamics of the plant at any instants of time.

In the next section, an overview of existing modelling tools are presented. These tools are used for general cyber-physical system development, but also can target digital twin.

5   Modelling Tools

Table 3 summarises various types of modelling tools available which target general-purpose discrete and continuous systems as well as more application specific fields. It is not possible to cover all of them here, but we selected some of the notable tools currently available in the market and academia.

Tools like Scilab, Modelica, and Matlab/Simulink provide general-purpose, numerical computing environment for modelling a wide range of systems such as mechanical and electrical systems, fluid dynamics, and etc. The SCADE Suite is a model-based development environment for mission critical embedded software with Lustre as its core language. ANSYS Simplorer and Digital Twin Builder provide multi-domain, co-simulation environment with support for VHDL-AMS, Modelica, C/C++, and SPICE languages along with MIL (Model-in-the-Loop), and SIL (Software-in-the-Loop) capabilities. The model can be connected to various industrial IoT platforms such as PTC ThingWorx, GE Predix, and SAP Leonardo.

There are also tools equipped with formal models of computation. For example, synchronous reactive languages such as Esterel, Lustre, and Céu and Petri-Net based IOPT and CPN Tools. Building Controls Virtual Test Bed (BCVTB) is a software environment based on Ptolemy II project [6], to couple different simulation programs for co-simulation.

Modelling tools which target hybrid systems have direct support for capturing both discrete and continuous dynamics and transition between these modes. For example, Compositional Interchange Format (CIF) is a automata-based language for the specification of discrete event, timed, and hybrid systems. HyST and SL2SX do source-to-source transformation to enable evaluation of HA models using different tools. Model checking tools for HA models also exist, for instance SpaceEx and Flow*.

Flexsim is a simulation software for manufacturing factories including 3D visualisation and statistical reporting and analysis features. The Integrated Tool Chain for Model-based Design of Cyber-Physical Systems (INTO-CPS) is an integrated tool chain for comprehensive model-based design of cyber-physical systems. It aims to provide a framework for model-based design and analysis by

Table 3. A summary of modelling tools

Tools	License	Formal MoC	Code generation
SCADE Simplerer[a]	Commercial	Multi-paradigm	–
SCADE Suite[b]	Commercial	Synchronous dataflow	✓
ANSYS Twin Builder[c]	Commercial	Multi-paradigm	–
SCILAB[d]	GPLv2	–	via third-party plugins: X2C, Project-P
Modelica families[e]	Open source and commercial	–	✓ (some implementations)
MATLAB/Simulink[f]	Commercial	–	✓
BCVTB[g]	Modified BSD	Actor-based	–
INTO-CPS[h]	Open source	VDM, SysML	✓
CIF[i]	MIT	HA	✓
Flow*[j]	GPL	HA	–
Flexsim[k]	Commercial	–	–
HyST[l]	LGPL	HA	✓ (To other HA models)
SL2SX[m]	GPLv3	–	✓ (Simulink to SpaceEx)
SpaceEx[n]	GPLv3	HA	–
IOPT[o]	Free (Web-based)	Petri-Net	✓
CPN Tools[p]	GPLv2	Coloured Petri-Net	–
Ptolemy II[q]	Mixed	Actor-oriented on top of heterogenous MoC	✓
Esterel[r]	Mixed and commercial	Synchronous reactive	✓
Lustre[s]	Free and commercial	Synchronous dataflow	✓
Céu[t]	MIT	Synchronous reactive	✓

[a] https://www.ansys.com/products/systems/ansys-twin-builder
[b] http://www.esterel-technologies.com/products/scade-suite/
[c] https://www.ansys.com/products/systems/ansys-twin-builder
[d] https://www.scilab.org/
[e] https://www.modelica.org/
[f] https://www.mathworks.com/products/matlab.html
[g] https://simulationresearch.lbl.gov/bcvtb
[h] https://into-cps.github.io/
[i] http://cif.se.wtb.tue.nl/index.html
[j] https://flowstar.org
[k] https://www.flexsim.com/
[l] http://www.verivital.com/hyst/
[m] https://github.com/nikos-kekatos/SL2SX
[n] http://spaceex.imag.fr/
[o] http://gres.uninova.pt/IOPT-Tools/login.php
[p] http://cpntools.org/
[q] https://ptolemy.berkeley.edu
[r] http://www-sop.inria.fr/esterel-org/files/Html/News/News.htm
[s] http://www-verimag.imag.fr/Sync-Tools.html?lang=en
[t] http://www.ceu-lang.org/

combining multiple models generated from different tools using the Functional Mock-up Interface (FMI) standard [5].

In the next section, a case study called the IMPACT manufacturing line is introduced where an initial concept of the digital twin modelling is presented.

6   Case Study: The IMPACT Manufacturing Line

To illustrate the use of heterogeneous models and discuss open issues, we propose developing a cyber-physical production system case study called the IMPACT line shown in Fig. 4. It consists of four linear modules with parallel conveyors and seven processing stations for manufacturing smart phones. The following outlines the operation of each station:

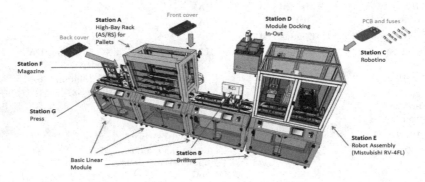

Fig. 4. The IMPACT line – a testbed for future manufacturing

1. *High-Bay Rack* – When there is a request from an external source for manufacturing a product, a cartesian robot is triggered to pick-up a workpiece pallet. The pallet is then placed on the conveyor belt. A motor for the conveyor belt is turned on to move the pallet to the drilling module
2. *Drilling Module* – Two drilling spindles are advanced in the Z and X directions to make two pairs of holes into the workpiece.
3. *Robot Assembly Module* – The 6-axis arm picks up the rear panel from the pallet and place it on the processing bay. The arm places a PCB on the panel and switches to a smaller gripper so that it can pick up and install a fuse into the PCB. The arm switches to the original gripper to place the rear panel with the finished PCB back to the pallet.
4. *Mobile Station* – This module delivers boxes of PCBs to the IMPACT line.
5. *Robotino* – This automated guided vehicle transfers a box of PCBs from the Mobile Station to the Robot Assembly Module.
6. *Magazine Module* – This module places a front panel on the PCB.
7. *Pressing Module* – This module applies pressing force to seal the product.

This CPPS has a number of characteristics for demonstrating the need for digital twin development: (1) modelling continuous dynamics such as the 6-axis arm and cartesian robot movements, (2) choosing the right modelling strategies for the machines with different observabilities, (3) detecting faults such as unsatisfactory drilling operations due to wear and tear of a drill bit and misplacement of fuses on a PCB, (4) and real-time closed-loop control.

6.1   Modelling Continuous Dynamics of the Factory

This section focuses modelling the motion of the conveyor belt on the linear modules and the cartesian robot arm in the High-Bay Rack for the illustration purpose. The first model of the conveyor belt is shown in Fig. 5. This is the simplest possible case where the conveyor belt operates in either one of two macro states: *Idle* or *On* mode. When *TurnOn* signal is set high by the controller, the machine makes transition to state *On* after setting $v = 0.03$, which indicates the speed of the conveyor belt. The conveyor belt stays on as long as an incoming workpiece WP resets a timer via *Reset*. It goes *Idle* mode when *TurnOn* signal is unset by the controller or there were no incoming workpieces for the last x time period indicated by *TimeOut*.

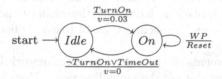

Fig. 5. An FSM model of the conveyor belt

The cartesian robot arm in the High-Bay Rack (HBR) is able to move in x, y, z directions simultaneously. Let us assume a designer has chosen Coloured Petri-Net (CPN) to model the robot since it features both concurrency and data manipulation for capturing the position of the arm in the cartesian space. The corresponding CPN model is shown in Fig. 6a. This CPN has four colours (data types) and two variables defined as follows.

```
type dir = | x | y | z
type pos = int
type U = dir * pos
type E = e
var d : dir
var i : pos
```

The three outgoing arcs from q_1 indicate the robot arm can move in x, y, z directions simultaneously when it is requested via input signals inM_x, inM_y, and inM_z. The initial marking at q_1 shows there are three tokens of type U. The plus sign indicates the tokens are combined into a multiset. Consider a token

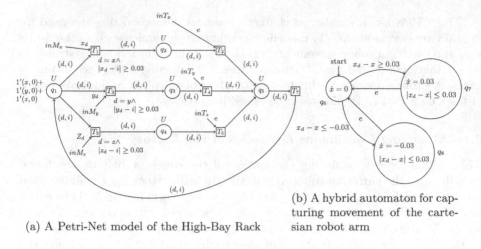

(a) A Petri-Net model of the High-Bay Rack

(b) A hybrid automaton for capturing movement of the cartesian robot arm

Fig. 6. Modelling the High-Bay Rack

travelling from q_1 to q_5 via transitions T_1 and T_2. The guard on T_1 ensures that it is only enabled when there is a token of type U in q_1 whose first element is x. When there is a request to move the arm in x direction, i.e. when $|x_d - i| \geq 0.03$, a token is added to the place q_2 indicating the model is now in the "moving" state. The colour set U on q_2 specifies type of tokens which may reside on the place.

One of the requirements of the digital twin framework is to provide a real-time view of the current state of the modelling plant. However at this point, the designer realises that he/she cannot easily capture continuous dynamics of the arm movement using CPN since it does not support the flow of continuous variables. Assume that the tool allows to mix different models so that the designer does not have to redesign the robot arm from scratch. In this case, HA can be added that runs together with the previously designed CPN as shown in Fig. 6b. Here, the HA makes a transition from q_6 to q_7 or q_8 when the final position x is greater or smaller than the current coordinate, respectively. States q_6 and q_7 show continuous evolution of variable x using its derivative $\dot{x}$, which is equivalent to i of the token (x, i) in q_2 in Fig. 6a. When the arm reaches its destination, i.e. $|x_d - x| \leq 0.03$, the HA makes transition back to q_6 while generating an event e. This event enables transition T_2 in Fig. 6a and results in returning of the token back to q_1 for serving the next request for x direction movement.

By supporting different levels of abstraction, a model can be enhanced further to incorporate finer details of operating modes. For example, after turning on a conveyor from the idle state, it may take some time until the motor reaches full rotational speed. Thus, the original conveyor belt modelled in an FSM can be further refined using HA, which is shown in Fig. 7a. Here, the system starts with the state Acc where the speed increases according to the flow variable $\dot{v} = 0.5$. When the speed reaches 1, a jump condition is satisfied that results in a state transition to $Const$. The system stays in this state as long as the next workpiece

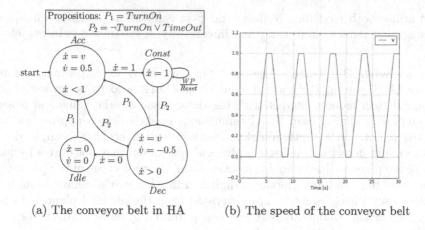

(a) The conveyor belt in HA   (b) The speed of the conveyor belt

Fig. 7. The conveyor belt refined

arrives before *TimeOut* or a controller resets signal *TurnOn*. The state *Dec* decelerates the speed of the conveyor belt until it reaches zero and the system stays in *Idle* until *TurnOn* signal is set by the controller. The change of speed of the conveyor belt over the period of 30 s is shown in Fig. 7b, which is modelled in Modelica. Similar approaches can be applied to model rest of the stations of the IMPACT line.

6.2   Open Problems

Addressing Discrepancy in a Model. Discrepancy between a model and a physical system may arise due to several reasons. For example, increase in complexity, choosing an inadequate modelling strategy, accumulation of errors over time, lack of documentation about the system, and lack of observable states as explained in Sect. 4. Unlike traditional software development process, where a set of test cases can be executed on a single development computer, functionalities of digital twins cannot be easily validated unless they are tested and compared with the real system, which is often difficult and time consuming. Moreover, it is unrealistic to validate every aspect of physical phenomenon of the twinned system – should a designer consider all the circuitries, properties of the materials used, geometry, multibody, and etc. of the IMPACT line? How much of the physical system can be abstracted without causing significant discrepancy? For example, after deploying the digital twin for the IMPACT line, discrepancies between the physical plant and the twin might be found based on feedback data collected from the two. In this case, there should be a facility to minimise the error by automatically adjusting the parameters of the twin or even modify the model during runtime. If the error cannot be minimised, the corresponding issue can be reported and possible solutions may be suggested to the user. To realise a faithful digital twin, therefore, the development framework should utilise both modelling (offline) and post-calibration (online) techniques to manage and reduce discrepancy and uncertainty in the digital twin model.

Interplay with Big Data. Arguably, big data plays an important role in Industry 4.0. However, there are still many questions need to be answered on how digital twin models interact with big data: what are the gains and losses when employing digital twin based simulations or data-driven approaches for predictive maintenance, decision making, fault detection, etc. For example, data analytics might detect anomalies in a physical system but may not have a formal model of the plant to draw possible solutions and the root-cause of the problem. On the other hand, a formal model of digital twin itself may not have an ability to deduce useful insights from data generated from the physical plant or high-fidelity simulation. Undoubtedly, there is a potential synergy between the big data and formal modelling of digital twin. Recently, big data topic in digital twin modelling has been recognised in several literature [11,28,38]. However, a concrete use-case scenarios need to be further investigated.

A concept of Data-driven and Model-based Design (DMD) is discussed in [35] which is an extension of the Model-Based Design (MBD) with elements of data-driven approaches such as machine learning and model learning. The main focus of DMD is to leverage the advances of AI while preserving merits of MBD approaches such as mathematical formalism and analysability. In particular, model learning [36] can be useful for building formal models of legacy (black-box) models or for analysing complex systems when there is a lack of tools. Nevertheless, scalability issue when increasing number of states in the system and its applicability for building hybrid system are still in question.

Integration of Heterogeneous Models. There should be a consistent way to combine heterogeneous models to support design of the "mixed-fidelity" digital twin. This requires the formal modelling framework that can capture physical behaviour in different levels of abstraction. In case of designing the IMPACT line, it would be easier for a designer to first model a behaviour of the system in coarser level, e.g. flow of workpieces between modules using Petri-Nets or abstracting continuous dynamics using macro states in FSM, and further refine individual modules using high-fidelity models as required. In this case, a consistent method for exchanging information between different models should be developed. For example, when combining two models in Fig. 6, it is crucial that the event e generated from the HA model is always captured in the Petri-Net model. This implies that the models should synchronise whenever the invariant condition $|x_d - x| \geq 0.03$ becomes unsatisfied. Implementation-wise, the FMI standard [5] can be employed for interconnecting the heterogeneous models and implementing a deterministic mechanism for synchronisation and data exchange.

Time-Critical Systems. Some of the cyber-physical production systems are time-critical systems, for example Surface-Mount Technology (SMT) placement equipment. In this case, the worst-case response time for communication between the twin and the physical system must be guaranteed and within a bounded time. Furthermore, the worst-case execution time of the twin and its controller should also be bounded and analysable. Many digital twin architectures found in literature rely on information flow through the cloud and the non time-critical network interfaces, which is not suitable to build time-critical applications. A software architecture that comprises time-critical components are required for certain types of application.

Security. Since digital twins are tightly coupled with physical environment, an attack on a such cyber-physical system may endanger people's safety and result in significant economic loss. Applications interact with digital twins to access sensor data and actuate the physical system when necessary (see Sect. 3). Since user applications can be a major source of security threat, a secure access control mechanism needs to be implemented for those that access digital twins. In summary, security aspects of digital twin should be studied in the areas of malicious activities detection, cryptography, resiliency to cyber attacks.

6.3 An Architecture for Digital Twin

To address the aforementioned issues, the desired capabilities of digital twin need to be clearly defined first which will be the basis for the development of the underlying software/hardware architecture (see Fig. 2). More specifically, we anticipate that through digital twin, users should be able to (1) *control* physical object, (2) *monitor and analyse* data for minimising discrepancy and uncertainties in a model, and (3) *simulate* the physical counterparts by instantiating digital twins in a cyber space. To achieve this, a basic design block will be introduced namely a digital twin component (DTC). It consists of a twin itself, a virtual controller, database for storing cyber and physical data, and a digital twin runtime that manages data collection and synchronisation between the twin and the physical object. Furthermore, DTC should support incremental update of the twin as well as the controller to handle discrepancies and uncertainties as much as possible. Multiple DTCs can be combined to create a bigger system and we plan to adopt Globally Asynchronous Locally Synchronous paradigm for their integration. On the highest level of the architecture, we plan to provide a set of services, for example DTC repository, DTC management (i.e. creation and disposal), analytics, and data access etc., with which more intelligent applications such as prognostic and health management and virtual commissioning can be developed. The digital twin framework therefore will consist of a tool and the architecture that enables the aforementioned capabilities for CPPS.

7 Conclusions

In this paper, we presented an overview and open research questions in digital twin development for cyber-physical production systems (CPPS). Digital twin is still a relatively new concept that requires more researches in the fields of modelling and integration with other technologies. We propose development of a tool that supports modelling CPPS in various levels of abstraction underpinned by formal mathematical models. The result is a mixed-fidelity digital twin which is a trade-off between accuracy and scalability. In future work, we plan to develop formal semantics for translating different models into an intermediate representation for analysis and code generation and implement a digital twin architecture described in Sect. 6.3 that enables control, monitoring, and simulation of physical plant in the cyber space.

References

1. Alam, K.M., El Saddik, A.: C2PS: a digital twin architecture reference model for the cloud-based cyber-physical systems. IEEE Access **5**, 2050–2062 (2017)
2. Alur, R., Dill, D.: The theory of timed automata. In: de Bakker, J.W., Huizing, C., de Roever, W.P., Rozenberg, G. (eds.) REX 1991. LNCS, vol. 600, pp. 45–73. Springer, Heidelberg (1992). https://doi.org/10.1007/BFb0031987
3. Berry, G., Gonthier, G.: The ESTEREL synchronous programming language: design, semantics. Implement. Sci. Comput. Program. **19**(2), 87–152 (1992)
4. Bliudze, S., Furic, S., Sifakis, J., Viel, A.: Rigorous design of cyber-physical systems. Softw. Syst. Model. 1–24 (2017)
5. Blochwitz, T., et al.: The functional mockup interface for tool independent exchange of simulation models. In: Proceedings of the 8th International Modelica Conference, Technical University, Dresden, Germany, pp. 105–114. No. 063, Linköping University Electronic Press (2011)
6. Brooks, C., et al.: Heterogeneous concurrent modeling and design in Java. Introduction to Ptolemy II, vol. 1. Technical report, Department of Electrical Engineering and Computer Science, California University, Berkeley (2008)
7. Fehling, R.: A concept of hierarchical Petri nets with building blocks. In: Rozenberg, G. (ed.) ICATPN 1991. LNCS, vol. 674, pp. 148–168. Springer, Heidelberg (1993). https://doi.org/10.1007/3-540-56689-9_43
8. Fritzson, P.: Principles of Object-Oriented Modeling and Simulation with Modelica 2.1. Wiley (2010)
9. Generic Electric: Digital Wind Farm. https://www.ge.com/renewableenergy/wind-energy/technology/digital-wind-farm
10. Glaessgen, E., Stargel, D.: The digital twin paradigm for future NASA and US air force vehicles. In: 53rd AIAA/ASME/ASCE/AHS/ASC Structures, Structural Dynamics and Materials Conference 20th AIAA/ASME/AHS Adaptive Structures Conference 14th AIAA, p. 1818 (2012)
11. Grieves, M., Vickers, J.: Digital twin: mitigating unpredictable, undesirable emergent behavior in complex systems. In: Kahlen, F.-J., Flumerfelt, S., Alves, A. (eds.) Transdisciplinary Perspectives on Complex Systems. LNCS, pp. 85–113. Springer, Cham (2017). https://doi.org/10.1007/978-3-319-38756-7_4
12. Henzinger, T.A.: The theory of hybrid automata. In: Inan, M.K., Kurshan, R.P. (eds.) Verification of Digital and Hybrid Systems, pp. 265–292. Springer, Heidelberg (2000). https://doi.org/10.1007/978-3-642-59615-5_13
13. Hoare, C.A.R., Jifeng, H.: Unifying Theories of Programming, vol. 14. Prentice Hall Englewood Cliffs, Upper Saddle River (1998)

14. Jensen, K., Kristensen, L.M.: Colored petri nets: a graphical language for formal modeling and validation of concurrent systems. Commun. ACM **58**(6), 61–70 (2015)
15. Kagermann, H., Helbig, J., Hellinger, A., Wahlster, W.: Recommendations for implementing the strategic initiative INDUSTRIE 4.0: securing the future of German manufacturing industry. Final report of the Industrie 4.0 working group. Forschungsunion (2013)
16. Larsen, P.G., et al.: Integrated tool chain for model-based design of cyber-physical systems: the INTO-CPS project. In: 2016 2nd International Workshop on Modelling, Analysis, and Control of Complex CPS (CPS Data), pp. 1–6. IEEE (2016)
17. Lee, E.A.: Cyber physical systems: design challenges. In: 2008 11th IEEE International Symposium on Object Oriented Real-Time Distributed Computing (ISORC), pp. 363–369. IEEE (2008)
18. Li, C., Mahadevan, S., Ling, Y., Wang, L., Choze, S.: A dynamic Bayesian network approach for digital twin. In: 19th AIAA Non-deterministic Approaches Conference, p. 1566 (2017)
19. Lopez, F., Shao, Y., Mao, Z.M., Moyne, J., Barton, K., Tilbury, D.: A software-defined framework for the integrated management of smart manufacturing systems. Manuf. Lett. **15**, 18–21 (2017)
20. MacDonald, C., Dion, B., Davoudabadi, M.: Creating a digital twin for a pump. ANSYS Advant. Issue **1**, 8 (2017)
21. Magargle, R., et al.: A simulation-based digital twin for model-driven health monitoring and predictive maintenance of an automotive braking system. In: Proceedings of the 12th International Modelica Conference, Prague, Czech Republic, 15–17 May, pp. 35–46. No. 132, Linköping University Electronic Press (2017)
22. Malik, A., Salcic, Z., Roop, P.S., Girault, A.: SystemJ: a GALS language for system level design. Comput. Lang. Syst. Struct. **36**(4), 317–344 (2010)
23. MarketsandMarkets: Digital twin market by end user (Aerospace and Defense, Automotive and Transportation, Home and Commercial, Electronics and Electricals/Machine Manufacturing, Energy and Utilities, Healthcare, Retail and Consumer Goods), and Geography (August 2017). http://www.reportsnreports.com/reports/1175159-digital-twin-market-by-end-user-aerospace-defense-automotive-transportation-home-commercial-electronics-electricals-machine-manufacturing-energy-utilities-healthcare-retail-consumer-goods-and-ge-st-to-2023.html
24. Moreno, A., Velez, G., Ardanza, A., Barandiaran, I., de Infante, Á.R., Chopitea, R.: Virtualisation process of a sheet metal punching machine within the industry 4.0 vision. Int. J. Interact. Des. Manuf. (IJIDeM) **11**(2), 365–373 (2017)
25. Negri, E., Fumagalli, L., Macchi, M.: A review of the roles of digital twin in CPS-based production systems. Procedia Manuf. **11**, 939–948 (2017)
26. Peterson, J.L.: Petri Net Theory and the Modeling of Systems. Prentice Hall PTR, Upper Saddle River (1981)
27. Potok, M., Chen, C.Y., Mitra, S., Mohan, S.: SDCWorks: a formal framework for software defined control of smart manufacturing systems. In: Proceedings of the 9th ACM/IEEE International Conference on Cyber-Physical Systems, pp. 88–97. IEEE Press (2018)
28. Qi, Q., Tao, F.: Digital twin and big data towards smart manufacturing and industry 4.0: 360 degree comparison. IEEE Access **6**, 3585–3593 (2018)
29. Ramchandani, C.: Analysis of asynchronous concurrent systems by Petri Nets. Technical report, Massachusetts Institute of Technology, Cambridge, Project MAC (1974)

30. Scaglioni, B., Ferretti, G.: Towards digital twins through object-oriented modelling: a machine tool case study. IFAC-PapersOnLine 613–618 (2018)
31. Schluse, M., Priggemeyer, M., Atorf, L., Rossmann, J.: Experimentable digital twins-streamlining simulation-based systems engineering for industry 4.0. IEEE Trans. Ind. Inf. **14**(4), 1722–1731 (2018)
32. Siemens: Digital twins bring real-life success. https://www.siemens.com/global/en/home/markets/machinebuilding/references/bausch-stroebel.html
33. Tao, F., Cheng, J., Qi, Q., Zhang, M., Zhang, H., Sui, F.: Digital twin-driven product design, manufacturing and service with big data. Int. J. Adv. Manuf. Technol. **94**(9–12), 3563–3576 (2018)
34. Tao, F., Zhang, M.: Digital twin shop-floor: a new shop-floor paradigm towards smart manufacturing. IEEE Access **5**, 20418–20427 (2017)
35. Tripakis, S.: Data-driven and model-based design. In: 2018 IEEE Industrial Cyber-Physical Systems (ICPS), pp. 103–108. IEEE (2018)
36. Vaandrager, F.: Model learning. Commun. ACM **60**(2), 86–95 (2017)
37. Wang, X.V., Kemény, Z., Váncza, J., Wang, L.: Human-robot collaborative assembly in cyber-physical production: classification framework and implementation. CIRP Ann. **66**(1), 5–8 (2017)
38. Zhuang, C., Liu, J., Xiong, H.: Digital twin-based smart production management and control framework for the complex product assembly shop-floor. Int. J. Adv. Manuf. Technol. **96**(1–4), 1149–1163 (2018)

Simulation and Tools

Subjecting Legacy Simulink Models to Timing Specifications

Andreas Naderlinger[✉]

Department of Computer Sciences, University of Salzburg, Salzburg, Austria
andreas.naderlinger@cs.uni-salzburg.at

Abstract. The interest in the logical execution time (LET) paradigm
has recently experienced a boost, especially in the automotive industry. This is because it is considered a practical candidate for migrat-
ing concurrent legacy software from single- to multi-core platforms by
introducing deterministic intra- and inter-core communication. In many
cases, the implementation of these individual software components roots
in MATLAB/Simulink, a modeling and simulation environment, where
the controller functionality is described with a block-oriented formalism
and simulated with synchronous reactive semantics. Considering LET
already in the modeling and simulation phase instead of deferring this to
the integration phase, as it is done now, is an important step towards the
idea of models being the single source of truth and to estimate the effect
of LET on end-to-end timing in cause-effect-chains at an early stage.
This paper presents two approaches of simulating software components
with LET semantics in Simulink. In contrast to previous work, which
deals with clean slate top-down approaches, we focus on legacy software
(in the form of Simulink models) that does not satisfy some of the initial
assumptions of the LET programming model.

Keywords: Timing specification · Simulink · Logical execution time

1 Introduction

Embedded real-time systems are proliferating. They find their way into almost
any area. In other sectors, where they have been around for decades, their amount
and complexity is ever increasing, and so are the costs for their development [9].
In order to cope with this growth in complexity, and to reduce development time
while at the same time increasing the quality of the software, model-based design
(MBD) processes have been proposed. The model-based methodology moves
away from manual low-level coding and is centered around abstract mathematical models. It aims at providing appropriate levels of abstraction and promotes
a clear separation between design and implementation level. Before code generators transform the model into executable (e.g., C-) code, the correctness of the
behavior is typically assessed in simulations. There is a variety of methodolo-
gies and model-based development tools with simulation capability, e.g. MAT-
LAB/Simulink, Scade, or UML-based ones such as SysML. In this work we focus

© Springer Nature Switzerland AG 2019
R. Chamberlain et al. (Eds.): CyPhy 2018/WESE 2018, LNCS 11615, pp. 51–70, 2019.
https://doi.org/10.1007/978-3-030-23703-5_3

on Simulink [23], an environment based on the synchronous block diagram (SBD) formalism, which is prevalent for modeling, simulating, and generating code for control systems, especially in the automotive and aerospace sector.

Here, the above mentioned increase of complexity and the accompanied growing demand for computing power has eventually led to a platform shift towards multi-core processors. Soon the performance of single-core processors won't be sufficient to keep pace with the needs of powertrain control systems, for example [6]. Along with this hardware migration, a substantial effort is required to migrate also the software. Control and software engineers are thus faced with the necessity of parallelizing single-core legacy code. At this, arising data consistency issues must be tackled properly and provisions must be made to guarantee the correct behavior along cause-effect chains.

The Logical Execution Timing (LET) programming model [7] was recently identified as a potential candidate to facilitate the migration from single- to multi-core architectures in the automotive sector [2, 6, 11]. Amongst other benefits, LET is a timing specification that introduces time- and value-deterministic inter-task communication across multiple cores. As the LET model clearly separates functionality from timing, it matches also well with principal ideas from MBD. Indeed, right from its introduction, LET was intended to be integrated with available MBD tools [4, 8].

For several years now, model-based design forms an established development approach in the field of embedded real-time systems and is considered best practice in many domains. Therefore, industries such as automotive have piled up huge amounts of legacy software, not only in the form of code, but also as (Simulink) models. In this work, we look at the question of how to subject such legacy Simulink artifacts to LET or other timing specifications. The remainder of this paper is structured as follows: We start with a comparison of assumptions made in the original LET model and typical characteristics of legacy systems. The section continues with a short introduction to Simulink. Subsequently, we discuss the applicability of an existing LET-based timing specification language called TDL and its Simulink integration in the context of legacy models in Sect. 2. In Sect. 3, we present a new approach, which is different in several respects. Section 4 concludes the paper.

1.1 The LET Programming Model vs. Legacy Systems

The Logical Execution Time (LET) paradigm, as introduced in Giotto [7], establishes an additional level of abstraction on top of the physical execution of computational tasks. It associates with each periodic task a logical execution time, that is equal to the task's period. All inputs are read only at the start of the LET (called the *release* time) and buffered locally. The actual (physical) execution of the task is started (and potentially preempted) any time during the LET at the discretion of the scheduler, but it must be (physically) finished before the end of the LET (called the *terminate* time). Only at the end of the LET, the task updates its outputs. Thus, the LET achieves a platform-independent observable temporal behavior, since input values used in a task do not change during execution and its output values remain constant between successive LET end points, regardless of potential preemptions or execution time variations. One approach for ensuring LET semantics at run-time is a virtual machine implementation (called E-Machine) that interprets a compiled version of the timing specification (called E-Code) [7]. The quintessence of the LET paradigm is extensive buffering. This ensures time- and value determinism [9].

As outlined in [18], the LET paradigm, which was proposed as a top-down development process for purely time-triggered systems, cannot be applied to legacy software systems without modifications. Typical legacy systems combine time- and event-triggered tasks with mixed priorities. Furthermore, they use shared memory (global variables, potentially updated by multiple tasks) for efficiency reasons, while the LET paradigm assumes variables that have a task-level scope. In order to be useful for industrial applications, the requirements for the LET model must be aligned with performance-oriented concerns of legacy systems, such as low latencies. Subsequent refinements of the LET model such as described in [17] and later also in [10] abandon the restriction that the LET is equal to the period, allowing much more flexible timing patterns and thus more realistic applications. As the LET of multiple tasks with the same period, for example, can now be staggered, the introduced end-to-end latencies are reduced. This is one of the variations to the original LET model that the presented approaches make use of. The plea for low memory overhead is another performance-oriented concern of legacy systems that is due to limitations of available memory in embedded devices.

1.2   Model-Based Development with Simulink

Simulink is a block-based modeling environment for dynamic systems, which supports the combination of a continuous representation of the physical plant together with discrete blocks that represent the controller functionality. In addition to a variety of predefined blocks, it is possible to add also custom blocks by implementing the so-called *S-Function* interface. During simulation, Simulink constantly evaluates the whole model and updates the individual signals according to the *synchronous reactive (SR)* model of computation [12] based on a fixed order of blocks derived during initialization. For the discrete controller part, a block (or a subsystem consisting of multiple and potentially further nested blocks) is either activated at periodic time instants based on its *sample time* parameter or *triggered* by the occurrence of a certain event, such as the transition of a data signal or the reception of a *function-call* signal. In particular since the widespread introduction of the AUTOSAR [1] standard also in model-based development, the top-level architecture of Simulink models tend to be based on or at least compatible with the triggered approach. This allows for AUTOSAR-compliant software architectures where every individual runnable of a software component (SW-C) is implemented by one triggered Simulink subsystem. As an alternative to triggered subsystems, also function-call subsystems or so-called *Simulink Function* blocks (not to be confused with S-Function blocks) can be used.

Typical legacy applications consist of a considerable amount of control functions (called runnables in the AUTOSAR context) which are distributed over a multitude of different models. The functional correctness of individual components is assessed in simulations under the *synchrony hypothesis* (zero execution/simulation time) before automatic code generators turn the blocks into C code functions. On the target platform, some real-time operating system schedules these functions, which now have varying execution times and concurrently operate on global variables, potentially on multiple cores. Thus additional provisions must be made at the model level or at the system integration level in order to ensure data consistency and time determinism [5]. We continue with how to achieve these properties by subjecting the model to the LET semantics defined in a timing specification, which is enforced also by a run-time system on a target platform.

2 Applicability of the TDL/Simulink Approach for Legacy Models

In the following discussion, we consider a specific Giotto inspired LET-model, namely the one of the Timing Definition Language (TDL). TDL takes over the general principles of Giotto, but makes several changes to the original model in order to increase its flexibility and its applicability in real-world scenarios. In the following we concentrate on features that are especially relevant for an application to legacy systems, and refer to the TDL report [22] for a detailed description and an explicit list of all syntactic and semantic differences to Giotto. The timing specification features of TDL have already been successfully applied to subject C-based legacy systems (using an FPP real-time OS such as OSEK or AUTOSAR OS) to LET semantics [18] with a specially developed Eclipse-based tool-chain. The Simulink integration [16], however, is based on the original TDL tool-chain which was mostly intended to be applied in clean slate top-down approaches, but not to legacy systems. In this section, we discuss the suitability of the TDL/Simulink integration and its representation of the LET run-time system in the context of legacy systems with characteristics as outlined above including event-triggered tasks and variables with multiple writers. Since the tool and the whole model generation- and development process is strongly dependent on assumptions that are originally taken from Giotto, the original specification format, and the corresponding compiler, this involves also a discussion about these aspects.

In Giotto computations are performed in *tasks* running logically in parallel and all data is stored and communicated over *ports*, i.e., typed variables in a global namespace. While TDL introduces a component model with separate namespaces, it takes over the concept of tasks and ports, which are partitioned into disjoint sets of *sensor* ports, *actuator* ports, and *task ports* for input, output, and state. Sensor ports are updated by the environment, while actuator and all task ports are updated by the (potentially multi-modal) TDL program. Data communication with the environment and between tasks is performed by dedicated *driver functions*, which are assumed to execute (logically) in zero time. They copy the value of a task output port or sensor port to a task input port or actuator port. Both LET models assume task-level scoped data (e.g., a task can only update its own output ports), while legacy systems typically assume globally visible and accessible variables. TDL introduces *global ports* that can be written by different tasks of the same mode. In principle, this allows two or more legacy functions to write to the same variable. However, the LET of these tasks must not overlap, which makes it unsuitable for the general case. The same principle holds also for actuator ports, as it must never occur that an actuator is written by two different tasks at the same logical time.

2.1 Flexible Time- and Accessory Event-Triggered Tasks in TDL

Besides being limited to time-triggered tasks only, the LET of a Giotto task is identical to its period and no offset can be specified. Most legacy systems in contrast, have time- as well as event-triggered tasks, and task precedencies can be defined by explicitly offsetting a task or by assigning different priorities to them. In Giotto, all tasks run logically in parallel and the timing specification of a periodic activity such as a task invocation is based on the mode period Π and the activity's frequency f. The task is then invoked f times per mode period, and the LET of all invocations is implicitly given by Π/f. In order to support task precedences and introduce a more flexible timing, TDL separates the LET of a task from its period. The LET interval of a TDL task must start at or after the beginning of the period (i.e., with an offset) and must end before or at the end of the period. This is expressed by a feature called *slot-selection*, which relaxes this rigid execution pattern by splitting the mode period into a sequence of slots $(s_1, \ldots, s_f)$ where each slot s_i has length (duration) Π/f. A task invocation is then associated to non-overlapping groups of contiguous slots.

Finally, TDL introduces so-called *asynchronous activities* to describe event-triggered tasks and their communication with periodic tasks. However, as opposed to periodic tasks, besides not having an associated LET, asynchronously executed tasks are treated as non-realtime activities with lower priority. This is in contrast to typical legacy systems with mixed priority and criticality level among both time- and event-triggered task sets. The limitation to low-priority event-triggered tasks is not immediately considered a decisive factor in the Simulink setting: Since TDL dismisses event-triggered functions as non-realtime activities, legacy priorities cannot be respected one to one. However, this holds true with priorities in Simulink in general. The role of priorities in RTOS-based legacy systems and Simulink models differs. In the former, the priority of a task might be a result of its rate. It is further used, for example, as a means for task precedencies and flow preservation, or to schedule task sets with mixed criticality. Simulink blocks have a priority property that influences the appearance of the block in the block update order, but only as long as the resulting order doesn't conflict with data-dependencies. Since without any further provisions (e.g., as done in [13]) Simulink executes functions in zero time, there is no need to ensure reactivity and schedulability via priorities. In a LET context, flow preservation among time-triggered tasks is ensured by appropriate LETs. TDL allows asynchronous activities of different priority. They can be taken over from the legacy event-triggered functions. However, all LET tasks will be executed with higher priority. In Simulink this is only recognized at time instants where a LET start or end coincides with the occurrence of an interrupt triggering an asynchronous activity.

2.2 Supporting Independent Task Periods and Offsets

In order to model a legacy application with the existing TDL/Simulink approach, the execution patterns of the legacy tasks must be expressible by TDL's slot selection notation. Note that this kind of realization introduces dependencies between the timing specification of all activities in a mode and the mode period. It may also have non-obvious implications on the size of the E-Code.

In general, there exist different strategies to derive a TDL mode specification for a set of legacy tasks initially described by their period and their offset, as soon as a LET has been defined for each. As a first possibility, all tasks are allocated to a single TDL module with one mode. The mode period Π is the hyperperiod of all time-triggered legacy tasks, i.e., the lcm of their individual periods. Inside the *mode declaration*, for each legacy task T_i with period π_i, offset o_i, and LET L_i, we define a task invocation for this very task with an execution frequency $f_i = \frac{\Pi}{\gamma_i}$, where $\gamma_i = \gcd(o_i, \ o_i + L_i)$ and from the resulting slots $S = (s_1, s_2, \ldots, s_{f_i})$, we select a series of individual slots $s_{\frac{o_i}{\gamma_i}+1}, s_{\frac{o_i+p_i}{\gamma_i}+1}, \ldots$ or a series of slot intervals (called groups) $[s_{\frac{o_i}{\gamma_i}+1}, s_{\frac{o_i+L_i}{\gamma_i}}], [s_{\frac{o_i+p_i}{\gamma_i}+1}, s_{\frac{o_i+L_i+p_i}{\gamma_i}}], \ldots$ to match the original execution pattern (see the example below). Pooling together all tasks in a single module/mode may result in a large E-Code representation because of mixing frequent and infrequent tasks. At the other extreme, we may declare for each task T_i a separate module M_i, with a mode period equal to the task period ($\Pi_i = \pi_i$) and a single slot $\frac{o_i}{\gamma_i} + 1$. This results in a set of i minimal individual E-Code structures, which the E-Machine works off in parallel.

2.3 Supporting Multiple Writers in a Single-Writer Model

Aside from the timing aspect, also the data-dependencies between legacy functions must be expressible in TDL. In a scenario, where a particular variable is written only by a single legacy function, the LET specification of TDL is close to its designated use. Every legacy time- and event-triggered function f is covered by a dedicated TDL task. A legacy variable v that is read/written by legacy function f is represented by an input/output port of the TDL task of f. Alternatively, instead of a task output port, a global port can be used. The execution pattern of a time-triggered function is specified in a TDL mode declaration using slot selection as described above. The *asynchronous declaration* section is used to connect a task representing an event-triggered function to a particular *interrupt ID*. Data-flow is expressed with function parameters inside the mode and asynchronous specifications.

The far more realistic scenario is however the case where one legacy variable is allowed to be written by multiple tasks. Since TDL does not allow to have ports written by multiple tasks at one particular time instant, we do not introduce a representation of the legacy variable inside the TDL program, but in what the language report [22] calls the *environment*. We still achieve data consistency and deterministic behavior with LET semantics, by wrapping the legacy functions into tasks with in- and output ports and imposing the access to the legacy variable on dedicated TDL sensors and actuators. A sensor or actuator defines a read-only or write-only variable which represents a particular value or controls the setting of a particular value in the physical environment, respectively. The connection between the TDL ports and the environment is established by external getter or setter functions that are called at particular times according to the timing specification. While typically they operate some A/D or D/A device, in our case they access a memory area that represents a particular legacy variable. Since similar restrictions regarding multiple accesses for updating output ports apply also to actuator updates, we typically require a bunch of different actuators all accessing the representation of one and the same legacy variable in the setter function.

Consequently, a valid TDL realization for a particular legacy specification defines for every legacy function a TDL task declaration with one input port for every variable that is read and one output port for every variable that is written by the function. Additionally, it defines for each task input port a separate sensor port that is used as data source for the release driver of the task and a separate actuator port that is updated by an explicit actuator update at every LET end of the task. While this is the most stable realization with respect to changes in the timing specifications, it adds even more ports and drivers and thus run-time and memory overhead to the LET middleware. A more efficient configuration shares sensors/actuators for a particular variable between tasks that never start/end at the same logical time. Likewise, global output ports can be used jointly instead of individual task-level output ports for tasks with non-overlapping LETs.

Multiple coinciding drivers of the same category (e.g., terminate drivers that are executed at LET ends) appear in the E-Code in the order in which the corresponding TDL constructs (e.g., tasks) were declared. This corresponds to priorities of drivers (within the same category) and allows one to influence from which task a legacy variable should be updated last at a particular logical time in the multi-writer case. Note that due to the period-equals-LET semantic of Giotto multiple coinciding LET ends are inevitable, while in TDL such cases can be avoided by design.

2.4   Example

We consider a simple example with a single legacy variable a that is accessed by two time-triggered tasks $t6$ ($\pi = 6, o = 2, L = 3$) and $t8$ ($\pi = 8, o = 1, L = 2$), and one event-triggered task $t0$ activated by some event (interrupt $ir0$) with low priority (0). While $t6$ and $t8$ both read and write the variable, $t0$ only writes to it. Figure 1 shows the LETs for the time-triggered tasks and a sample activation

Listing 1.1. TDL program (.tdl) for a single variable accessed by three tasks.

```
module M {
  sensor double sens_a uses get_a;

  actuator double act_a_t6 uses set_a_t6;
  actuator double act_a_t8 uses set_a_t8;
  actuator double act_a_t0 uses set_a_t0;

  public task t6 {
    input double in_a;
    output double out_a;
    uses t6(in_a, out_a);
  }

  public task t8 {
    input double in_a;
    output double out_a;
    uses t8(in_a, out_a);
  }

  public task t0 {
    output double out_a;
    uses t0(out_a);
  }

  start mode m [period=24 ms] {
    task [freq=24, slots=3−5|9−11|15−17|21−23] t6 {in_a := sens_a;}
    task [freq=24, slots=2−3|10−11|18−19] t8 {in_a := sens_a;}
    actuator [freq=24, slots=3−5|9−11|15−17|21−23] act_a_t6 := t6.out_a;
    actuator [freq=24, slots=2−3|10−11|18−19] act_a_t8 := t8.out_a;
  }

  asynchronous {
    [interrupt=ir0, priority=0] t0(); act_a_t0 := t0.out_a;
  }
}
```

point of the event-triggered task. A valid and minimal TDL program for this setup is given in Listing 1.1. Note that *t6* and *t8* have a LET end at the same time instant, which requires separate actuator ports.

2.5   Simulink Representation

Once a valid TDL program has been derived for a given legacy application using the mapping strategy presented above, the TDL/Simulink tool-chain [15] can be used to generate the simulation model containing a Simulink implementation of the LET run-time system. This tool-chain assumes an empty Simulink model where the timing behavior is specified with a graphical editor that is integrated and synchronized with Simulink, similarly to the Stateflow extension. The graphical editor is syntax driven and geared to the TDL semantics described in [22]. Optionally, one can import the timing specification from a textual description in .tdl format (see Listing 1.1). The Simulink integration is compatible with TDL version 1.5 and hence supports the features described above (global output ports, slot selection, asynchronous activities). A Simulink model that implements the TDL program in Listing 1.1 is shown in Fig. 2. The green blocks stem from the

TDL-Simulink library, they represent a TDL module (M) and a TDL interrupt ($ir0$) for triggering an asynchronous activity. Blocks in gray are used to trigger the asynchronous task function $t0$ and to visualize variable a in a Scope block. The blocks in orange represent elements that must be added specifically for the usage with legacy systems and are described further below.

The LET run-time model, which is generated automatically inside the subsystem M by the TDL tool-chain, is shown in Fig. 3. For a clearer arrangement, signals are routed through Goto/From blocks. The right part of the figure shows an E-Machine implementation consisting of two parameterized S-Functions implementing the E-Code interpreter and a series of control-flow signals for triggering subsystems on the left. The splitting in two S-Functions together with well placed unit delay blocks avoids data dependency violations (aka algebraic loops) while guaranteeing the correct timing behavior [16]. The driver area contains all necessary port copy operations, which are implemented in triggered subsystems that simply forward the inputs to the outputs. Triggering such a subsystem corresponds to executing a function containing a sequence of assignments. Each section corresponds either to a release driver, a terminate driver, or a driver to access a sensor or actuator. The task function area contains one triggered subsystem for each task. They are implemented by the user and may represent subsystems containing legacy components. There is another area that simply maps signals to different names. While this whole section is unnecessary in this particular example, in general it implements multi-mode support. TDL is a language for specifying multi-rate multi-mode systems. It supports tasks to be executed with mode specific LETs and actuators with different update frequencies. Executing a task in different modes, for example, leads to additional drivers that write to the same port. As Simulink does not allow multiple blocks to write to the same signal directly, instead the drivers and assignments are translated into static single assignment (SSA) form [20], where the Φ-function for choosing the right signal path is implemented by a *Merge* block. We use the same principle to represent legacy variables implemented by the orange blocks in Fig. 2. Sensors and actuators that belong to the same legacy variable have to be connected. Essentially, this resulting signal implements the getter/setter functions to connect to the same data item (i.e., variable a in this example).

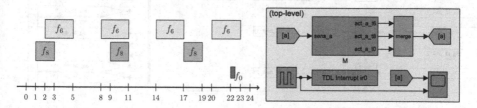

Fig. 1. LETs for f_6 and f_8 and activation time for f_0.

Fig. 2. Simulink model for the example in Listing 1.1. (Color figure online)

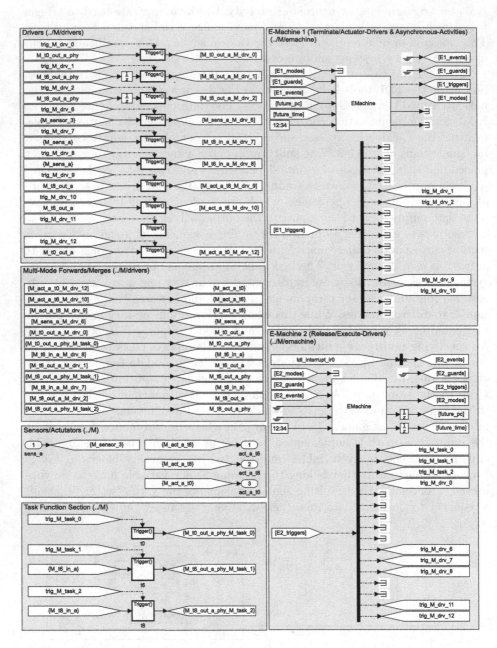

Fig. 3. The generated LET run-time for the example in Listing 1.1 (i.e., the content of subsystem M of Fig. 2).

To summarize, with the exception that event-triggered tasks cannot have a LET and that priorities between time- and event-triggered tasks cannot be fully preserved at LET boundaries in the general case, the TDL/Simulink approach is capable of simulating legacy systems with multiple writers to the same variable. However, considering that the legacy system contains a single variable that is accessed by three tasks, the generated LET model is disproportionately complex. It involves 13 different drivers and around 40 signals referring to one single legacy variable. At least, the TDL-based implementation supports legacy systems with a multi-mode timing specification with no further effort. Some indications on the model size and the simulation overhead that comes with this approach for a real application are discussed in Sect. 3.6.

3   A Puristic Approach: LET4Simulink (with Spec/c)

This section presents a new approach to simulate LET behavior in Simulink. As a first important difference, it is not based on an existing LET-based DSL such as TDL. This makes it particularly flexible and amenable to represent legacy systems. The presented workflow follows a specification-driven approach, which may start out with a minimal description of a legacy configuration describing the existing functions and their access to data. This specification is then augmented and refined in further iterations, for example, by introducing LETs for individual functions. The application to a Simulink model is then only one (final) step in the development process that we envision to be centered around one single source of information. For this reason, we have conceived a minimalistic specification language and a plug-in based compiler infrastructure called *Spec* and *Spec/c*, respectively. It must be noted however, that for the realization of LET semantics in Simulink, the usage of the Spec format is not a requirement.

3.1   Specification-Driven Development with Spec/c

The *Spec* language is not tailored to this particular use-case of specifying legacy systems and their timing behavior. So per se there are no keywords that introduce variables or functions, for example. Instead, the keywords and thus the allowed items as well as their mandatory or optional properties are described in a meta specification in the same format. A main feature is the extensibility and the ability for the specification to be refined during the development process (if the setting of the meta configuration allows to do so). Allowing the specification to be developed in an incremental way, rudimentarily gives consideration to the different competences that are involved in the process. It also reflects the fact that information about a particular system becomes available at different points in time during the development. Individual Spec/c plug-ins may add to the specification and may also introduce new meta-information. This stepwise extension and refinement allows us, for example, to separate information about the general architecture of the LET run-time system from platform-specific aspects such as a concrete implementation in Simulink. The individual steps in the development process, for example, are implemented by separate plug-ins. The same holds true for different simulation environments. In addition to Simulink, other simulation environments that have an appropriate API to generate models programmatically include Ptolemy or Scicos/Xcos.

In the following we start with a short illustration of the Spec language by reconsidering the example from Sect. 2.4. We continue with a LET run-time system that is based on periodic drivers and optimized w.r.t. the number of required buffers. We further outline a Simulink implementation of the run-time system, which differs from the one presented in Sect. 2 in several respects. For example, it is not based on classic Simulink signals. Instead it uses *Data Store* blocks to represent legacy variables. Also, it does not use an E-Machine implementation that, although it is a standardized approach for realizing LET-behavior across different platforms, hides the actual triggerings and program logic in a customized and proprietary *S-Function*. In lieu thereof, this approach is based exclusively on standard Simulink blocks. It must be noted, however, that this design decision is not carved in stone and that the current triggering, for example, could be easily replaced by an E-Machine implementation.

3.2   Refining a Legacy Specification with LET

As a first prerequisite, we specify language elements that will allow us to express the required information of our legacy system with the meta specification in Listing 1.2. This meta information introduces a number of valid specification elements together with their mandatory and optional properties. For example, a **data** element represents a particular legacy variable, whereas **function** is used to describe legacy functions together with their **input**- and **output** variables taken from the list of defined **data** elements as well as further standard properties. The @ sign is used to restrict the set of allowed elements. Alternatively, those data dependencies can also be described in separate elements that *refine* existing functions (see below). The **extern** attribute is used as an indicator for the code generation in later steps. Finally, the **event** element is used to introduce events and associate them to functions. The keyword **modifier** and **int** represent predefined elements. Each element in the meta section introduces a separate namespace in which all defined elements must have a unique identifier.

Listing 1.2. Spec: Meta section for the description of the legacy system.

```
meta {
  data [optional=(extern@modifier)];
  function [optional=(priority@int, period@int, offset@int,
                      in@data, out@data, extern@modifier)];
  event [required=(target)];
}
```

In the following, we consider the example from Sect. 2.4. The specification for the legacy system is given in Listing 1.3. Note that the highlighted keywords are not defined in the core language, but in the meta specification of Listing 1.2 above.

Listing 1.3. Spec: Legacy specification for the example above.

```
extern data a; /* legacy variable */

extern function [in=(a), out=(a)] { /* legacy functions */
  f6 [period=6, offset=2, priority=3];
  f8 [period=8, offset=1, priority=4];
}

extern function f0 [priority=2, out=(a)]; /* legacy function */

event ir0 [target@function=f0]; /* event for triggering functions defined above */
```

Later in the development process, some of the previously defined functions can be refined to follow LET semantics. Listing 1.4 extends the meta information and introduces an additional LET attribute to the two time-triggered functions. This refinement of the system specification completes the input to the process. Further additions and refinements to the specification for the described example are exclusively generated by Spec/c compiler plug-ins as described below.

Listing 1.4. Spec: LET refinement for Listing 1.3 (incl. an additional meta element)

```
meta LET@function [required=(refine@modifier, let@int)];

refine LET {
  f6 [let=3];
  f8 [let=2];
}
```

3.3 A LET Run-Time with Optimal Buffers and Periodic Drivers

Typically, ensuring LET semantics is based on extensive buffering. Therefore, the default *(buffer everything)* approach, leads to a non-negligible memory overhead [18]. This is especially true, when mapping a legacy system to a LET model that assumes function-local memory and (rightly) restricts the write-access to ports as described in Sect. 2, such that additional sensor- and actuator ports need to be introduced atop of the already required task ports. Each sensor, each actuator, and each task input port result in one additional variable and each task- or global-output port in even two additional variables (one private and one that is updated at the LET end only). One can readily see for this toy example with a single legacy variable that for an embedded platform the default approach is not applicable to industrial-sized systems with several thousand variables. In [18,19] we presented a systematic transformation approach of a legacy system written in C to satisfy the LET constraints with a special focus on memory efficiency. The presented buffer analysis method is also applicable and useful in the Simulink setting, although for a simulation environment, the additional memory introduced for buffering is not as much of a concern as on an embedded platform. Most importantly, we obtain a Simulink implementation that matches the implementation on the target platform, which is particularly beneficial.

In conventional C-based systems, the run-time to ensure LET semantics consists of a set of variables implementing the buffers, and a set of functions that perform copy operations between the individual variables. These functions are then triggered at the correct times (e.g., at LET start/end). A platform-independent Spec representation of the run-time system of the above example is given in Listing 1.5 (the meta section is omitted). The run-time consists of a list of buffers that are derived from a buffer analysis that takes the LET placements of reader and writer tasks of a particular variable into account [18]. Furthermore, the analysis determines if functions can use the original legacy variable instead of a buffer without violating the specified behavior, or if multiple functions can share a single buffer. The output of this analysis is a minimal set of buffers required to ensure LET semantics. It further optimizes the number of actual program variables that are required to implement these buffers. In the particular LET placement of the example in Sect. 2.4, every function indeed needs a distinct buffer that each must be implemented by a separate variable (*implVar*). The drivers for each function fall into three categories: *release, execute,* and *terminate*. The release and the terminate driver assigns each output variable the value of the input variable at the matching index in the lists *in* and *out*. The execute driver calls the given function and conceptually uses the values of the list of input variables as actual parameters and assigns the return values to the respective variables in the list of output variables. Release and terminate drivers can be thought of the same, however with $|out| = |in|$ and using the identity as the function being called.

Listing 1.5. Spec: The generated LET run-time.

```
buffer [variable=(a)] {
  f6_a [function=(f6)];
  f8_a [function=(f8)];
}

implVar f6_a [buffer=(f6_a)];
implVar f8_a [buffer=(f8_a)];

driverType {release; execute; terminate;}

driver {
  rel_f6 [out=(f6_a), in=(a), type=release];
  exec_f6 [out=(f6_a), in=(f6_a), call=f6, type=execute];
  term_f6 [out=(a), in=(f6_a), type=terminate];
  rel_f8 [out=(f8_a), in=(a), type=release];
  exec_f8 [out=(f8_a), in=(f8_a), call=f8, type=execute];
  term_f8 [out=(a), in=(f8_a), type=terminate];
}
```

The triggering mechanism of the drivers is implementation specific. In an E-Machine based approach, the drivers would be called as specified by the E-Code. In this work, we follow a different strategy, by using a periodic timer for each individual trigger (see Listing 1.6). All triggers for a function execute with the function period. The trigger for the release driver has an offset equal to the function offset, while the terminate trigger is additionally shifted by the function's LET. The offset of the execute trigger must be within the closed interval starting with the release and ending with the terminate trigger.

Listing 1.6. Spec: A sample trigger declaration for the drivers in Listing 1.5.

```
trigger@driver [period=6] { rel_f6 [offset=2]; exec_f6 [offset=2]; term_f6 [offset=5]; }
trigger@driver [period=8] { rel_f8 [offset=1]; exec_f8 [offset=1]; term_f8 [offset=3]; }
```

3.4   Spec Generation: Simulink Representation

The Simulink representation of the system is obtained by building a model where the conceptual elements from above, such as *data* or *driver*, are mapped to standard Simulink blocks. This is done in two steps. In a first step, the specification is augmented by additional elements that are tailored to Simulink, such as a notion for a Simulink block, signal, or library component. The purpose of this step, is to obtain a compact representation of the final Simulink model, where relevant (functional) properties are separated from layouting properties, which are specified in separate *refine* Spec elements, for example. This allows us to have a textual representation of the model providing benefits for versioning and model comparison. In a second (trivial) step, the derived specification is turned into a Simulink model, for example, by translating it into a MATLAB (.m) file containing the commands for building the model. A Simulink model for the example above is shown in Fig. 4. The blue areas are generated automatically. The gray blocks are added by hand to trigger the execution of the event-triggered task and to show the value of the legacy variable for debugging purposes. The green area shows the legacy Simulink system. Since the legacy functions $f6, f8, f0$ and the legacy variable a were marked as *extern* in the specification, no extra (mock) blocks have been created for them in the transformation process. We assume that functions in the legacy specification correspond to *Simulink Functions*, which were introduced in MATLAB R2014b. They accommodate a software/code-oriented rather than a data-flow/signal-based modeling view. However, the presented approach is independent of the representation of the task implementations. Legacy variables as well as buffers are represented by a *Data Store Memory* block. A trigger for executing a driver is realized as a *Pulse Generator* with an appropriately set period and phase delay. The drivers themselves are implemented in triggered subsystems being activated at the rising edge of the trigger. Note that the signals between triggers and drivers have been routed via pairs of From/Goto blocks for debugging purposes. For triggers that execute at time zero (offset $= 0$), it must be ensured that the *initial trigger signal state* property is changed to zero. Otherwise, for compatibility reasons, Simulink does not evaluate the trigger in the first evaluation.

The implementation of the drivers is shown in Fig. 5. On activation, the release and terminate drivers perform the copy operations. Each assignment corresponds to a connection between a *Data Store Read* block and a *Data Store Write* block with inherited sample time. These two blocks implicitly read/write data from/to the data store memory block with the corresponding label at the top-level without requiring signal connections. An execute driver contains a *Function Caller* block that has its input arguments and return values connected to data store read and write blocks, respectively. It is important to note that the access to the data stores must be performed inside the triggered subsystem and that there are no In-/Outport connections to the surrounding subsystem (as, for example, in the signal-based approach described in Sect. 2). In contrast to *From/Goto* blocks, data store blocks do have an autonomous sample time that would lead to a wrong behavior in almost all cases, if not contained in a triggered subsystem. A sample implementation of the legacy functions and the resulting output for the duration of one hyperperiod (24) for the given LET configuration is shown in the lower part of Fig. 5, where the blue signal shows the value of variable a and the red signal shows the activation of the interrupt $ir0$ at time 22. For comparison, the dashed black line shows the value of variable a with standard Simulink semantics (zero execution-time, without LET buffers and drivers).

Execution Order and Priorities. Since multiple drivers can execute at the same simulation time, the order of execution is important. The LET paradigm dictates the order of actions at one logical time instant as follows: *task terminations (output port updates)* → *actuator updates* → *task releases (input port updates)* → *task executions*. In an E-Machine based implementation, this order is readily enforced by the E-Code. In an implementation with triggers represented by multiple individual blocks, as in our case, it must be ensured that the block order that Simulink derives during initialization complies with the required sequence of actions. Primarily, the block order depends on data-flow and whether the block is of type Moore or Mealy (called direct- or non-direct-feedthrough), but is unpredictable for independent blocks (they execute *"in no particular order"* [23]). However, one can explicitly assign priorities to blocks, which the simulation engine will honor unless data-dependencies are violated. In the LET model section, it is enough to prioritize the triggered subsystem blocks in order to enforce the correct LET semantics. A valid order of the remaining blocks is then automatically derived by the simulation engine. It is important to note that in a setup, where variables might be written by multiple tasks, also the execution order of individual terminate drivers is relevant, if LET end times coincide or also when an event-triggered task writes to the same variable. Values of higher priority drivers (having a lower block order) are overwritten by those produced by low priority drivers (having a high block order). As a consequence, priorities should by all means be explicitly set in the specification. Note that a lack of an explicitly set priority property does not necessarily result in a low priority (later block execution). That is why care must be taken when adding additional data store read blocks that are driving a scope block for debugging purposes, for example, as it makes a difference if the drivers executed before or afterwards at a particular time instant. This motivates the automatically generated *Debug* area in Fig. 4.

3.5   Beyond Single-Mode, Single-Core, and Zero-Execution-Time

In a standard E-Machine based approach, multiple modes are represented by multiple sections in the E-Code. During simulation, solely the E-Machine, which periodically evaluates mode switch conditions and then jumps between these sections, is responsible for implementing the multimodal behavior. Depending on the current section, the E-Machine either executes the drivers at different times or even executes an alternative set of drivers. The approach with standard

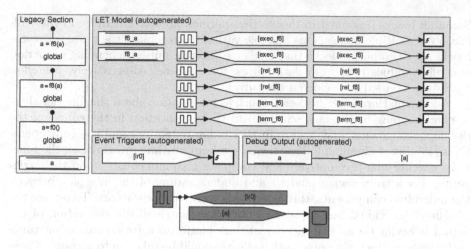

Fig. 4. Simulink model with legacy functions/variables (green area), the generated LET run-time (blue area), and user-added (gray) blocks for triggering *ir*0 and debugging. (Color figure online)

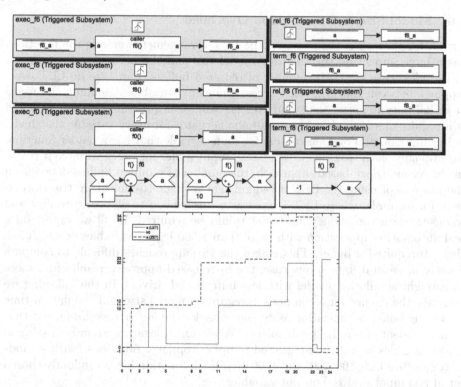

Fig. 5. Auto-generated contents of the individual subsystems of Fig. 4 (blue areas), a sample implementation for the legacy functions (green areas), and values for variable *a* with LET (blue signal) and without LET (dashed black signal) over one hyperperiod. (Color figure online)

Simulink blocks described in this section permits greater flexibility in the realization of multiple modes. One possible variant is to replace the pulse generator blocks by customized blocks that generate variable pulses depending on period and offset values read from data stores, for example. Alternatively, *Stateflow blocks* can be used to decide on the current mode.

Adding platform-specific details (such as information about the functionality-to-core mapping or the task schedule) to the specification in the course of the development process, may lead to further buffer reductions and less copy operations [19]. Since Simulink follows the zero-execution-time principle, all the functions execute non-preemptively and complete instantaneously upon their triggering. For a truly deeper analysis and understanding of the interplay between the individual components, this behavior is rather unsatisfactory. To retrace the benefit of individual buffers, and to obtain a more realistic simulation of the actual behavior on an embedded real-time platform, software execution times and scheduling including preemption effects should be taken in to account. These two aspects can be combined with the presented approach and are described for software-in-the-loop simulations in [13, 14] or in [3].

3.6 Model Size and Simulation Overhead

For both approaches, the choice of the LET arrangements among the functions has a large impact on the resulting model size and the performance overhead. In the ideal case w.r.t. the number of required buffers, there are no LET overlappings between functions that access the same variable. Assuming the usage of global output ports, the standard LET approach presented in Sect. 2 would still require one such global port and one actuator for every variable that has a writer function and one sensor port for each variable that has a reader function. Additionally, each task requires one task input buffer for every variable it reads. In the second (Spec-based) approach, the number of required buffers depends on the purpose of using the LET paradigm. For a single-to-multi-core transformation, for example, where LET is used as a mechanism to enforce causality and to ensure data consistency, no buffer would be required. In [6] we report on a real automotive application with more than 1,500 legacy variables of which less than 10 required a buffer. This makes the two approaches difficult to compare exactly in general, but in any case, the Spec-based approach results in a more lightweight simulation model with less buffers and drivers. In the following we still take the chance for a comparison regarding model size and simulation time by setting buffer optimization aside and consider the *buffer everything* case that is independent of any LET alignment. We assume a legacy system consisting of 1,500 variables and 9 time-triggered (empty) top-level functions (with periods of $1, 2, 5, 10, 20, 50, 100, 200$, and $1000\,ms$). Each function has a randomly chosen set of 300 input and 150 output variables.

The generated TDL/Simulink model consists of more than 45,000 model elements (29,624 blocks and 16,211 signals). Simulation runs (in *Normal* mode) for 1, 10, 50, and 100 s simulation time take approximately 12, 15, 28, and 44 s of real-time. The generated Spec model consists of about 10,000 model elements (7,321 blocks and 2,754 signals). The simulation of this model takes approximately 4, 8, 25, and 48 s of real-time, respectively. The data suggests that the simulation initialization, which includes determination of block order etc, is more efficient for the smaller Spec model. However, the simulation loop of the E-Machine based TDL/Simulink approach slightly outperforms the chosen run-time implementation of the Spec approach. As a first cause, tests showed that the usage of data store blocks instead of plain signals has a negative impact on the performance. For a sound performance discussion however, detailed tests are required where all the available optimization parameters are considered. As mentioned above, these results don't take the optimization potential of the Spec based approach w.r.t. the number of required buffers into account.

4   Conclusion

The Logical Execution Time (LET) paradigm is well on the way to facilitate a smooth transition from single- to multi-core platforms in the automotive industry. While the exact implications on the development process, which involves many different parties from diverse professions in circular dependencies, are not clear to date, an involvement of MATLAB/Simulink, as the de-facto development and simulation environment in this domain is indisputable. While the first integration approach of the LET semantic in Simulink goes back to 2003 [21] and recently LET has been applied also to legacy systems on the C-code level [18], the relevance of legacy artifacts in a model-driven development process (e.g., Simulink models) has been neglected so far. In this paper, we discussed on an existing LET-based language called TDL and its tool-chain, which bases on a clean slate approach, and its applicability for legacy models. We presented an alternative approach that is more flexible and allows developers to subject legacy models to the LET semantics in an efficient and transparent way. The approach is based on a concise specification language supporting incremental refinements, which aims to address the dependencies and the stepwise evolution observed in this interweaved development process.

References

1. AUTOSAR (2018). http://www.autosar.org
2. Beckert, M., Möstl, M., Ernst, R.: Zero-time communication for automotive multi-core systems under SPP scheduling. In: Proceedings of Emerging Technologies and Factory Automation (ETFA), Berlin, Germany, September 2016
3. Cremona, F., Morelli, M., Di Natale, M.: TRES: a modular representation of schedulers, tasks, and messages to control simulations in simulink. In: Proceedings of the 30th Annual ACM Symposium on Applied Computing, SAC 2015. ACM, New York (2015)
4. Derler, P., Naderlinger, A., Pree, W., Resmerita, S., Templ, J.: Simulation of LET models in simulink and ptolemy. In: Choppy, C., Sokolsky, O. (eds.) Monterey Workshop 2008. LNCS, vol. 6028, pp. 83–92. Springer, Heidelberg (2010). https://doi.org/10.1007/978-3-642-12566-9_5

5. Di Natale, M., Guo, L., Zeng, H., Sangiovanni-Vincentelli, A.: Synthesis of multi-task implementations of simulink models with minimum delays. IEEE Trans. Ind. Inform. **6**(4), 637–651 (2010)
6. Hennig, J., von Hasseln, H., Mohammad, H., Resmerita, S., Lukesch, S., Nader-linger, A.: Towards parallelizing legacy embedded control software using the LET programming paradigm. In: 2016 IEEE Real-Time and Embedded Technology and Applications Symposium (RTAS), WIP, Vienna, Austria, April 2016
7. Henzinger, T., Horowitz, B., Kirsch, C.: Giotto: a time-triggered language for embedded programming. Proc. IEEE **91**, 84–99 (2003)
8. Henzinger, T., Kirsch, C., Sanvido, M.A.A., Pree, W.: From control models to real-time code using Giotto. IEEE Control Syst. Mag. **23**(1), 50–64 (2003)
9. Henzinger, T.A., Sifakis, J.: The embedded systems design challenge. In: Misra, J., Nipkow, T., Sekerinski, E. (eds.) FM 2006. LNCS, vol. 4085, pp. 1–15. Springer, Heidelberg (2006). https://doi.org/10.1007/11813040_1
10. Kloda, T., d'Ausbourg, B., Santinelli, L.: EDF schedulability analysis for an extended timing definition language. In: Proceedings of the 9th IEEE International Symposium on Industrial Embedded Systems, SIES 2014, Pisa, Italy, 18–20 June 2014, pp. 30–40 (2014)
11. Kluge, F., Schoeberl, M., Ungerer, T.: Support for the logical execution time model on a time-predictable multicore processor. SIGBED Rev. **13**(4), 61–66 (2016)
12. Lee, E.A., Seshia, S.A.: Introduction to Embedded Systems - A Cyber-Physical Systems Approach, 1 edn (2010)
13. Naderlinger, A.: Simulating execution time variations in MATLAB/Simulink. In: 2017 Winter Simulation Conference (WSC), pp. 1491–1502, December 2017
14. Naderlinger, A.: Simulating preemptive scheduling with timing-aware blocks in Simulink. In: Design, Automation and Test in Europe Conference and Exhibition, DATE 2017, Lausanne, Switzerland, 27–31 March 2017, pp. 758–763 (2017)
15. Naderlinger, A., Pree, W., Templ, J.: Visual modeling of real-time behavior. In: Proceedings of Symposium on Automotive/Avionics Systems Engineering (SAASE) (2009)
16. Naderlinger, A., Templ, J., Pree, W.: Simulating real-time software components based on logical execution time. In: SCSC 2009: Proceedings of the 2009 Summer Computer Simulation Conference (2009)
17. Pree, W., Templ, J., Hintenaus, P., Naderlinger, A., Pletzer, J.: TDL - steps beyond Giotto: a case for automated software construction. Int. J. Softw. Inf. **5**(1–2), 335–354 (2011)
18. Resmerita, S., Naderlinger, A., Huber, M., Butts, K., Pree, W.: Applying real-time programming to legacy embedded control software. In: 2015 IEEE 18th International Symposium on Real-Time Distributed Computing, pp. 1–8, April 2015
19. Resmerita, S., Naderlinger, A., Lukesch, S.: Efficient realization of logical execution times in legacy embedded software. In: Proceedings of the 15th ACM-IEEE International Conference on Formal Methods and Models for System Design, MEMOCODE 2017, Vienna, pp. 36–45 (2017)
20. Rosen, B.K., Wegman, M.N., Zadeck, F.K.: Global value numbers and redundant computations. In: Proceedings of the 15th ACM SIGPLAN-SIGACT Symposium on Principles of Programming Languages, pp. 12–27 (1988)
21. Stieglbauer, G.: Model-based development of embedded control software with TDL and Simulink. Ph.D. thesis, University of Salzburg (2007)
22. Templ, J.: Timing Definition Language (TDL) 1.5 specification. University of Salzburg, Technical report, July 2009. http://www.softwareresearch.net
23. The MathWorks: Simulink Reference, R2018a (2018)

Model-Implemented Hybrid Fault Injection
for Simulink (Tool Demonstrations)

Mehrdad Moradi[1,2]($\boxtimes$) (iD), Bert Van Acker[1,2] (iD), Ken Vanherpen[1,2],
and Joachim Denil[1,2] (iD)

[1] Antwerpen University, Prinsstraat 13, 2000 Antwerp, Belgium
{Mehrdad.Moradi,Bert.VanAcker,Ken.Vanherpen,
Joachim.Denil}@uantwerpen.be
[2] Flanders Make, Oude Diestersebaan 133, 3920 Lommel, Belgium

Abstract. The increasing complexity and certification needs of cyber-physical systems (CPS) requires improved methods of dependability analysis. Fault injection (FI) is an experimental-based way for safety analysis of a system which is mainly divided in *model-based*, *software-based* and *hardware-based* techniques. For safety analysis during model-based development, FI mechanisms can be added directly into models of hardware, models of software and/or models of the system. This approach is denoted as *model-implemented hybrid FI*. The availability of a modelling environment such as Simulink allows for early stage verification of FI experiments to analyze the correct behavior of the system-under-design. This results in a reduced time and cost by testing at early stages of the development process. This paper presents an automated framework to inject faults in the Simulink model. The framework is not only limited to injection at the model-in-the-loop (MiL) level but is also applicable at other approximation levels in model-based testing such as hardware-in-the-loop (HiL). The modeler instruments the model with FI blocks to specify which faults need to be injected and when they should be injected. This model is converted to a fault-injected model and a FI orchestrator that allows the FI experiment to run automatically. The framework is completely build upon the generative technique of model transformation, allowing it to be ported to other formalisms and tool environments.

Keywords: Cyber-physical system · Model-implemented fault-injection ·
Model transformation · Safety analysis

1 Introduction

Humans use their cognitive abilities to make their lives more comfortable. By merging embedded systems with electro-mechanical systems, automation of time consuming or error prone tasks became available. This resulted in e.g. advanced automobiles, trains, medical technology and manufacturing plants. With the increase of market pressure and increased need for more features such as autonomous decision making, safety regulation and more efficiency in terms of power and cost, novel methods, techniques, and tools are required to create this next generation of CPS.

© Springer Nature Switzerland AG 2019
R. Chamberlain et al. (Eds.): CyPhy 2018/WESE 2018, LNCS 11615, pp. 71–90, 2019.
https://doi.org/10.1007/978-3-030-23703-5_4

CPS are systems that combine computational and networking components together with physical components [1]. The computational part of a CPS has different components which have a predefined task that comprises e.g. controlling mechanical actuators, computing the new state of the system or monitoring the system context using a set of physical and virtual sensors. Designing a CPS therefore also requires a multi-disciplinary approach.

Because of this complexity and the huge impact on our daily lives, most of the current and future CPS are also dependable systems. Dependable system, and more specifically safety critical system, are systems that need to be reliable and resistant to failures, specially failures that can endanger or damage humans, environment or equipment. To keep the complexity of the system design at bay, engineers adhere to standardized processes to create more dependable systems. These standards define process constraints on all levels of the process such as design, development and testing, etc. to assure that the final product is safe and reliable [2]. An example of such standard is the ISO 26262 standard [3]. It is intended to be applied to safety-related systems that include one or more electrical and/or electronic (E/E) systems and that are installed in series production passenger cars. The ISO 26262 standard specifies that FI could be used in the development process. This recommendation raised the issue of the role of FI in the design phase, which is a difficult problem that has not been fully investigated.

FI is a well-studied verification technique that has been applied to many different targets, e.g. operating systems (OS), embedded software, and more recently at the model level. In safety engineering, the use of FI is twofold [4, 5]:

- FI is used for testing different fault tolerant mechanisms that are embedded in the system. The safety standard is requirement driven, this means that all requirements have to be verified and that each line in the software can be traced to a (set of) requirement(s). To allow the testing of these fault-tolerance mechanisms, FI techniques at both the level of the hardware (or their models) and the software (and their models) are a necessity.
- Second, FI can be used as a supporting technique to hazard and risk analysis: It allows to identify the different fault modes during fault identification. By analyzing the traces of the FI, the propagation of errors can be seen. This leads to the detection of possible new failure modes and the cause for this failure.

However, this raises the question which faults have to be injected when and where, as it is impossible to inject all possible faults, at all different possible places, in all different scenarios and time windows. A structured technique to reason about a FI experiment is the FARM model [6]. The FARM model describes the set of **F**aults to be injected, the **A**ctivation of the faults, the **R**eadouts of the experiments and finally the **M**easures or analysis of the readouts. The conceptual FARM model can be applied at each level of the design process but as mentioned.

In this paper we model the FARM concept explicitly within a Simulink model such that a domain-expert can easily setup FI experiments without the need for other tooling. The contributions of the paper can be summarized as follows:

- Modelling of FI experiments at the model level using the same visual notation that the engineer is comfortable with.

- The generation of FI experimental setups for both MiL and HiL simulation.
- The consideration of real-time behavior of the application when instrumenting the model for HiL simulation such that the tasks do not overrun its real-time deadline. This is to avoid that faults emerge in the behavior of the system that cannot be traced to the experiments defined by the user.

The rest of the paper is organized as follows. Section 2 introduces the background needed to understand the contributions presented in this paper. Section 3 introduces the running example which is used to show the contribution of this paper. Section 4 shows the approach followed in this paper to instrument the model and create the experimental setups for a FI experiment. Afterwards, in Sect. 5 we discuss the approach. Section 6 gives an overview of the work related to this work. Finally, we conclude in Sect. 7.

2 Background

2.1 Fault Injection

FI is a verification technique that has been available since the 80's–early 90's. Today, FI has been applied to many different targets: OS, middleware, web services, web servers, embedded systems, etc. [2]. FI is an experimental approach to evaluate dependability. Dependability is particularly important when system/software being developed is safety critical, where failure can cause a serious hazard or even loss of life. FI techniques can be classified as physical or simulation-based. Based on the implementation of FI mechanisms, the techniques can be classified as hardware-implemented FI (HIFI) or software-implemented FI (SWIFI) techniques [7].

In hardware-based FI, faults are injected at the physical level by controlling the environment parameters. Real-life faults are emulated by injecting voltage sags, disturbing the power supply, heavy ion radiation, electromagnetic interference, etc. Radiation result in the change of data in parts of the memory like microprocessor internal register, program memory and data memory. Production defects and component wear-out can potentially increase latency to execute tasks, wrong measurements and loss of response (for example in sensors). Interface problems will create package loss, latency and even full loss of communication when a short-circuit occurs.

Software-based FI refers to techniques that inject faults by implementing it in the software. Different types of faults can be injected with software-based FI, for example register and memory faults, error conditions and flags, irregular timings, missing messages, replays, corrupted memory, etc. Data memory changes in source code lead to control flow errors [8]. Technically, faults are injected within the application or between the software application and the operating system (OS)/middleware. In case where the target is the OS itself, faults are embedded within the middleware/OS [9]. The faults within the application or middleware/OS are inserted either at compile-time or at run-time. Software implemented FI methods can be adapted to inject faults on various trigger mechanisms such as exception, traps, time-out, code-modification [10].

Finally, simulation-based FI involves constructing a simulation model of the system-under-test and adding faults in this model. In most of the literature, the system-under-test is the computational hardware. In that case, hardware description languages such as VHDL are injected with faults [7]. With the advent of CPS, the techniques of simulation-based FI are also applied to other systems and formalisms. Mostly, a simplified model of a CPS consists of a plant and controller which are connected to each other in feedback loop.

In safety engineering there needs to be a way to establish if a failure occurs (failure mode) when doing FI experiments. One way is to explicitly model the safety requirement of system. These safety requirement models can be co-simulated together with the FI experiments to verify the defined safety properties. We will assume that the safety properties of the system are modelled using an appropriate language that can detect these failures. An example of such a language is a temporal logic such as signal temporal logic (STL). Monitors for STL can automatically be generated for Simulink [11]. Another technique is to compare the trace of a correct system with the trace of the experiment run (where a fault is injected). If there is a difference between traces (using an error metric), the trace has to be further examined by the expert to define if this result in an unsafe or incorrect behavior.

2.2 Model-Based Techniques

Model-based systems engineering together with model-based design is gaining more interest for the design and development of software-intensive and CPS. This results in a development shift from hand-written code to models from which implementation code is automatically generated through model-to-text transformations (also known as code generation). Furthermore, various disciplines are involved in designing a CPS such as mechanical engineering, control engineering, software engineering, integration engineering [12].

The major advantage of using model-based techniques is that verification and validation steps can be front-loaded. This means that users can use their previous experience and/or other developer's knowledge during the development process of the new system-under-design. In traditional design processes, the verification and validation of the system behavior can only be done when all components are designed and integrated. Model-based techniques allow to check system-level properties much earlier in the design process.

Today, MATLAB/Simulink is a popular tool used in the design, simulation, and verification of software-intensive and CPS. Thanks to extensive automatic code generation facilities, developers often use Simulink as a control programming language based on the causal block diagram (CBD) formalism. Simulink uses two basic entities: blocks (with ports) and links. Blocks represent (signal) transfer functions, such as arithmetic operators, integrators, or relational operators. Links represent the time-varying signals shared between connected blocks. Figure 1 shows the meta-model of a Simulink model. All models in the Simulink language follow the structural rules defined by the type model. The semantics of continuous-time causal blocks diagrams map to ordinary differential equations.

Model-based techniques are also applied for the testing of systems. Zander in [13] defines model-based testing as the technique where the test specification is derived in whole or in part from both the system requirements and a model that describe selected functional aspects of the system-under-test. In the literature different test execution

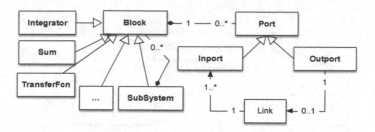

Fig. 1. Simulink meta-model

platforms are defined where the integration with the real computational platforms is increasing. MiL is the first integration level where the control model is attached to a plant model. It is done for testing purposes. Software-in-the-loop (SiL) uses the implementation code in closed loop with the plant model for testing. Processor-in-the-loop (PiL) uses the production microcontroller to execute the control model in closed-loop with the plant model. Finally, HiL simulation, in which the real-time embedded system has interactive simulation with the plant model [14]. Because of its rapidness and high precision, it has been widely used in the testing and verification of embedded systems such as automobiles, ships and aircrafts [15–18].

2.3   Model Transformation

With the advent of more models in the design of systems, a systematic way to manipulate models is required. During the process of design, models have to be converted between different representations (in possibly different modelling languages) that allow different features such as code generation, model checking, simulation, performance checking, etc. MTs systematically modify models. Rule-based MT languages work on typed, attributed, and directed graphs that represent the model. The transformation rule language can automatically be generated from the meta-model of the languages [19]. A transformation rule represents a manipulation operation on the represented model. Figure 2 shows such a MT's schema. A rule consists of a left-hand side (LHS) pattern representing the pre-condition for the applicability of the rule. The right-hand side (RHS) pattern defines the outcome of the operation. A set of negative application condition (NAC) patterns block the application of the rule. A unique label in the pattern elements of the LHS, RHS, and NAC refers to the matched elements. The transformation execution decides the outcome of the rule based on these unique labels.

We design the Simulink MT in this work using the Simulink language based on the tool presented in [20]. The transformation language in this tool is based on the T-Core MT language framework [21]. The Simulink MT scheduling language is a simple branch-condition-loop language modelled in Simulink. The Simulink transformation language supports multiple scheduling blocks that have different effects on the model:

- ARULE: The atomic rule matches a single instance of the precondition pattern in the model and rewrites it.

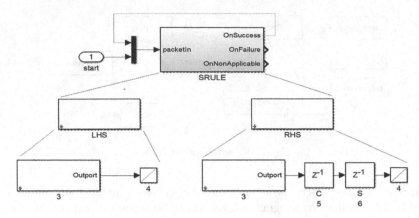

Fig. 2. Example of Simulink transformation

- FRULE: The for-all rule matches all the instances of the precondition pattern in the model and rewrites all of them in one pass. This can create consistency issues when patterns are overlapping because part of the model is already rewritten.
- SRULE: The SRULE is similar to the FRULE but does not create consistency issues. It basically executes the ARULE in a loop until no more instances can be found in the model.

The schedule is shown at the top level. The schedule emulates an SRULE application using a simple loop with an ARULE. The schedule block contains two subsystems, one for the LHS and one for the RHS. Opening the subsystems allows us to specify the pre and post condition patterns. The pre-condition pattern matches all combinations of a constant and product block. The post-condition pattern changes the matched constant product block into a gain block (removing the product and constant block). The parameters of the gain block are set based on the attributes of the matched product and constant block. The color of the new gain block is set to red. The *Pre_InportOfBlock* and *Post_InportOfBlock* (as well as the *Pre-* and *Post_OutportOfBlock*) are abstract blocks. They explicitly refer to the input port of the block. To re-attach the post-condition pattern in the model to the previous (respectively next) blocks in the model, the MT language needs these constructs. Other abstract blocks can match any block, any block with an input port and/or output port, or even only discrete blocks [22].

3 Running Example

We will use a running example to show the contribution of this paper. The example is a case study in Simulink which implements a power window. The model contains the *DRV_Control, Object_DRV, Debounce_DRV, PW_DRV* and the *plant model* in a feedback loop as shown Fig. 3. *DRV_Control* and *Object_DRV* are blocks for providing system inputs. *Debounce_DRV* and *PW_DRV* are our controller. By using FI mechanisms, the safety properties of the control model will be verified. The verification of the plant model will not be examined in this paper.

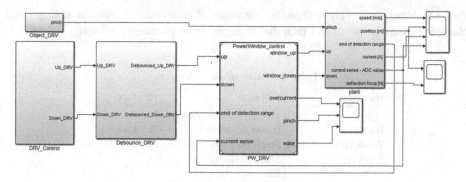

Fig. 3. Use case model

Our framework considers two possible instrumentation levels, MiL and HiL. For HiL experiments, we use a real-time hardware simulator, more specific the dSPACE SCALEXIO HiL box, which enables us to simulate the plant model and interact with the real embedded hardware. The controller is implemented on an Atmel board.

4 Fault Injection Framework

The goal is to inject faults into the executable model. This framework will be described in three main parts. First, we look into the fault library for models in Simulink. Second, we focus on the workflow and experiment orchestrator for MiL. Finally, we show the additional workflow steps when applying our framework in a HiL setting.

4.1 Fault Library

By studying possible faults at the hardware level and software level in the literature [5, 10], we came up with a list of faults that can be injected at the model level. Because most of these techniques are either for hardware or software, not all are applicable at the model level. For example, for hardware-based FI we cannot emulate power surge, bridging, sporous current and changing program memory or internal hardware component specification at the model level. Also, for software-based FI we cannot introduce compile time faults. However, we can cover other faults and inject them at the model level. We distinguish four categories (data faults, latency faults, open links, code insertion) at three levels of the computational stack (hardware, software and interface). Also, the faults have three different types of nature including permanent fault, temporary fault and intermittent fault. Permanent fault remains until end of each simulation, while temporary change the model in only a short time. Finally, intermittent fault is something between permanent and temporary and they repeat periodically.

Data. Data changing comes from changes of data in memory or when data transfer between layers in the computational stack. Reasons of changes in the data are shown in Table 1. Generally, changes in the data could be permanent or transient phenomena. At the model level in Simulink, we can easily mimic data changing manipulating blocks.

These manipulations include changing the value of parameters directly or adding small changes in the computational path that changes these parameter values.

Table 1. Cause of data changing

Hardware	Software	Interface
Noise	Developer/user mistake	Noise
Bit flip	Buffer overflow	Stuck at 0/1
Wrong measurement	Small memory	Bus contention
Stuck at 0/1	Share resource	
	Resource starvation	

Latency. Cause of latency faults are described in Table 2. Delay does not have a permanent nature. In hardware, latencies are normally intermittent and are transient in interface and software. Adding a delay block enables us to manipulate timing behavioral of hardware and software.

Table 2. Cause of latency

Hardware	Software	Interface
Component wear out	Work load	Busy line
Busy component	Synchronizing	Bus contention
	Share *resource*	

Open Link. These faults come from broken wires or broken component in the system. It accrues in hardware and interface not in software. Its nature is permanent, and it remains faulty until end of simulation.

Code Insertion/Drop. This type of faults happens in software only. It can originate from developer's mistakes and/or manual introduced bugs e.g. missing parameter incrementation within a loop control structure. By adding and/or dropping certain parts of the execution path, framework create control flow errors in software. In Simulink, blocks can be added to define a different control flow or blocks can easily be short-circuited.

4.2   MiL Fault Injection Workflow

Figure 4 shows the workflow needed to create a MiL FI experiment in Simulink. We use UML activity diagrams to depict the workflow [23]. The process starts at the black circle and ends with the black dot in a circle. White round tangles indicate manual activities and yellow round tangles are automatic actives within the framework. Diamonds show control flow decisions (in our case for looping the different experiment runs within a single experiment). The black bar represents a fork and join node. In between the fork and the join node, the activities are concurrently executed.

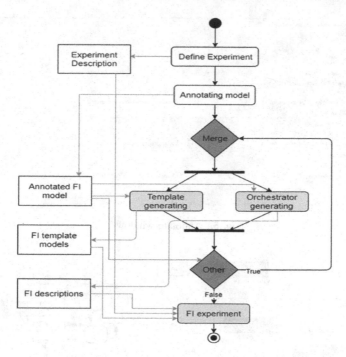

Fig. 4. FI framework workflow (Color figure online)

Define Experiment. Before starting to annotate the model with FI blocks, the goals of the experiment should be clear. The user must define these goals by modelling the properties she/he wants to check. As previously mentioned, temporal logics can be used to define such properties. The properties and its monitoring of the control model explicitly models readouts and measures of the FARM model. The input scenario also must be selected (or modelled) such that a complete simulation is possible. These models are a small but important part of the activation part of the FARM model.

Annotation. The objective of our instrumentation problem is to create an instrumentation of the elements of the Simulink model that are marked for FI. We instrument a block in the Simulink model at the output ports. The framework enables the user to indicate which blocks should be instrumented, with what different types of faults, and the time at which to inject the fault (explicit time, range and/or simple conditions). The activity takes the control model as input. The output is a new annotated model with user defined parameter for the FI experiment. For annotating, custom FI blocks that can be configured, shown in Fig. 5, are available. Users need to dedicate a special ID for each instrumentation block. In addition to the set of faults, users define parameters for each of the selected faults. This includes FI orchestrator settings for activating the saboteur blocks. Saboteurs are the faulty blocks that replace the annotation and are responsible for injection the fault at the correct time instant. In Fig. 6 you can see power window controller which annotated by user.

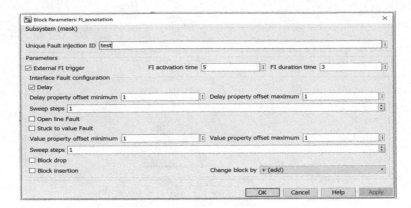

Fig. 5. Annotate window

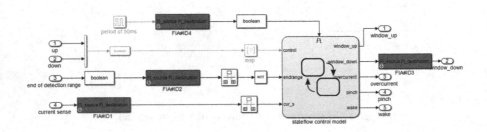

Fig. 6. Annotated controller

Generate Injection Model. This activity transforms the annotated model into a model with the saboteurs added to the model. As an input, the model with the fault types and parameters is used. The orchestrator goes over each annotation block and adds the correct saboteur blocks in the model. Internally, each of the faults in the fault library has an associated transformation rule attached to it. Figure 7 shows a part of the transformation rule library in our framework that transforms a changing parameter, an open line and does code insertion. Each saboteur can be activated by the switch block that either takes the normal (without fault) path or the faulty path. These trigger blocks are activated by the experiment FI orchestrator.

Generate Model Orchestrator. The orchestrator is generated concurrently with the generation of the annotated model. The activity that generated the orchestrator also uses the annotated model as input. As output it generates an activity diagram and parameter files that are an explicit representation of the experiment that will run. From this activity diagram the framework generates a MATLAB m-script that is used for the MiL experiment. Again, MT are used to generate the activity diagram. For this, each fault library rule from the previous activity has a sister rule to generate the orchestrator at the same time as the fault injected model. The next subsection shows some more information about the orchestrator.

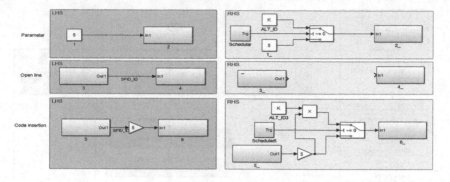

Fig. 7. Part of fault library for MT regarding open line and code insertion

FI Execute Experiment. Finally, the experiment can be run using the generated m-script from the activity diagram. The property models provide information about the requirements that are met or violated when faults are injected.

Fault Injection Orchestrator. The Orchestrator is responsible for activating the different saboteurs in the correct experiment run. As previously shown, each saboteur has an input which is triggered by the orchestrator. An abstraction of the fault orchestrator is shown in Fig. 8. The following activities are shown:

Initializing Orchestrator. The orchestrator must load some files to execute the different simulations. First, the FI description contains some fault's parameter such as range and step size of the latency of a saboteur. Second, the stimuli description contains information of triggering time (or triggering condition). Finally, the property description file contains the requirements, condition or functions which fulfilled. The modeled properties in Simulink allow to automate the process of property checking.

Preparing FI Parameter. In this step, the orchestrator gets the fault parameter description according to the template and the FI scenario, defined within the experiment. This contains the information on how to activate the correct saboteur.

Load FI Template Model. In this phase, the orchestrator prepares the FI template model for the experiment by loading the parameter into the FI template model. The experiment setup is almost complete and can be executed to produce the traces for further analysis.

Reset FI Model. Before executing the experiment, the orchestrator first resets the plant model and controller model.

Simulate FI Model. According to the parameterized model and the stimuli description, the orchestrator runs the simulation from the start to stop time.

Store Readouts. The results or readouts of the experiment are logged in a MATLAB file, used for further offline analysis.

FI Model Clean-Up. After running the simulation, the orchestrator will clean and reset the model for the next simulation run. Next, the orchestrator will check its parameters

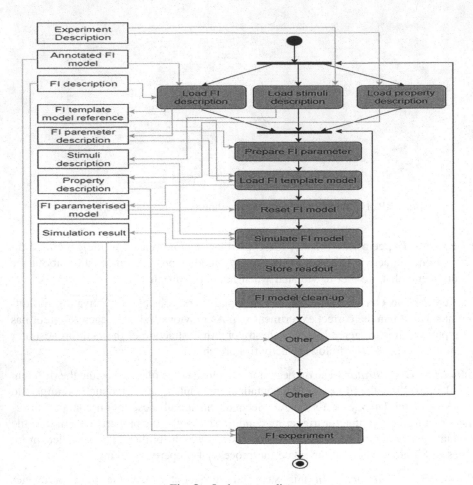

Fig. 8. Orchestrator diagram

to find out if it is sweeping a parameter finished or not. If there are more sweep parameter, the orchestrator will prepare new FI parameter and execute the sweep of the parameter. Finally, the orchestrator checks if there is another saboteur for execution. If so, it will do the experiment runs of the other faults.

Analyze Readouts. At the end of each experiment, an analysis of the results or readouts is needed. This process is offline and is activated by the orchestrator after the complete experiment suite is simulated. To enable this, all the readouts are stored for each experiment.

Figure 9 shows the results of an experiment run. The left-hand side figure is the result of a model without faults and the right-hand figure shows the result from a fault within model. The first row, second row and last row are in inputs from the up button, down button and output from current sensor which will be active when there is something between window and door's frame or if there will be external force toward window. We can see in normal operation that the window position is changing logically when the up button is active. The window position is increasing until the time that the current sensor will be active, then the window stops and goes down for a certain time. Afterward, by pushing the up and down button we see that window position is changing. In the faulty injected model, the window position is not changing anymore.

4.3 HiL Fault Injection

In this subsection we look at the differences in the framework when using it for HiL FI. In HiL, we consider the deployment of the control model onto the hardware platform.[1] This also requires that the orchestrator is either run on the embedded platform or run from an experiment box e.g. the HiL real-time target simulator. Synchronization between the plant model running on HiL box and the controller should be provided such that the plant model and control model are reset and started at the correct times. We implement the orchestrator on the embedded board and synchronize with the HiL box using a dedicated general-purpose input/output (GPIO) pin on the hardware. Furthermore, we consider the real-time properties of the control task such that it does not overrun its real-time bounds, as this could create additional faults that are hard to trace to the injected fault.

Extra Workflow Steps: To allow for HiL FI, we need to add some extra steps in the workflow model of Fig. 4. These steps have to be done before starting the MiL workflow.

- **Define hardware deployment.** The hardware deployment model is needed to allow us to model the injection of representative faults that occur at the interface level and other hardware faults (e.g. faulty sensor readings). A custom deployment block set in Simulink allows the modeler to model the deployment of the control models onto the defined hardware setup. This extra deployment information is used to add extra FI annotation to the system model.
- **Generating hardware FI deployment model.** This step generates the deployment model automatically by referring to the hardware model and deployment description. Deployment descriptions contain information about the timing of the system components for example, the deadline and worst-case execution time. The output of this step is a model with annotation block. In this phase, the framework determines the place for annotation block and generates a new model.

Figure 10 contains FI deployment model from the use case. In this model, the annotation blocks have been added at the interconnections (which they are physical part). These boxes are between inputs, plant and controller indicate hardware-based faults such as stuck to value.

---

[1] Note that the hardware setup can contain multiple interconnected hardware platforms and by this, the control model is distributed over these hardware platforms.

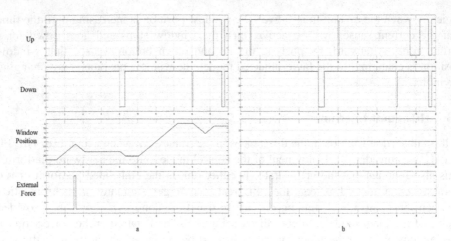

Fig. 9. MiL sample result (a) Normal model behavioral (b) Faulty model behavioral

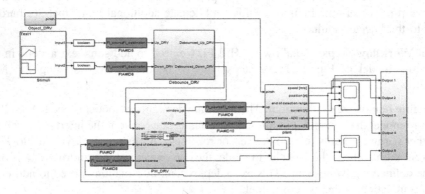

Fig. 10. FI deployed model

Generation of the Orchestrator. As previously mentioned, a different implementation of the experiment orchestrator is needed so it can run on the embedded hardware. This can be done by transforming the activity model into C-code. We build upon the OSEK (Open Systems and their Interfaces for the Electronics in Motor Vehicles) as our real-time OS (RTOS) for running the control model. This is reflected in the generated code.

For representing an example of the generated code, we show a part of orchestrator as pseudo as follow:

```
TASK(InputTaskPeriodic)
{
    if (simtime<=SIM_stop){
        if (simtime==0)
        {
            FIOrchestrator();
        }
        simtime = simtime+stepsize;
    }else{
        if (FI_block <= FI_blockcount){
            simtime = 0;
        }
    }
    TerminateTask();
}
```

The **FIOrchestrator()** function is called within a periodically triggered task and initializes the FI and overall simulation parameters. This orchestrator function will take care of the synchronization between the plant model, running on the HiL box and the controller, running the embedded hardware and will reset them both when needed. This synchronization is a very important step for valid HiL FI simulations. The real-time constraint of the control system tasks is also critical for validity of HiL FI simulations. Despite of the additional FI blocks and the FI activation of different saboteurs, the tasks must assure to finish before the defined deadline, otherwise real-time behavior of system is not met and, as previously mentioned, faults can originate from this real-time constraint violation.

Real-Time Constraints for HiL. For HiL instrumentation in a real-time environment we want to test the behavioral of model without introducing extra fault because of real-time constraints. Therefore, we must assure that real-time behavior of system is not violated. We use the slack parameter to define how much extra blocks can be added to the execution of the Simulink model. The slack time is explicitly modelled during the modelling of the deployment. Figure 11 shows an example of slack time of a task that needs to be instrumented with FI. Both "control task 1" and "to instrument task" have the same period (we assume that the deadline of the task is equals the period). The "to instrument task" and "the control task 1" are both released at times n × T1 (with n = 1...∞). In our example, "task control 1" has the highest priority and runs first. Afterwards, the "to instrument task" runs. Because there is some time left in between the end of the execution of "to instrument task" and the start of the new period, this extra time is available for instrumentation. Note, that we use worst-case execution timings for both tasks. The creation and/or extension with other properties, such as memory consumption, is similar.

Our model for extending the framework with real-time properties is straightforward. The execution model of Simulink is based on [24]. We characterize each FI pattern (by transformation rules) to add saboteurs to the application. These saboteurs add execution time to the application and this execution time needs to be taken into account in order to fulfil the real-time constraints of the application. In certain cases, this is quite small because stateless paths in the Simulink model execution will not compute when the

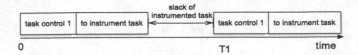

Fig. 11. Slack in execution of tasks

other path is chosen. Stateful paths however need to be updated and compute every execution step of the Simulink model. The condition blocks also always execute every step.

When all MT rules are characterized, a greedy approach to defining the experiment is created. To avoid overruns, the experiment is no longer one schedule with one model, but rather a set of schedules and its instrumented models. Now, the slack mapper towards creating the FI enabled Simulink model and schedule count the added execution times when applying a rule. It will use a greedy approach for selecting the next instrumentation to apply to the model. When there is no possibility anymore to apply an instrumentation transformation (the slack become too small), a new orchestrator and model with saboteurs is created. The process repeats until all instrumentation requests are fulfilled. For seeing the HiL's result you can refer to [25].

5 Discussion

In our approach, the readouts and measures of the FARM model are represented by the modelling of (safety) properties that can be traced to the safety requirements. The modelling can, in Simulink, be done by the use of explicit blocks that monitor a combination of signals in the model. Another approach is to model these properties using another formalism. Appropriate formalisms for detecting complex temporal patterns are temporal logics such as STL and linear temporal logic (LTL) [11, 26]. However, the abstraction level which to specify these logics is at a wrong abstraction level. Therefore, we need express these properties at that same level of abstraction as the model itself. ProMoBox is such a technique that allows engineers to model properties at a more domain-specific level [27]. Properties also specifies what needs to be observed after a specific period, in safety properties referred to tolerance time interval. The simulation orchestrator can take this time into account to check if the properties are violated or not and reduce the simulation time. The detection using STL can be done either online or offline on the traces of the model.

In this work, we only modelled part of the activation concept of the FARM model. The time to activate an event is underspecified in our case. It just uses an explicit list of times to inject the fault or a range of injection timings by specifying a start time and stop time with discrete steps. If we want to cover all scenarios, experimenting overhead will increase and make the approach infeasible. To solve this, domain-knowledge needs to be added to the injection time. This can be done using the same property language. The temporal logic can be used to create fine grained control over the injection time as it is possible to specify the conditions when a fault is activated. For real-time simulation in HiL, we can deploy the monitor on the target or on the HiL box that simulates the plant model. If the monitor is deployed on the target, we need to take the computation time of the STL monitor into account when experimenting. When it is deployed on the HiL box, all the necessary signals must be exposed to the HiL box which is not always feasible.

The proposed method uses MT techniques to implement the injection of faults. However, the Simulink language and its features allows for a much simpler solution by embedding the sabotage blocks immediately in the parametrized fault library block or by using code generation. We have several reasons not to do this. The most important reason is that our method is generic and not depending on language features such as hierarchy, scripting and parametrization. Not relying on such language features but using the generic approach of MT allows us to port the technique to other formalisms and tools. As each formalism is modelled using a type-model or meta-model, the generic technique of ramification can be applied to the meta-model and MTs can be created for this language. The added benefit of the explicit transformation is that the intermediate model can more easily be analyzed for additional properties such as timing or memory consumption. Finally, it also helps in extending the fault library more easily. When using the hierarchy with scripting approach, the expert needs to create scripts in a possibly new language. When using code generation, code generation capabilities of the block have to be altered which is in the solution domain, rather than in the problem domain. The transformation approach is probably closest to the mental model of the expert and thus most appropriate.

6 Related Work

Methods in [28] and [29] are the closest approach to our framework. This tool tries to use model-based FI at the beginning level of design to decrease the cost. The main advantage of this tool is providing minimal cut set for hardware-based FI and software-based FI. MODIFI does this by inspiration of hardware fault types. Our framework hasn't provided minimal cut set, but it has two more advantages. First, we considered software FI method as well as hardware FI. We have code inserting and code drop as well as latency (it could be considered as shared fault type between hardware-based and software based). Secondly, our framework covers a wide sweep range for each parameter of fault types. The user can set start point, end point and steps for sweeping data and latency which enables the user to have a better evaluation of dependency while MODIFI covers only 30 different faults. In [30] authors try to combine software-based technique with model-based FI separately. So, this work doesn't cover different aspect of FI, but they focused more on efficiency.

7 Conclusion and Future Work

For having a fast FI-based for dependability evaluation, there are three main approaches: (i) workload-based FI [31, 32], (ii) sample-spread-based FI [9, 33], or (iii) introducing error behavioral functions [34] and we are going to use these techniques and combine them to framework to increase efficiency.

In addition, we are going to determine fault types and their values in a matured approach based on system dynamic feature, system architecture and cut set analysis. Adding these techniques will enable user and framework to choose fault wisely in model and increase fault coverage of system as well as fast instrumentation.

Also, in current framework, one fault per model is implemented and triggered. A better approach is that a framework does not limit the user to inject faults. In the next version, we try to add capability of mix FI and activation.

In conclusion, for each type of fault in hardware and software level of design there are a lot of tools, platforms and environments which focus on one or several fault types. You can find them in [35], but there is no such comprehensive environment to automate process specially in beginning of development.

Acknowledgment. This work is partly supported by INES (Innovation in the Development of Electrical Systems For Aeronautics) under project no. 11172. We thank our colleagues at Siemens Industry Software in Leuven, Belgium for supporting us: Stefan Dutre, Jef Stegen, Sweety Pate, Jonathan Menu and Satya Prakash Jha.

References

1. Lee, E.: Cyber physical systems: design challenges. In: 11th IEEE International Symposium on Object Oriented Real-Time Distributed Computing (ISORC), pp. 363–369. IEEE (2008)
2. Pintard, L., Toulouse, D.E.: Des Analysis de securite a la validation experimentale par injection de faults – le CAS DES systems embarques automobiles. Doctorat de l' université de toulouse (2012)
3. ISO Homepage. https://www.iso.org/standard/54591.html
4. Project page. http://www.eurekanetwork.org/project/id/11172
5. Ziade, H., Ayoubi, R., Velazco, R.: A survey on fault injection techniques. Int. Arab J. Inf. Technol. **1**(2), 171–186 (2004)
6. Arlat, J., et al.: Fault injection for dependability validation: a methodology and some applications. IEEE Trans. Softw. Eng. **16**(2), 166–182 (1990). https://doi.org/10.1109/32. 44380
7. Rana, R., Staron, M., Berger, C., Hansson, J., Nilsson, M., Törner, F.: Improving fault injection in automotive model-based development using fault bypass modeling. In: GI-Jahrestagung, pp. 2577–2591 (2013)
8. Kooli, M., et al.: Software testing and software fault injection (2016)
9. Wang, W., Trivedi, K.S., Profeta, J.A.: The impact of fault expansion on the interval detection coverage estimate for fault. In: Proceedings of IEEE 24th International Symposium on Fault-Tolerant Computing, pp. 330–338 (1994). https://doi.org/10.1109/FTCS.1994. 315627
10. Hsueh, M.C., Tsai, T.K., Iyer, R.K.: Fault injection techniques and tools. Computer **30**(4), 75–82 (1997). https://doi.org/10.1109/2.585157
11. Balsini, A., Di Natale, M., Celia, M., Tsachouridis, V.: Generation of Simulink monitors for control applications from formal requirements. In: Proceedings of the 12th IEEE International Symposium on Industrial Embedded Systems (SIES) (2017). https://doi.org/ 10.1109/sies.2017.7993389

12. Vanherpen, K., Denil, J., Vangheluwe, H., Meulenaere, P.: Model transformations for round-trip engineering in control deployment co-design. In: SpringSim (TMS-DEVS), pp. 55–62 (2015)
13. Zander, J.: Model-based testing of real-time embedded systems in the automotive domain. Ph.D. thesis, TU, Berlin (2009)
14. Luo, A., Wu, C., Shen, J., Shuai, Z., Ma, F.: Railway static power conditioners for high-speed train traction power supply systems using three-phase V/V transformers. IEEE Trans. Power Electron. **26**(10), 2844–2856 (2011)
15. Hasanzadeh, A., Edrington, C.S., Stroupe, N., Bevis, T.: Real-time emulation of a high-speed microturbine permanent-magnet synchronous generator using multiplatform hardware-in-the-loop realization. IEEE Trans. Ind. Electron. **61**(6), 3109–3118 (2014)
16. Ou, K., et al.: MMC-HVDC simulation and testing based on real-time digital simulator and physical control system. IEEE J. Emerg. Sel. Top. Power Electron. **2**(4), 1109–1116 (2014)
17. Zhang, H., Zhang, Y., Yin, C.: Hardware-in-the-loop simulation of robust mode transition control for a series-parallel hybrid electric vehicle. IEEE Trans. Veh. Technol. **65**(3), 1059–1069 (2016)
18. Yang, X., Yang, C., Peng, T., Chen, Z., Liu, B., Gui, W.: Hardware-in-the-loop fault injection for traction control system. IEEE J. Emerg. Sel. Top. Power Electron. **6**(2), 696–706 (2018). https://doi.org/10.1109/JESTPE.2018.2794339
19. Kühne, T., Mezei, G., Syriani, E., Vangheluwe, H., Wimmer, M.: Explicit transformation modeling. In: Ghosh, S. (ed.) MODELS 2009. LNCS, vol. 6002, pp. 240–255. Springer, Heidelberg (2010). https://doi.org/10.1007/978-3-642-12261-3_23
20. Denil, J., Mosterman, P.J., Vangheluwe, H.L.M.: Rule-based model transformation for, and in Simulink. In: Proceedings of the Symposium on Theory of Modeling and Simulation - DEVS Integrative (DEVS 2014), no. 1, p. 4 (2014)
21. Syriani, E., Vangheluwe, H.: A modular timed graph transformation language for simulation-based design. Softw. Syst. Model. **12**(2), 387–414 (2013). https://doi.org/10.1007/s10270-011-0205-0
22. Denil, J., Kashif, H., Arafa, P., Vangheluwe H., Fishmeister S.: Instrumentation and preservation extra-functional properties of Simulink models. In: Proceedings of the Symposium of Theory of Modelling and Simulation (2015)
23. UML Homepage. http://www.uml.org/
24. Di Natale, M., Guo, L., Zeng, H., Sangiovanni-Vincentelli, A.: Synthesis of multitask implementations of Simulink models with minimum delays. IEEE Trans. Ind. Inf. **6**(4), 637–651 (2010). https://doi.org/10.1109/TII.2010.2072511
25. https://www.youtube.com/channel/UCvfwLU_G0FrbSl1Ef7fbHUg?view_as=subscriber
26. Bartocci, E., Ferrère, T.: Localizing faults in Simulink/Stateflow models with STL. In: Proceedings of the 21st International Conference on Hybrid Systems: Computation and Control (Part of CPS Week) (HSCC 2018), pp. 197–206. ACM, New York (2018). https://doi.org/10.1145/3178126.3178131
27. Meyers, B., Wimmer, M., Vangheluwe, H., Denil, J.: Towards domain-specific property languages: the ProMoBox approach. In: Proceedings of DSM 2013, pp. 39–44 (2013). https://doi.org/10.1145/2541928.2541936
28. Svenningsson, R., Vinter, J., Eriksson, H., Törngren, M.: MODIFI: a MODel-implemented fault injection tool. In: Schoitsch, E. (ed.) SAFECOMP 2010. LNCS, vol. 6351, pp. 210–222. Springer, Heidelberg (2010). https://doi.org/10.1007/978-3-642-15651-9_16
29. Svenningsson, R., Eriksson, H., Vinter, J., Törngren, M.: Model-implemented fault injection for hardware fault simulation. In: Proceedings - 2010 Workshop on Model-Driven Engineering, Verification, and Validation (MoDeVVa), pp. 31–36 (2011). https://doi.org/10.1109/modevva.2010.11

30. Guthoff, J., Sieh, V.: Combining software-implemented and simulation-based fault injection to a single fault injection method. In: Twenty-Fifth International Symposium on Fault-Tolerant Computing. Digest of Papers (II), pp. 196–206 (1995). https://doi.org/10.1109/ftcs. 1995.466978

31. Goswami, K.K.: DEPEND: a simulation-based environment for system level dependability analysis. IEEE Trans. Comput. **46**(1), 60–74 (1997)

32. Kanawati, G.A., Kanawati, N.A., Abraham, J.A.: FERRARI: a flexible software-based fault and error injection system. IEEE Trans. Comput. **44**(2), 248–260 (1995)

33. Powell, D., Martins, E., Arlat, J., Crouzet, Y.: Estimators for fault coverage evaluation. IEEE Trans. Comput. **44**(2), 261–273 (1995)

34. Imén, M., Ohlsson, J., Torin, J.: On microprocessor error behavior modeling. In: Proceedings of IEEE 24th International Symposium on Fault-Tolerant Computing (FTCS-24), pp. 76–85. IEEE Computer Society (1994)

35. Yu, Y., Johnson, B.W.: Fault Injection Techniques and Tools for Embedded Systems Reliability Evaluation. Springer, Heidelberg (2003)

A Component-Based Hybrid Systems Verification and Implementation Tool in KeYmaera X (Tool Demonstration)

Andreas Müller[1]([envelope]) [ORCID], Stefan Mitsch[2] [ORCID], Wieland Schwinger[1],
and André Platzer[2] [ORCID]

[1] Department of Cooperative Information Systems, Johannes Kepler University,
Altenbergerstr. 69, 4040 Linz, Austria
{andreas.mueller,wieland.schwinger}@jku.at
[2] Computer Science Department, Carnegie Mellon University,
Pittsburgh, PA 15213, USA
{smitsch,aplatzer}@cs.cmu.edu

Abstract. Safety-critical cyber-physical systems (CPS) should be analyzed using formal verification techniques in order to gain insight into and obtain rigorous safety guarantees about their behavior. For practical purposes, methods are needed to split modeling and verification effort into manageable pieces and link formal artifacts and techniques with implementation. In this paper we present a tool chain that supports component-based modeling and verification of CPS, generation of monitors, and systematic (but unverified) translation of models and monitors into executable code. A running example demonstrates how to model a system in a component-based fashion in differential dynamic logic (dL), how to represent and structure these models in the syntax of the hybrid systems theorem prover KeYmaera X (which implements dL), and how to prove properties in KeYmaera X. The verified components are the source for translation into executable C code, which can be run on controlled components (e.g., a robot). Additionally, we demonstrate how to generate monitors that validate the behavior of uncontrolled components (e.g., validate the assumptions made about obstacles).

1 Introduction

To ensure safe operation of cyber-physical systems (CPS), their behavior should be analyzed in safety analysis using formal verification techniques. However, monolithic models and their analysis become unnecessarily complex with increasingly large systems. Hence, techniques are needed to split both modeling and verification effort into more manageable pieces. At the same time, the correctness properties that are verified formally for a model also have to hold for the actual

This research was sponsored by the Defense Advanced Research Projects Agency (DARPA) under grant number FA8750-18-C-0092 and FA8750-12-2-0291, AFOSR FA9550-18-1-0120, and by the Austrian Science Fund (FWF) P28187-N31.

R. Chamberlain et al. (Eds.): CyPhy 2018/WESE 2018, LNCS 11615, pp. 91–110, 2019.
https://doi.org/10.1007/978-3-030-23703-5_5

implementation. When translating a model into an implementation, however, any gaps need to be overcome between modeling concepts beneficial for verification (e.g., nondeterministic control and real numbers) and those appropriate for implementation (e.g., deterministic control and machine floating points) in a way that preserves correctness (assuming correct C compilation).

Formal verification has been used successfully for hybrid system models, both using model checking [6] and theorem proving [17] techniques. For more complex applications, monolithic hybrid systems models are impractical compared to models that provide more structuring principles into smaller submodels. The real gain of component-based hybrid systems modeling techniques is realized, however, when the division into smaller components of less responsibilities is not just available when describing the models but also exploited during their formal verification by compositional proofs [14]. Finally, the full benefit of component-based hybrid system modeling needs a way of correctly implementing the components in a way that faithfully fits the intended interactions of the model.

Sound axiomatizations [15,16], verification tools [9], cross-verification in other provers [3], and provably correct compilation tools to executables [4] are known for hybrid systems themselves. While these are compositional in the programming language operators of hybrid programs [15–17], extensions to component-based hybrid system models remain an important challenge.

Thus, this paper takes a useful step toward these goals by developing a component-based hybrid systems modeling and verification tool built into the KeYmaera X prover for hybrid systems [9]. No soundness-critical extensions are needed for the verification in KeYmaera X, because the implementation is in tactics outside its soundness-critical kernel [8]. We take a pragmatic approach for component-based implementation of hybrid systems by generating C code that is informally inspected to be correct, but does not yet provide the degree of rigor of generating implementations of hybrid systems correctly and bridging floating point vs. real arithmetic using a chain of theorem provers [4]. Given the added value of generating code in the well-known C language, we argue that our pragmatic choice is useful in practice to enable an easy integration into an existing infrastructure of embedded and cyber-physical systems. In addition to the challenges of nondeterminism in the models, we tackle the challenges specific to component-based systems: generating code for ownsystem components with sensing/actuation interfaces to external components (e.g., obstacles). As in [4], our main ingredient to obtain correct integration with external control components is the provably correct monitor synthesis from ModelPlex [13].

2   Preliminaries

Differential Dynamic Logic (dL). For specifying and verifying correctness statements about hybrid systems, we use *differential dynamic logic* (dL) [15–17], which is a real-valued first-order dynamic logic for hybrid systems and supports *hybrid programs* as a program notation for hybrid systems.

Operators of dL and their informal meaning, are summarized in Table 1, and comprise the usual comparison operators, boolean operators and quantifiers.

Table 1. Operators of differential dynamic logic (dL) formulas

dL	Operator	Meaning
$\theta_1 \sim \theta_2$	comparison	true iff $\theta_1 \sim \theta_2$ with $\sim \in \{>, \geq, =, \neq, \leq, <\}$
$\neg\phi$	not	true iff ϕ is false
$\phi \wedge \psi$	and	true iff both ϕ and ψ are true
$\phi \vee \psi$	or	true iff ϕ is true or if ψ is true
$\phi \rightarrow \psi$	implies	true iff ϕ is false or ψ is true
$\phi \leftrightarrow \psi$	equivalent	true iff ϕ and ψ are both true or both false
$\forall x\, \phi$	universal quant.	true iff ϕ is true for all values of variable x in $\mathbb{R}$
$\exists x\, \phi$	existential quant.	true iff ϕ is true for some values of variable x in $\mathbb{R}$
$[\alpha]\phi$	$[\cdot]$ modality	true iff ϕ is true after all runs of hybrid program α
$\langle\alpha\rangle\phi$	$\langle\cdot\rangle$ modality	true iff ϕ is true after at least one run of α

Table 2. Hybrid program statements (Q is a formula, α, β are hybrid programs)

Statement	Effect
$\alpha;\ \beta$	Sequential composition where β starts after α finishes
$\alpha \cup \beta$	Nondeterministic choice, following either alternative α or β
α^*	Nondeterministic repetition, repeating α n times for any $n \in \mathbb{N}$
$x := \theta$	Discrete assignment of the value of term θ to variable x (jump)
$x := *$	Nondeterministic assignment of an arbitrary real number to x
$(x_1' = \theta_1, \ldots,$	Continuous evolution of x_i along the differential eq. system
$x_n' = \theta_n \& Q)$	$x_i' = \theta_i$ Restricted to remain in evolution domain Q at all times
$?Q$	Test if formula Q holds at current state, otherwise abort

Additionally, dL supports modalities to reason about the state after at least one, respectively all runs of a hybrid program. The syntax and informal semantics of hybrid programs are summarized in Table 2. For example, a hybrid program

$$\alpha \equiv (y := *;\ ?y \leq z;\ t := 0;\ \{x' = y, t' = 1\ \&\ t \leq 10\})^* \tag{1}$$

picks any real value for y that does not exceed z, resets time t to zero, and then in the ODE continuously evolves the value of x according to the fixed slope y while simultaneously increasing the value of t with constant slope 1. The ODE stops nondeterministically at any time, but before $t \leq 10$ becomes false; then the program repeats by the * operator. A corresponding dL formula

$$x = 0 \wedge z < 0 \rightarrow [\alpha]x \leq 0 \tag{2}$$

states that starting in a state, where x is 0 and z is negative, each run of the above program α leads to a state, where x is less or equal 0.

KeYmaera X. KeYmaera X [9] is an automated and interactive theorem prover for dL and hybrid programs. KeYmaera X is implemented in Scala, expands upon functionality by introduction of tactics [8] and is based on a significantly smaller soundness-critical core than other hybrid systems verification tools, which makes it easier to ensure correct verification results. The valid example formula (2) can, for instance, be verified in KeYmaera X. We will introduce the concrete ASCII syntax of KeYmaera X later alongside our running example in Sect. 3.

3 Component-Based Verification Tool

As the complexity of CPSs increases, monolithic models and analysis techniques become unnecessarily challenging. As already established for discrete software, decomposition into subsystems with contracts is essential in taming the complexity of larger systems. Thus, we have explored compositional modeling and verification techniques for hybrid systems [14] that conclude safety of the entire system from separate isolated safety arguments about its components and their interaction with the environment. The KeYmaera X hybrid system theorem prover allows us to bundle and analyze the ingredients of our component-based approach—component models, specifications, and lemmas of satisfied proof obligations—in a single input format.

ASCII Syntax. Models and specifications are provided to KeYmaera X in the dL ASCII syntax, which is a straightforward ASCII rendition of Tables 1 and 2, e.g., using A->B for $A \rightarrow B$ and using A&B for $A \wedge B$. The ASCII notation alpha++beta is used for alpha$\cup$beta. For improved readability in longer examples, braces {...} are used for grouping differential equation systems and other program operators. Like in C programs, assignments etc. end with explicit semicolons.

The dL ASCII syntax is the basis for named entries in .kyx files, which consist of an optional **SharedDefinitions** block, with global definitions for the entire archive, and multiple named **ArchiveEntry** blocks, which themselves consist of optional definitions (**Definitions**), system variables (**ProgramVariables**), a (safety) specification in dL (**Problem**), and optional tactic scripts[1] (**Tactic**). Each of these blocks must be closed with an **End** statement.

```
ArchiveEntry "Example Formula (2)"
  Definitions      /* constants, functions, properties, programs */
    Real z;
    HP a ::= { {y:=*; ?y<=z; t:=0; {x'=y, t'=1 & t<=10} }* };
  End.
  ProgramVariables Real x, z; End.      /* variables */
  Problem x=0 & z<0 --> [a;]x<=0 End.    /* specification in dL */
  Tactic "Auto Proof"   /* tactic script, produces proof/lemma */
    master
  End.
End.
```

---

[1] The tactics language Bellerophon [8] for verification of hybrid systems provides a way to convey insights by programming hybrid systems proofs.

The symbols defined in the `Definitions` and the variables defined in the `ProgramVariables` can be used in the `Problem` block or in other definitions. The named `Tactic` blocks, if provided, each list a Bellerophon [8] tactic to verify the current `Problem`.

3.1   Running Example

To illustrate the concepts of our component-based verification approach and to demonstrate the capabilities of our verification tool, we use a running example of a *robot* that has to avoid collision with an *obstacle*, see Fig. 1.

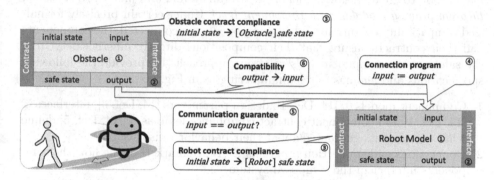

Fig. 1. Running example: robot collision avoidance

The speed of the obstacle is limited to at most S. The robot regularly receives the obstacle's position to ensure that it stays at a safe distance from the obstacle. Additionally, the robot can receive desired speed suggestions (e.g., from a remote control, or by a user, which will not be modeled as part of the example), which guide the robot's speed. In our example, the difference between updates of the speed suggestion is limited to avoid sudden speed changes. The overall *safety property* of the system is that robot and obstacle should never crash. If they meet, the robot must be stopped.

Shared Definitions. Shared definitions in the beginning of a `.kyx` file are used to define global constants, facts, and programs, which can be accessed in all archive entries. The components in the example share facts about constants, such as the maximum difference `D()` between speed suggestions, the speed limit `S()` of obstacles, each ≥ 0, and the maximum control cycle time `ep()>0` that limits the plant runtime (i.e., the time until the next controller run and sensor update). They also define program `skip` as the trivial test that always passes.

```
SharedDefinitions
  Real D();              /* maximum change in desired speed request */
  Real S();                            /* speed limit */
  Real ep();                   /* maximum control cycle time */
  Bool globalFacts <--> ( D()>=0 & S()>=0 & ep()>0 );    /* facts */
  HP skip ::= { ?true; };              /* skip as trivial test */
End.
```

3.2 Component-Based Deductive Verification by Contracts

Our component-based deductive verification approach [14] bases on individual *components* with *interfaces* and local *contracts*, which are *composed* in a *compatible* fashion to create a safe model of the overall system and *make hybrid system theorem proving modular on a component level*. Under certain precisely formalized compatibility conditions on how components are connected, the components and their contracts ensure that their compositions directly inherit safety from the safety of the components. Users of our approach [14] provide the following specifications and lemmas (circled numbering as in Fig. 1):

1. Component models ① [14, Def. 1], design parameters [14, Def. 3], interfaces ② [14, Def. 4] and component contract compliance lemmas ③ [14, Def. 5] define what components guarantee about their behavior in isolation.
2. Connections and connection programs ④ [14, Remark 1] define how the components interact in the composed system.
3. Communication guarantee lemmas ⑤ [14, Def. 7] and compatibility lemmas ⑥ [14, Def. 8] ensure that the interaction in the system happens between compatible components.

The component composition tactic in KeYmaera X then combines these individual lemmas into a safety proof of the overall composed system. In the following, we briefly recap the necessary definitions of previous work [14] and apply our component-based verification approach to the robot example.

Components, Interface and Contract Compliance

Components. As usual, each component combines a model of the dynamic behavior with an interface defining how the component receives inputs and provides outputs through ports. The component behavior model consists of a control *ctrl* (comprising exclusively discrete computations), a physical plant *plant* and internal communication *cp* between the sub-components of non-atomic components (skip for atomic components). Components do not share any variables, except for global constants accessed throughout the system.

  The robot example consists of two components: Both measure time t in their plant. The obstacle C_o (3) nondeterministically chooses speed s_o in its controller and moves its position p_o as defined in the plant. If safe according to formula (5) (i.e., distance to measured obstacle position $\hat{p}_o$ large enough), the robot C_r (4)

sets its speed s_r to the received speed suggestion $\hat{d}$ and moves its position p_r accordingly in the plant (i.e., position changes according to speed and time evolves linearly, for at most maximum control cycle time ε); otherwise it stops. These components are atomic, so have trivial internal communication $cp \equiv \texttt{skip}$.

$$C_o = (\overbrace{s_o := *; ?(0 \leq s_o \leq S)}^{ctrl_o}, \overbrace{t' = 1, p_o' = s_o}^{plant_o}) \tag{3}$$

$$C_r = (\underbrace{\text{if}\,(\text{Drive})\, s_r := \hat{d}\,\text{else}\,s_r := 0}_{ctrl_r}, \underbrace{t' = 1, p_r' = s_r \ \&\ t - t^- \leq \varepsilon}_{plant_r}) \tag{4}$$

$$\text{Drive} \equiv \hat{p}_o - p_r > (\hat{d} + S) \cdot \varepsilon \tag{5}$$

Components in ASCII Syntax. When specifying components in KeYmaera X, we declare all component variables and define the hybrid programs for the component controller, plant, and internal connections. For example, the obstacle C_o (3) has real-valued variables for its current position p_o (po), its previous position p_o^- (po0), and its speed s_o (so), and it will keep track of time t (t) and plant start time t^- (t0) in the contracts that we develop subsequently.

```
Real po;     /* current obstacle position */
Real po0;    /* previous obstacle position */
Real so;     /* speed of obstacle */
Real t;      /* time */
Real t0;     /* time before plant's present control cycle */
```

In ASCII syntax, the component programs are the controller $ctrl_o$ written as ctrlobs, the plant $plant_o$ as plantobs with ASCII evolution domain constraint true (which can also be omitted in dL), and glue code cp_o as cpobs.

```
HP ctrlobs  ::= { so:=*; ?(0<=so&so<=S()); }; /* obstacle control */
HP plantobs ::= { {t'=1, po'=so & true} };    /* obstacle plant */
HP cpobs    ::= { skip; };                     /* obstacle glue code */
```

Interfaces. Possible interaction points of a component are described in its interface, which defines input ports V^{in} and output ports V^{out}, together with input assumptions π^{in} and output guarantees π^{out} that stipulate the expected respectively guaranteed range of values on each port. We use $\mapsto$ to associate assumptions and guarantees with ports.

In the robot example, the obstacle outputs its position p_o, whose change is bounded by the maximum speed S and the time $(t - t^-)$ that has passed since the last position information transmission (6). The robot comes with two input ports (7) that take a speed suggestion $\hat{d}$, which must not deviate from its previous value $\hat{d}^-$ by more than D (to avoid too sudden speed changes), and an obstacle position $\hat{p}_o$, with an input assumption that, for simplicity, exactly matches the output guarantee of the obstacle's single output port.

$$I_o = (\overbrace{\{p_o\}}^{V_o^{out}}, \overbrace{p_o \mapsto |p_o - p_o^-| \leq S \cdot (t - t^-)}^{\pi_o^{out}}) \tag{6}$$

$$I_r = (\underbrace{\{\hat{p}_o, \hat{d}\}}_{V_r^{in}}, \underbrace{(\hat{p}_o \mapsto |\hat{p}_o - \hat{p}_o^-| \leq S \cdot (t - t^-), \hat{d} \mapsto |\hat{d} - \hat{d}^-| \leq D))}_{\pi_r^{in}} \quad (7)$$

Interfaces in ASCII Syntax. The variable and property declarations of interfaces translate into hybrid programs and formulas [14, Def. 6]. The obstacle (6) has a single output port for its position p_o, so we define a port memory program `deltaobs` that stores the position in `po0`. The obstacle does not have input ports, so `inobs` is `skip`. The obstacle output guarantee π_o^{out}, which specifies that the position change $|p_o - p_o^-|$ over duration $(t - t^-)$ cannot exceed maximum speed S (referred to with nullary constant function symbol `S()`, is defined in `safeobs`. The boolean predicate `safeobs` takes real-valued position and time arguments. Additionally, in `initobs` we define under which initial conditions obstacles will meet their output guarantees, which will become important for verifying contract compliance.

```
HP deltaobs ::= { po0:=po; };                    /* port memory */
HP inobs    ::= { skip; };                        /* read input ports */
Bool safeobs(Real po, Real po0, Real t, Real t0) <->
    ( abs(po-po0) <= S()*(t-t0) );                /* safety property */
Bool initobs(Real po, Real po0, Real so) <->      /* initial state */
    ( po=po0 & so=0 );
```

Contract Compliance. Contracts are dL formulas that tie together a component's behavior with its interface. The contract compliance proof obligations [14, Def. 5] that users have to show follow the structure in the obstacle contract compliance example below:

$$(\overbrace{S \geq 0 \wedge D \geq 0}^{\Omega} \wedge \overbrace{s_o = 0 \wedge p_o = p_o^-}^{\phi_o}) \rightarrow [(\overbrace{p_o^- := p_o}^{\Delta_o}; \overbrace{s_o := *; ?(0 \leq s_o \leq S)}^{ctrl_o};$$

$$\underbrace{t^- := t; \{t' = 1, p_o' = s_o\}}_{plant_o}; \underbrace{skip}_{in_o}; \underbrace{skip}_{cp_o})^*]\underbrace{|p_o - p_o^-| \leq S \cdot (t - t^-)}_{\Pi_o^{out}} \quad (8)$$

From global facts Ω about system parameters as well as initial conditions ϕ (here: initially the obstacle is stopped $s_o = 0$ and the port memory bootstrapped $p_o = p_o^-$), users must prove that all runs of a component ensure the interface output guarantees Π^{out}. The component behavior is stitched together as a hybrid program from the component specification according to [14, Def. 5] as follows:

- Δ updates the port memory (here: remember the position of the obstacle)
- *ctrl* runs the component controller (here: choose a new obstacle speed s_o, but at most maximum speed S
- $t^- := t; \{t' = 1, plant\}$ measures time and describes the effect of the control decision (here: the obstacle moves according to the chosen speed)
- *in* reads values from the component input ports (here: `skip` since obstacle has no inputs)

– *cp* transfer values between the subcomponents of the current component (here: `skip` since the obstacle is not built from smaller components)

The obstacle contract compliance proof obligation (8) follows in a straightforward way from the ASCII definitions.

```
Problem  /* obstacle contract */
  t=t0 & globalFacts() & initobs(po,po0,so) -> [{
    deltaobs; ctrlobs; t0:=t; plantobs; inobs; cpobs;
  }*]safeobs(po,po0,t,t0)
End.
```

Robot contract compliance (9) assumes that the robot is stopped initially. It stores both initial port values (Δ_r) and nondeterministically chooses values for its input ports (in_r). The robot has no output ports, but guarantees that its local safety property ψ_r^{safe} holds, which ensures that the robot will never actively crash into the obstacle.

$$
(\Omega \wedge \overbrace{\hat{p}_o = \hat{p}_o^- \wedge \hat{d} = \hat{d}^- \wedge s_r = 0 \wedge \varepsilon > 0}^{\phi_r}) \rightarrow [(\overbrace{\hat{p}_o^- := \hat{p}_o; \hat{d}^- := \hat{d}; ctrl_r; t^- := t;}^{\Delta_r}
$$
$$
\{t' = 1, plant_r\}; \underbrace{\hat{p}_o := *; ?\pi_r^{in}(\hat{p}_o); \hat{d} := *; ?\pi_r^{in}(\hat{d})}_{in_r}; cp_r)^*](\underbrace{s_r > 0 \rightarrow \hat{p}_o \neq p_r}_{\psi_r^{safe}})
$$

$$(9)$$

Verifying Contract Compliance in KeYmaera X. In order to ensure contract compliance, both contracts must be formally verified. The proof automation of KeYmaera X can complete the component proofs of the running example fully automatically. But to illustrate our component-based approach we provide proof scripts to store the lemmas that are required for deriving system safety upon composition. Such proof scripts can be included as tactics in the archive entry, using the Bellerophon tactics language [8]. The KeYmaera X web user interface [12] supports point-and-click creation of proof scripts (see Sect. 3.3). The tactics language provides a number of predefined named tactics (e.g., `andL` – simplify a conjunction on the left-hand side of the sequent). Most of these tactics must be applied at certain positions of the sequent (e.g., `andR(1)` – apply the tactic to the first formula on the right-hand side of the sequent) and some require additional parameters (e.g., `loop(invariant,1)` – prove a nondeterministic repetition at position 1 using loop induction with the provided `invariant`). A *semicolon* concatenates tactics, i.e., `t1;t2` executes tactic `t2` after `t1`. If a proof requires the verification of multiple proof goals (e.g., loop induction requires the verification of three branches, i.e., `invariant` holds initially, `invariant` implies target property, `invariant` is inductive) a *less-than sign* indicates that the following *comma-separated* tactics are applied to the respective branches (e.g., `t1 <(t2,t3)` – after `t1`, tactic `t2` is applied to the first branch and `t3` is applied to the second branch).

The proof script to verify the obstacle contract is straightforward: First, the implication is resolved (`implyR(1)`). Then, loop induction uses the safety property as invariant, and the resulting branches (base case, use case and induction step) are proved by general proof automation (`master`). The statement `done({'message'},{'id'})` creates lemmas to verify each branch (can be referred to with the provided ID). We will need these lemmas later, when we apply our composition theorem.

```
Tactic "Proof Obstacle Contract Compliance (Create Lemmas)"
  implyR(1);
  loop({'safeobs(po,po0,t,t0)'},1); <(
    master; done({'Base case done'}, {'Obstacle Base Case Lemma'}),
    master; done({'Use case done'}, {'Obstacle Use Case Lemma'}),
    master; done({'Step done'}, {'Obstacle Step Lemma'}) )
End.
```

Composition. To safely compose individual components, [14, Def. 6] introduces a quasi-parallel, associative and commutative *composition operation* (true parallel *plant* composition and coarse-grained *ctrl* composition without interleaving) to create systems from components. The composition operation is configurable with a *connection program* to account for different options how to transfer values between ports (e.g., lossless connection vs. estimation from sensors with some uncertainty). A notion of *compatibility* ensures that connections are made only between ports whose assumptions and guarantees fit.

Connection Program. A user-defined connection program determines how values are passed between ports. For example, lossless, instantaneous connection[2] directly copies the value of an output port v to an input port $\hat{v}$: $con_{ll}(v) \equiv \hat{v} := v$. The corresponding HP `con` in ASCII syntax is listed below.

```
HP con ::= { por:=po; };    /* connection program */
```

These user-defined connection programs must provably provide certain communication guarantees [14, Def. 7]: a connection program *con* must be executable ($\langle con \rangle true$) and its effect must be expressible in a first-order logic formula ζ by relating the connected ports without side effects ($[con]\zeta$). The direct assignment in a lossless, instantaneous connection is obviously executable and its effect is trivial equality between the port values, i.e., $\zeta_{ll}(\hat{v}, v) \equiv \hat{v} = v$. To ensure that the communication guarantees hold, both properties are formally verified from the ASCII syntax specifications below.

```
Problem
  <con;>true  /* connection program is executable */
End.
Tactic "Proof Connection Program Executable"
  master; done({'Executable'},{'Connection Executable Lemma'})
End.
```

---

[2] See [14] for further examples of connection programs.

The effect of a lossless, instantaneous connection is summarized with the formula **Bool zeta(Real por, Real po) <-> (po=por);** and used in the communication guarantee effect proof below.

```
Problem
  [con;]zeta(por,po)        /* communication effect */
End.
Tactic "Proof Communication Effect"
  master; done({'Effect'}, {'Communication Effect Lemma'})
End.
```

Compatibility. When connecting ports, users must prove that the connections between the components are compatible, so that an output port exclusively supplies values that are accepted by the connected input port, so formally: $\zeta(v^-, \hat{v}^-) \wedge \Omega \rightarrow [con(v)]\left(\pi_j^{out}(\hat{v}) \rightarrow \pi_i^{in}(v)\right)$. In our robot example, the sole connection transfers the obstacle position to the robot (the desired speed suggestion port remains unconnected), so we get one compatibility proof obligation:

$$\overbrace{(p_o^- = \hat{p}_o^-)}^{\zeta_{ll}(p_o^-, \hat{p}_o^-)} \wedge \overbrace{(S \geq 0 \wedge D \geq 0))}^{\Omega} \rightarrow$$

$$\underbrace{[\hat{p}_o := p_o]}_{con_{ll}(p_o)}\left(\underbrace{\left|p_o - p_o^-\right| \leq S \cdot \left(t - t^-\right)}_{\pi_o^{out}(p_o), \text{ see } (6)} \rightarrow \underbrace{\left|\hat{p}_o - \hat{p}_o^-\right| \leq S \cdot \left(t - t^-\right)}_{\pi_r^{in}(\hat{p}_o), \text{ see } (7)}\right) . \quad (10)$$

The compatibility proof obligation (10) includes the input assumption (7) and output guarantee (6) for the connected port, and the communication guarantee ζ about the connection program *con*. The compatibility proof obligation is verified automatically in KeYmaera X and the resulting lemma is again stored.

```
Definitions
  Bool zeta(Real por, Real po) <->       /* communication guarantee */
    ( po=por );
  Bool ObsPosOut(Real po, Real po0, Real t, Real t0) <->
    ( abs(po-po0) <= S()*(t-t0) );        /* output guarantee */
  Bool ObsPosIn(Real por, Real por0, Real t, Real t0) <->
    ( abs(por-por0) <= S()*(t-t0) );      /* input assumption */
End.
Problem                             /* compatibility proof obligation */
  zeta(por0,po0) & globalFacts() ->
    [por:=po;](ObsPosOut(po,po0,t,t0) -> ObsPosIn(por,por0,t,t0))
End.
```

After composing the components from the running example using lossless, instantaneous communication, we get a composite system component and interface. The system component (11) sequentially composes individual controllers and executes plants in parallel. Internally the obstacle position is transmitted using the connection program. The system component's interface (12) contains the remaining input port of the robot and indicates that previous values must be stored for connected and unconnected ports alike.

$$\overbrace{}^{ctrl_{sys}} \quad \overbrace{}^{plant_{sys}} \quad \overbrace{}^{cp_{sys}}$$
$$C_{sys} = \big((ctrl_{rc}; ctrl_r; ctrl_o), (plant_r, plant_o), (con_{ll}(\hat{p}_o))\big) \tag{11}$$

$$I_{sys} = \big(\underbrace{\{\hat{d}\}}_{V^{in}}, \underbrace{(\hat{d} \mapsto |\hat{d} - \hat{d}^-| \le D)}_{\pi^{in}}, \underbrace{\{\}}_{V^{out}}, \underbrace{()}_{\pi^{out}}, \underbrace{\{p_o^-, d^-, \hat{p}_o^-, \hat{d}^-\}}_{V^-}\big) \tag{12}$$

Composition Retains Safety. After verifying local contracts (8) and (9), compatibility among connected ports (10) and the communication guarantee for the applied connection program, the remaining question is whether the safety property holds for the composed system. [14, Thm. 1] ensures that, starting from an initial state where both initial conditions hold, all runs of the composed system satisfy the safety properties, here:

$$\vDash (t = t^- \wedge \Omega \wedge \phi_1 \wedge \phi_2 \wedge \zeta) \rightarrow$$
$$[(\Delta; ctrl; t^- := t; \{t' = 1, plant\}; in; cp)^*] \left(\psi_1^{safe} \wedge \Pi_1^{out} \wedge \psi_2^{safe} \wedge \Pi_2^{out}\right) \tag{13}$$

The proof of this theorem is implemented constructively in KeYmaera X to *automatically* derive a proof tactic that will verify that the system contract (13) holds from component proofs. This proof tactic takes the lemmas of component contract compliance, communication guarantees, and compatibility as input.

Summary. The user specifies and verifies contract compliance (based on component behavior and interface) for each component according to [14, Def. 5], defines a connection program with verified communication guarantees according to [14, Def. 7], and discharges the compatibility proof obligation for connected ports according to [14, Def. 8]. The results of verified contract compliance, communication guarantees, and compatibility are stored as named lemmas and fed to our tool to retrieve a tactic for proving safety of the composed system.

3.3   Web User Interface

KeYmaera X[3] comes with a web-based user interface (UI) [12] that supports the verification of dL formulas. If a .kyx file is loaded, the UI creates a proof attempt for each contained archive entry. If an archive entry includes a tactic, the UI calls the underlying KeYmaera X proof engine and attempts to prove the problem formula. Otherwise, the user can start a manual proof attempt and choose which sequence of tactics to apply. KeYmaera X automatically records the selected proof steps and exports the resulting proof script. Additionally, the UI allows textual input of proof steps. The proof scripts presented in this paper can be constructed with the UI, exported, and then fed into the component-based verification tool.

---

[3] http://www.keymaeraX.org.

4   Code Generation

For model debugging and testing purposes, KeYmaera X provides (*unverified*) *code generation* from the dL data structures. The code generation tools translate hybrid programs, which are often nondeterministic (nondeterministic assignments, choices, and repetitions), into deterministic C code. This translation requires to mimic nondeterminism with the deterministic language features of C. We aim for a translation that preserves safety, which means that we want the behavior of the resulting C program be *one of* the behaviors of the hybrid program, but need not necessarily preserve all possible behaviors of the hybrid program (such refinements are verifiable for hybrid programs with differential refinement logic [11], but here we bridge different languages). The translation is systematic but not verified; especially the translation of real arithmetic into floating point arithmetic does not preserve the semantics: verified compilation to machine code and interval arithmetic computations is supported through the VeriPhy pipeline [4].

Component-based hybrid systems typically model the interaction of controllers with their environment, and therefore combine ownsystem components (e.g., the robot) with environment components (e.g., obstacles). These components are fundamentally different in nature, which is reflected in their implementation: We generate *control code* from the controller models of the ownsystem components, and *monitoring code* to monitor whether or not the actual physical environment behaves according to the assumptions made in the model. Monitoring code can also be generated from the controller models of the ownsystem components, which is useful to sandbox untrusted control code (e.g., highly optimized controllers, or controllers that use learning).

4.1   Control Code

Static Semantics. In order to declare C data structures to represent constant system parameters and state variables, we analyze the static semantics of hybrid programs via their free and bound variables [16]. Uninterpreted function symbols and variables that are free but not bound in the program (and thus only read) become declared as system parameters. Bound variables that are chosen nondeterministically are interpreted as system inputs and must be provided, e.g., by the user, sensors, or through optimization procedures. All other bound variables are state variables and computed by the generated control code. Interpreted function symbols min, max, and abs are translated to library function calls.

```
typedef struct {      /* constant parameters that never change */
  long double ep;     /* reaction time bound */
  long double S;      /* obstacle maximum speed */
  long double D;      /* remote control maximum speed */
} parameters;
```

```
typedef struct {      /* component input variables */
  long double po;     /* obstacle position */
  long double dr;     /* desired speed (advisory) */
} inputs;
```

```
typedef struct {      /* state variables of controller and plant */
  long double pr;     /* robot position */
  long double sr;     /* robot speed */
  long double t;      /* time */
  long double por0;   /* previous obstacle position (port memory) */
  long double dr0;    /* previous desired speed (port memory) */
  long double t0;     /* plant start time */
} state;
```

The sensors and actuators are accessed from the generated control code through callback functions. Sensors provide the latest sensor values for each of the input variables, whereas actuators take as input the current and unmodifiable state including the control decisions of the controller.

```
typedef inputs (*Sensors)(void);
typedef void (*Actuators)(state const* const);
```

These data structures are used as arguments in the generated control code with signature

```
state ctrl(state const* const current,
           parameters const* const params,
           Sensors sense,
           Actuators actuate )
```

The implementation of the control code is derived using the translation rules discussed next.

Overview. In order to resolve nondeterminism in the execution paths of hybrid programs, the generated code uses backtracking and therefore operates on a copy of the state and tracks the success of statements in the following data structure:

```
struct { state state; bool success; } result = {
  .state = current, .success = false }
```

The effects (collected in **result.state**) of unsuccessful statements are reverted before attempting alternative executions with backtracking (e.g., the second branch of a nondeterministic choice). We use the notation $C(\cdot)$ to denote compilation of a dL formula, term, or hybrid program into C.

Terms and Formulas. The translation of terms and formulas from dL to C rests on an appropriate representation of real arithmetic in machine-executable floating point arithmetic. Even though unsound, here we opt for code readability and translate variables, number literals, and terms into double-precision floating point representations. Provable safety needs a sound translation of real arithmetic to floating/fixed point interval arithmetic as in VeriPhy [4].

Real-valued number literals n are compiled to double-precision floating point literals $C(n) \rightsquigarrow nL$, read-only constant variables c are compiled to system parameters $C(c) \rightsquigarrow params->c$, nondeterministically chosen variables x are compiled to the corresponding field in the inputs data structure $C(x) \rightsquigarrow sense()->x$, and deterministically computed state variables x are compiled to the corresponding field in the result state data structure $C(x) \rightsquigarrow result.state.x$. Terms are straightforward translations of the basic arithmetic operators, with exponentials and interpreted functions abs, min, and max translated to C math library calls. Formulas are straightforward translations of the boolean operators.

Deterministic Statements. Assignments $x := e$ are translated directly to C: `result.state.x = C(e); result.success = true;` where the success variable indicates that the assignment succeeded. Tests $?F$ are straightforward assignments to the program success flag: `result.success = C(F);` leaves the state unchanged. Conditionals if (F) a else b, which are syntactic sugar for $(?F; a) \cup (?\neg F; b)$, are straightforward C conditionals: `if (C(F)) C(a) else C(b)`. Sequential composition $a; b$ executes hybrid program b after successful execution of HP a, which is translated to `C(a); if (result.success) { C(b); }`.

Nondeterministic Statements. Nondeterministic assignments in hybrid programs are often used to model inputs to the controller, such as sensor values or optimization procedures when the controller has a variety of different options that are considered similar in terms of safety (e.g., controller is free to choose any acceleration if speeding up is safe). We therefore interpret nondeterministic assignments $x := *$ as control inputs to the generated controller by reading from the sensor input callback function: `result.state.x = sense()->x;`.

Nondeterministic Choice. Nondeterministic choices are resolved eagerly by executing the *first successful branch*, regardless of whether later branches would also be executable at the current state. This means, that source hybrid programs should be structured such that functionality that is important to achieve desired goals occur on the left-hand side branches of nonderministic choices (e.g., robot favors following remote control input over emergency stopping).

An integral feature of KeYmaera X is that tactics and proofs operate symbolically on terms, formulas, and programs and can therefore be used to transform their shape in a provably correct way. Here, we prepare the code transformation with a tactic that proves that executing eagerly is a safe implementation of a nondeterministic choice as follows: $[\alpha \cup \beta]P \rightarrow [(\alpha; s := 1 \cup s := 0);$ if $(\neg(s = 1))$ $\beta]P$. The success indicator s is a fresh variable mentioned neither in programs α, β nor the condition P. Note that the semantics of dL "discards" unsuccessful executions (e.g., if a test fails), which we implement by remembering the starting state, tracking the success of statements within programs, and resetting the state upon unsuccessful execution in the following translation template for the hybrid program $(\alpha; s := 1 \cup s := 0)$; if $(\neg(s = 1)) \; \beta$.

```
{ state reset = result.state;
  C(a);
  if (!result.success) result.state = reset;
}
if (!result.success) {
  state reset = result.state;
  C(b);
  if (!result.success) result.state = reset;
}
```

Nondeterministic Repetition. Similar to nondeterministic choice, we execute a nondeterministic repetition a^* until the first time the loop body program a is executed successfully: `while (!result.success) { C(a) }`.

Differential Equations. Differential equations are implemented by handing the current state to actuators, so just `actuate(result); result.success = true;`. In doing so, we exploit the structure of component contract compliance [14], which allows a single differential equation at a specific position in the component contract and hence guarantees that backtracking occurs only locally in control code and in the communication between sub-components, but never undoes the effect of differential equations.

4.2   Monitoring

In a readily composed system, only a subset of the components may describe system functionality and can be implemented by generating control code from the component model with above methods. Other components may describe environment behavior or agents (e.g., obstacles) that we cannot control. Nevertheless, the composed system makes crucial safety-relevant assumptions about the behavior of such environment components. Safety is provably guaranteed through ModelPlex [13] when we monitor the environment behavior for compliance with their model. The necessary monitoring conditions in dL are generated by proof [13]. The methods introduce above are applicable to generate executable monitor code. Here, we briefly discuss the nature of monitor conditions in C for debugging purposes and readability. The generated monitor conditions test for compliance between component environment model and true environment. Provably correct monitoring is available in our VeriPhy pipeline, which generates provably correct machine code [4] that witnesses compliance between a model and reality.

The monitor conditions generated by ModelPlex are formulas that describe how a current state of the program is related to the next state through the program statements. A monitor condition $P(x, x^+)$ compares two states for compliance with the program statements: variables in the previous state are identified by the program variable name x, whereas those in the next state are marked x^+. For example, the robot controller $ctrl_r$ (if (Drive) $s_r := \hat{d}$ else $s_r := 0$) is transformed by proof into a monitor condition $(\text{Drive} \wedge s_r^+ = \hat{d}) \vee (\neg\text{Drive} \wedge s_r^+ = 0)$ and represents assignments, tests, and nondeterministic choices as described below.

Assignments and Tests. Some of the statements are unambiguous computations that represent points in the state space: for example, assignment $s_r := 0$ only admits a specific new speed (0), and therefore the monitor condition will test speed with the formula $s_r^+ = 0$. Others represent regions in the state space and may refer to both states (e.g., testing whether stopping is necessary with Drive).

Nondeterministic Choices. Execution in a hybrid program splits into several paths at each nondeterministic choice, which result in disjunctions in the generated monitoring conditions (e.g., one disjunct describing how the robot chooses speed when following the remote control command, another disjunct for stopping). For example, the robot controller $ctrl_r$ results in the disjunction $(\text{Drive} \wedge s_r^+ = \hat{d}) \vee (\neg\text{Drive} \wedge s_r^+ = 0)$, which means that the monitor is satisfied either when the robot chooses a new speed $s_r^+ = \hat{d}$ when also the condition Drive was satisfied, or else chooses a new speed $s_r^+ = 0$. For provable runtime safety, the main result of ModelPlex [13] guarantees that the system at runtime enjoys the guarantees of the offline proof when the monitor conditions evaluate to true at runtime. The ModelPlex monitor conditions can be translated into C code using the control code transformations introduced above.

4.3   Using the Generated Code

The generated control code implements a control step that reads from sensors and writes to actuators, which are attached through hooks (signature repeated here for easy reference):

```
state ctrl(state const* const current,
           parameters const* const params,
           Sensors sense,
           Actuators actuate)
```

In the following code snippet, we implement the Sensors and Actuators callback functions to read from and modify the state of the system components according to a manually implemented simple simulator of the obstacle and robot motion, and a random desired speed suggestion of the remote control.

```
parameters sysParams = { .ep = 0.5L, .S=3.0L, .D=5.0L };
rcState rc           = { .dr = 0.0L };
obsState obs         = { .po = 10.0L, .so = 0.0L };
state robot = {
  .pr = 0.0L, .sr = 0.0L, .t = 0.0L,
  .por0 = 10.0L, .dr0 = 0.0L, .t0 = 0.0L
};

inputs readRobotInputs() {
  return ((inputs){ .po = obs.po, .dr = rc.dr });
}

void actuateRobotOutputs(state const* const out) {
  /* random time st in [0..ep] */
  long double st = randomDouble(0.0L, sysParams.ep);
  /* simulate robot */
  robot.sr = out->sr;
  robot.t = st;
  robot.pr = robot.pr + robot.sr*st;
  /* simulate obstacle: random so in [0..S] */
  obs.so = randomDouble(0.0L, sysParams.S);
  obs.po = obs.po + obs.so*st;
  /* simulate remote control: random dr in [0..D] */
  rc.dr = randomDouble(0.0L, sysParams.D);
}
```

In a real system, the sensor and actuator callback functions are used to interact with the system hardware through sensor and actuator drivers.

5   Related Work

Formal verification tools based on hybrid-automata, like SpaceEx [6], allow verification of parallel composed hybrid I/O automata, but either rely on soundness-critical extensions to support compositional reasoning or analyze a readily composed system in a monolithic fashion, which may lead to state space explosion. Modeling and simulation tools, such as Ptolemy [5] and Modelica [7], support component-based modeling of hybrid systems, but do not support verification or exploit the modular structure of the system for simulation. The model-driven development tool Simulink/Stateflow comes with a design verifier that allows a model analysis, but does not create proofs like KeYmaera X. Additional approaches allow formal verification of Simulink/Stateflow by translation into a other formalisms (e.g., timed automata [18], hybrid automata [1]), but thus rely on soundness-critical extensions. Conversely, [2] allow transformation of formally verified hybrid automata to Simulink/Stateflow, with follow-up code generation through (unverified) syntactic transformations. The CyPhyML paradigm [10], developed as part of the OpenMETA tool chain, supports component-based modeling of CPS. However, for analysis purposes (e.g., simulation, verification), the models must be translated to other formalisms, like Modelica.

In summary, the component-based verification and code-generation functionality of related tools extend the soundness-critical core of those tools. We, in contrast, analyze components separately and prove system safety from component safety in tactics [8] outside the soundness-critical core. For code generation, we follow a pragmatic approach similar to existing tools and use systematic transformations, but we strive for performing program transformations with proofs when possible: we exploit tactics to adapt the shape of hybrid programs from their nondeterministic nature to a deterministic implementation with proofs to prepare for emitting C code. The imperative nature of hybrid programs then makes inspecting the remaining syntactic transformations straightforward.

6 Conclusion

This paper demonstrates a tool chain that exploits the strict separation of tactics from the soundness-critical core in KeYmaera X in order to build component-based verification techniques. The input language, definitions, and lemma mechanism of KeYmaera X are a useful basis when structuring models into separate components and to combine separate component safety and connection compatibility proofs into a safety proof of a readily composed system.

For implementation of components and easy integration with embedded and cyber-physical systems, we take a pragmatic approach by generating C code with informally inspected program transformations. These transformations are designed to emit control code for components that describe implementable system functionality, and monitor code to monitor for violation of the assumptions that models make about environment behavior or agents outside the control of our own system. The transformations also address the gap between the nondeterministic operators of hybrid programs and the deterministic implementations in a way that preserves safety. We demonstrate how tactics can help implement these transformations by proof on the level of hybrid programs to prepare for emitting C code, so that only the final transformation step from hybrid programs into C is unverified. Fully verified machine code with a chain of theorem provers is available in KeYmaera X with VeriPhy [4].

References

1. Agrawal, A., Simon, G., Karsai, G.: Semantic translation of Simulink/Stateflow models to hybrid automata using graph transformations. Electr. Notes Theor. Comput. Sci. **109**, 43–56 (2004)
2. Bak, S., Beg, O.A., Bogomolov, S., Johnson, T.T., Nguyen, L.V., Schilling, C.: Hybrid automata: from verification to implementation. STTT (2017)
3. Bohrer, B., Rahli, V., Vukotic, I., Völp, M., Platzer, A.: Formally verified differential dynamic logic. In: Bertot, Y., Vafeiadis, V. (eds.) Certified Programs and Proofs - 6th ACM SIGPLAN Conference, CPP 2017, pp. 208–221. ACM, New York (2017)

4. Bohrer, B., Tan, Y.K., Mitsch, S., Myreen, M.O., Platzer, A.: VeriPhy: verified controller executables from verified cyber-physical system models. In: Grossman, D. (ed.) Proceedings of the 39th ACM SIGPLAN Conference on Programming Language Design and Implementation, PLDI 2018. pp. 617–630. ACM (2018)

5. Eker, J., et al.: Taming heterogeneity - the Ptolemy approach. Proc. IEEE **91**(1), 127–144 (2003)

6. Frehse, G., et al.: SpaceEx: scalable verification of hybrid systems. In: Gopalakrishnan, G., Qadeer, S. (eds.) CAV 2011. LNCS, vol. 6806, pp. 379–395. Springer, Heidelberg (2011). https://doi.org/10.1007/978-3-642-22110-1_30

7. Fritzson, P., Engelson, V.: Modelica—a unified object-oriented language for system modeling and simulation. In: Jul, E. (ed.) ECOOP 1998. LNCS, vol. 1445, pp. 67–90. Springer, Heidelberg (1998). https://doi.org/10.1007/BFb0054087

8. Fulton, N., Mitsch, S., Bohrer, B., Platzer, A.: Bellerophon: tactical theorem proving for hybrid systems. In: Ayala-Rincón, M., Muñoz, C.A. (eds.) ITP 2017. LNCS, vol. 10499, pp. 207–224. Springer, Cham (2017). https://doi.org/10.1007/978-3-319-66107-0_14

9. Fulton, N., Mitsch, S., Quesel, J.-D., Völp, M., Platzer, A.: KeYmaera X: an axiomatic tactical theorem prover for hybrid systems. In: Felty, A.P., Middeldorp, A. (eds.) CADE 2015. LNCS (LNAI), vol. 9195, pp. 527–538. Springer, Cham (2015). https://doi.org/10.1007/978-3-319-21401-6_36

10. Lattmann, Z., Nagel, A., Levendovszky, T., Bapty, T., Neema, S., Karsai, G.: Component-based modeling of dynamic systems using heterogeneous composition. In: Hardebolle, C., Syriani, E., Sprinkle, J., Mészáros, T. (eds.) Proceedings of the 6th International Workshop on Multi-Paradigm Modeling, MPM@MoDELS 2012, pp. 73–78. ACM (2012)

11. Loos, S.M., Platzer, A.: Differential refinement logic. In: Grohe, M., Koskinen, E., Shankar, N. (eds.) LICS, pp. 505–514. ACM, New York (2016)

12. Mitsch, S., Platzer, A.: The KeYmaera X proof IDE: concepts on usability in hybrid systems theorem proving. In: Dubois, C., Mery, D., Masci, P. (eds.) 3rd Workshop on Formal Integrated Development Environment, EPTCS, vol. 240, pp. 67–81. Open Publishing Association (2016)

13. Mitsch, S., Platzer, A.: ModelPlex: verified runtime validation of verified cyber-physical system models. Form. Methods Syst. Des. **49**(12), 33–74 (2016). Special issue of selected papers from RV 2014

14. Müller, A., Mitsch, S., Retschitzegger, W., Schwinger, W., Platzer, A.: Tactical contract composition for hybrid system component verification. STTT **20**, 615–643 (2018). special issue for selected papers from FASE 2017

15. Platzer, A.: Differential dynamic logic for hybrid systems. J. Autom. Reas. **41**(2), 143–189 (2008)

16. Platzer, A.: A complete uniform substitution calculus for differential dynamic logic. J. Autom. Reas. **59**(2), 219–265 (2017)

17. Platzer, A.: Logical Foundations of Cyber-Physical Systems. Springer, Switzerland (2018). https://doi.org/10.1007/978-3-319-63588-0

18. Yang, Y., Jiang, Y., Gu, M., Sun, J.: Verifying Simulink stateflow model: timed automata approach. In: Lo, D., Apel, S., Khurshid, S. (eds.) Proceedings of the 31st IEEE/ACM International Conference on Automated Software Engineering, ASE 2016, pp. 852–857. ACM (2016)

Formal Methods

Guaranteed Control Synthesis
for Continuous Systems in UPPAAL TIGA

Kim Guldstrand Larsen, Adrien Le Coënt[✉], Marius Mikučionis,
and Jakob Haahr Taankvist

Department of Computer Science, Aalborg University,
Selma Lagerlöfs Vej 300, 9220 Aalborg Øst, Denmark
{kgl,adrien,marius,jht}@cs.aau.dk

Abstract. We present a method for synthesising control strategies for
continuous dynamical systems. We use UPPAAL TIGA for the synthesis
in combination with a set-based Euler method for guaranteeing that
the synthesis is safe. We present both a general method and a method
which provides tighter bounds for monotone systems. As a case-study,
we synthesize a guaranteed safe strategy for a simplified adaptive cruise
control application. We show that the guaranteed strategy is only slightly
more conservative than the strategy generated in the original adaptive
cruise control paper which uses a discrete non guaranteed strategy. Also,
we show how reinforcement learning may be used to obtain optimal sub-
strategies.

Keywords: Continuous systems · Euler method · Control synthesis ·
Timed games

1 Introduction

The goal of this work is to introduce a new approach for the synthesis of *correct-by-construction* control strategies for continuous-time sampled switched systems,
based on the synthesis tool UPPAAL TIGA [2]. Sampled switched systems consti-
tute a sub-class of hybrid systems, and the synthesis problem for such systems
is still an important issue, particularly when considering safety critical systems.
The model of sampled switched systems has been used in various domains, such
as power electronics [9], green housing [17,25], automotive industry [23,30]. The
approach we develop is motivated by a cruise control application introduced in
[18]. In a few words, the objective of the case-study is to compute a controller
choosing the acceleration of a car (through the throttle and brake), in order to
avoid hitting the car in front of it. Obviously, one does not control the front car,
and such a system can easily be modelled as a two-player game. Furthermore, an
accurate modelling of the dynamics of the cars should be done with differential
equations. Our main goal is to ensure safety properties for the controlled system,
e.g., that the distance between the cars stays above a given limit. The system
can actually be formulated as a continuous-time switched system, however, the

© Springer Nature Switzerland AG 2019
R. Chamberlain et al. (Eds.): CyPhy 2018/WESE 2018, LNCS 11615, pp. 113–133, 2019.
https://doi.org/10.1007/978-3-030-23703-5_6

difficulty comes from uncontrollable components, which prevents us from using standard switched control synthesis methods.

Control synthesis for switched systems has been extensively studied in the past years. One of the current major approaches is symbolic methods, which basically aim at representing the continuous and infinite state-space of the system with a finite number of symbols, e.g. discrete points [11,29], sets of states [21], etc. This type of approaches is particularly adapted for safety critical systems, since it exhaustively ensures that an interest set is safe. However, dealing with uncontrollable components in this setting is particularly difficult. One could cite robust approaches [12], distributed computations [22], or contract-based design [31], but they usually consider the adversary as a bounded perturbation. In the case of the cruise control case-study, considering the front car as a bounded perturbation would be overly conservative, the reachability computations would lead to extremely pessimistic sets, and thus inapplicable controllers. Moreover, the state-space to be considered in the cruise control example is too large to be handled by most symbolic methods, using a discretisation or tiling based approach would be computationally infeasible.

The model of timed automata and games is particularly well suited for modelling the behaviour of the car. The tool UPPAAL TIGA allows to compute strategies for such systems, but for computability reasons, requires integers in the guards of the models. Thereby, the dynamics of the system should be described using only integers. A naive way of doing so is to discretise the system, for example with a numerical scheme, properly scaled or approximated so that the discrete approximation is described with integers. This is the approach which was used in [18]. The problem of this approach is that the properties are guaranteed only at discrete times, which compromises the safety of the controlled system. This is illustrated in Fig. 1, in which the true continuous distance can be compared to the integer approximation used in [18]. We clearly observe that the continuous distance between the cars goes below the integer approximation between two time steps. The safety property is not guaranteed in this case, since the cars could hit each other between two time steps.

We present an approach based on the synthesis tool UPPAAL TIGA, which allows to compute guaranteed safe strategies for timed game models of continuous dynamical systems. By merging safe reachability computations based on guaranteed numerical schemes, with state-of-the-art verification of timed automata and games, we extend the field of application of both continuous reachability computations, and timed game verification tools. The guaranteed solution of ordinary differential equations have been widely studied in the last decades. The main approaches rely on interval arithmetic, in the framework of Taylor series in [26,27], and Runge–Kutta schemes in [3,4,10]. In this paper, we choose to use a guaranteed Euler method, introduced in [20], because of its simplicity of implementation which allows its use directly in UPPAAL TIGA, without using any external libraries.

The principle of our approach is the following: instead of using a standard scheme or discretisation for computing successor states in the timed game model,

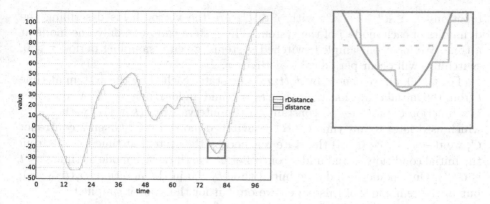

Fig. 1. The problem of using a discrete approximation for the dynamics as in [18]: the continuous distance (`rDistance`) can go below the integer approximation (`distance`) between the time steps.

we use a guaranteed set-based Euler scheme. Since we use a set-based approach, we need to use lower and upper over-approximations, this allows us to keep the continuous state in a convex set. The set-based approach is implemented in functions which take integers as inputs, and return integers, thus ensuring that we keep the decidability results of the verification tool. Since set-based methods usually lead to growing sets within time, we develop a refinement method for monotone systems in order to keep a tight approximation during long simulations. We then demonstrate the usability of the method by further exploring the safe strategies computed. In our case, we use a learning method implemented in the tool UPPAAL STRATEGO [7] to optimise the controller while keeping the strategy safe.

The paper is divided as follows. In Sect. 2, we present the synthesis tool UPPAAL TIGA, its underlying limitations, and the gap to be filled in order to synthesize safety controllers for continous-time switched systems. We present a set-based reachability method for continuous systems based on the Euler method in Sect. 3. In Sect. 4, we combine the latter to functions that can be handled by the UPPAAL framework, maintaining the associated decidability results and ensuring safety for the continuous system. We propose a refinement method for monotone systems in Sect. 5, allowing to tighten the reachability approximations. We further exploit the safe strategies in Sect. 6, in which we optimise the strategy with a learning algorithm. We conclude in Sect. 7.

Problem Statement

We are interested in continuous-time switched systems described by the set of nonlinear ordinary differential equations:

$$\dot{x} = f_j(x), \tag{1}$$

where $x \in \mathbb{R}^n$ is the state of the system, and $j \in U$ is the mode of the system. The finite set $U = \{1, \ldots, N\}$ is the set of switching modes of the system. The functions $f_j : \mathbb{R}^n \longrightarrow \mathbb{R}^n$, with $j \in U$, are the vector fields describing the dynamics of each mode j of the system. The system can be in only one mode at a time. We focus on sampled switched systems: given a sampling period $\tau > 0$, switchings will occur periodically at times $\tau, 2\tau, \ldots$

For $t \in [0, \tau)$, we denote by $\phi_j(t; x_0)$ the state reached by the system at time t from the initial condition x_0 at time $t_0 = 0$ and under mode $j \in U$. A controller is a function $C : \mathbb{R}^+ \longrightarrow U$, constant on the intervals $[k\tau, (k+1)\tau]$ with $k \in \mathbb{N}$, which associates to any time $t \in \mathbb{R}^+$ a switched mode $j \in U$. Given a controller C, we denote by $\phi_C(t; x_0)$ the state reached by the system at time $t \in \mathbb{R}^+$ from the initial condition x_0 and under controller C, i.e. the active mode at time $t' \leq t$ is $C(t')$. One should include the initial time $t_0 = 0$ in the notation: $\phi_j(t; t_0, x_0)$, but in the remainder of this paper, we omit it for the sake of simplicity.

We focus on synthesizing controllers for the class of system introduced, and we aim at ensuring safety properties. The safety properties we consider is defined as follows.

Definition 1. *Consider a switched system of the form* (1). *Consider a safety set* $S = [s_1^{min}, s_1^{max}] \times \cdots \times [s_n^{min}, s_n^{max}]$ *given as a box of* $\mathbb{R}^n$. *Given a controller* C, *system* (1) *is said to be safe with respect to* S *if, for any initial condition* $x_0 \in S$ *and for all time* $t \in \mathbb{R}^+$, *we have:*

$$\phi_C(t; x_0) \in S.$$

Case Study

To illustrate our approach, we consider a cruise control application introduced in [18]. Two cars *Ego* and *Front* are driving on a road shown in Fig. 2. We are capable of controlling *Ego* but not *Front*. Both cars can drive a maximum of 20 m/s forward and a maximum of 10 m/s backwards. The cars have three different possible accelerations: $-2\,\mathrm{m/s}^2$, $0\,\mathrm{m/s}^2$ and $2\,\mathrm{m/s}^2$, between which they can switch instantly. For the cars to be safe, there should be a distance of at least 5 m between them. Any distance less than 5 m between the cars is considered unsafe. *Ego*'s sensors can detect the position of *Front* only within 200 m. If the distance between the cars is more than 200 m, then *Front* is considered to be *far away*. *Front* can reenter the scope of *Ego*'s sensor with arbitrary velocity as it desires, as long as the velocity is smaller or equal to that of *Ego*.

In this example, the aim is to synthesize a strategy for controllable car *Ego* such that it always stays far enough from uncontrollable car *Front*. The contin-

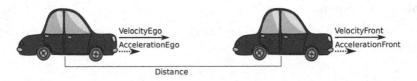

Fig. 2. Distance, velocity and acceleration between two cars [18].

uous dynamics of the resulting system is as follows:

$$\dot{v}_f = a_f \tag{2}$$
$$\dot{v}_e = a_e \tag{3}$$
$$\dot{d} = v_f - v_e \tag{4}$$

where a_f and a_e can take the values -2, 0, and 2, resulting in an 8-mode switched system of the form (1). The safety set to consider is thus $S = [-10, 20] \times [-10, 20] \times [5, 200]$. We suppose that the switching period of the system is $\tau = 1$. Note that the dynamics of this system is linear, therefore, given a controller C, we can analytically compute the exact trajectory of the system.

2 From Continuous Switched Systems to Stochastic Priced Timed Games

2.1 Modeling of the System

We model the system as a timed game in UPPAAL TIGA, later, in Sect. 6 we annotate the model with continuous behaviour and probabilities in UPPAAL STRATEGO [7] to be able to do performance optimisation. The system has two players, *Ego* and *Front*, with two different behaviors. We use an already existing model for these players, and we refer the reader to [18] for more information on this model. We see the two players in Figs. 4 and 5. We see that these two do not do anything except when they get a synchronisation call chooseEgo respectively chooseFront. In Fig. 3 we see a system component which waits one time unit and then sends the two signals. The fact that the controller only makes choices once every time unit means the system is a switched system as defined above.

In Fig. 3 we see that once every time unit we call updateDiscrete(). This function can be seen in Appendix A. A remaining question is the computation of function updateDiscrete(), which, given the current state of system (1) at time t, returns the successor state at time $t + \tau$. Using a proper scaling of the system, we can approximate system (1) by a discrete-time discrete-state system, where the state and time is described with integers. The approximate discrete system can be written

$$x(t + \tau) = F_j(x(t)), \tag{5}$$

where $x \in \mathbb{N}^n$ is the state, $t \in \mathbb{N}$ (with $\tau = 1$) and $F_j(x(t)) = x(t) + \int_0^\tau f_j(x(t))dt$.

2.2 Synthesis Using UPPAAL TIGA

As shown above, we model the system using only integers, and as shown in Fig. 1 this is not always safe as the continuous trajectory is not taken into account between discrete points. In Sect. 3 we introduce a method for calculating a tube in the state space, which we can guarantee the system will stay in. In the UPPAAL

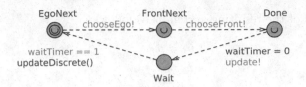

Fig. 3. Model of the system component.

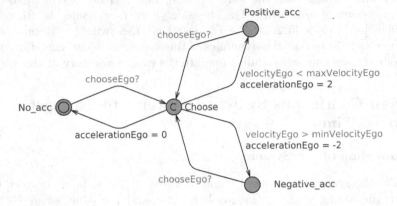

Fig. 4. Model of *Ego*.

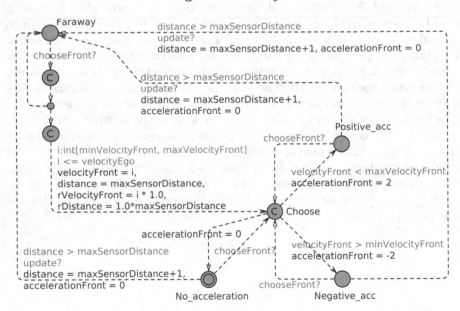

Fig. 5. Model of *Front*.

model we update the `updateDiscrete()` (see Appendix A) function to do the computation of this tube. We add the bounds of the tube to the state space in the form of arrays (vectors) containing the lower and upper guaranteed integer approximations. The function internally uses doubles. Generally, if real numbered variables (which are not clocks) are used, synthesis of strategies in timed games is undecidable. However, the doubles are *only* used in the calculation of the transition and the result of the function is integers[1]. This means the state space only contains integers, and as the model guarantees bounds on these integers the synthesis is possible.

As we now have guaranteed lower and upper bounds for the continuous state, we can ask UPPAAL TIGA to synthesize a strategy which ensures that the guaranteed lower and upper bounds always stay in the safety set S. It is clear that this is a conservative approach and if the guaranteed bounds are not reasonably tight, it might not be possible to synthesize a strategy. We will see in Sect. 5 how to tighten these bounds and in Sect. 6 we will explore the generated strategy using UPPAAL STRATEGO.

3   Reachability Tubes Using the Euler Method

3.1   Lipschitz and One-Sided Lipschitz Condition

We make the following hypothesis:

(*H0*)   For all $j \in U, f_j$ is a locally Lipschitz continuous map on S.

We recall the definition of locally Lipschitz:

Definition 2. *A function $f : A \subset \mathbb{R}^n \longrightarrow \mathbb{R}^m$ is* locally Lipschitz *at $x_0 \in A$ if there exist constants $\eta > 0$ and $M > 0$ such that*

$$\|x - x_0\| < \eta \rightarrow \|f(x) - f(x_0)\| \leq M\|x - x_0\|$$

As in [13], we make the assumption that the vector field f_j is such that the solutions of the differential equation (1) are defined, e.g. by assuming that the support of the vector field f_j is compact.

We denote by T a compact overapproximation of the image by ϕ_j of S for $0 \leq t \leq \tau$ and $j \in U$, i.e. T is such that

$$T \supseteq \{\phi_j(t; x_0) \mid j \in U, 0 \leq t \leq \tau, x_0 \in S\}.$$

The existence of T is guaranteed by assumption (*H0*) and the compactness of S. We know furthermore by (*H0*), Definition 2 and the compactness of the support of f_j that, for all $j \in U$, there exists a constant $L_j > 0$ such that:

$$\|f_j(y) - f_j(x)\| \leq L_j \|y - x\| \quad \forall x, y \in S. \tag{6}$$

---

[1] The method described actually calculates a box which is specified using reals, we then round these to obtain integers to make it possible to do the synthesis.

Let us define C_j for all $j \in U$:

$$C_j = \sup_{x \in S} L_j \|f_j(x)\| \quad \text{for all} \quad j \in U. \tag{7}$$

We make the additional hypothesis that the mappings f_j are *one-sided Lipschitz* (OSL) [8].
   Formally:

   ($H1$)   For all $j \in U$, there exists a constant $\lambda_j \in \mathbb{R}$ such that
   $$\langle f_j(y) - f_j(x), y - x \rangle \leq \lambda_j \|y - x\|^2 \quad \forall x, y \in T, \tag{8}$$

where $\langle \cdot, \cdot \rangle$ denotes the scalar product of two vectors of $\mathbb{R}^n$. Constant $\lambda_j \in \mathbb{R}$ is called one-sided Lipschitz (OSL) constant, and can also be found in the literature as Dahlquist's constant [32]. Note that in practice, hypotheses H0 and H1 are not strong. Hypothesis H0 just ensures the existence of solutions for the system, and constants L_j and λ_j can always be found if the state of the system stays in a compact set (e.g. the set T).

Computation of Constants λ_j, L_j and C_j. In the general case, computation of constants L_j, C_j, λ_j ($j \in U$) can be realised with constrained optimisation algorithms such as the "sqp" algorithm of Octave, applied on the following optimisation problems:

– Constant L_j:

$$L_j = \max_{x,y \in S, \ x \neq y} \frac{\|f_j(y) - f_j(x)\|}{\|y - x\|}$$

– Constant C_j:

$$C_j = \max_{x \in S} L_j \|f_j(x)\|$$

– Constant λ_j:

$$\lambda_j = \max_{x,y \in T, \ x \neq y} \frac{\langle f_j(y) - f_j(x), y - x \rangle}{\|y - x\|^2}$$

We could point out that such algorithms do not guarantee that an underapproximation of the constants is computed. However, some works have been done for computing over and under approximation of Lipschitz constants in [28], and could be used here. This approach can be extended to the OSL constant. Yet, for linear systems, constants L_j, C_j, λ_j ($j \in U$) can be computed exactly, such as in [19], and we use this approach for the cruise control example.

3.2   Euler Approximate Solutions

Having defined OSL conditions, we now present the method introduced in [20], allowing to compute reachability sets and tubes, relying on the Euler method. The introduction of OSL conditions actually allows to establish a new global error bound, permitting the computation of overapproximation of reachability sets and tubes, precise enough to be used for control synthesis. In the remainder of this section, we consider, without loss of generality, that $t_0 = 0$, and omit its notation in the trajectory ϕ_j.

Given an initial point $\tilde{x}_0 \in S$ and a mode $j \in U$, we define the following "linear approximate solution" $\tilde{\phi}_j(t; \tilde{x}_0)$ for t on $[0, \tau]$ by:

$$\tilde{\phi}_j(t; \tilde{x}_0) = \tilde{x}_0 + t f_j(\tilde{x}_0). \tag{9}$$

Note that formula (9) is nothing else but the explicit forward Euler scheme with "time step" t. It is thus a consistent approximation of order 1 in t of the exact trajectory of (1) under the hypothesis $\tilde{x}_0 = x_0$.

We define the closed ball of center $x \in \mathbb{R}^n$ and radius $r > 0$, denoted $B(x, r)$, as the set $\{x' \in \mathbb{R}^n \mid \|x' - x\| \leq r\}$.

Given a positive real δ, we now define the expression $\delta_j(t)$ which, as we will see in Theorem 1, represents (an upper bound on) the error associated to $\tilde{\phi}_j(t; \tilde{x}_0)$ (i.e. $\|\tilde{\phi}_j(t; \tilde{x}_0) - \phi_j(t; x_0)\|$).

Definition 3. *Let us consider a switched system verifying hypotheses (H0) and (H1), associated to constants* λ_j, L_j *and* C_j *for each mode* $j \in U$, *such that Eqs. (6), (7) and (8) hold. Let* δ *be a positive constant. We define, for all* $0 \leq t \leq \tau$, *function* $\delta_j(\rho, t)$ *as follows:*

- *if* $\lambda_j < 0$:

$$\delta_j(\rho, t) = \left(\rho^2 e^{\lambda_j t} + \frac{C_j^2}{\lambda_j^2} \left(t^2 + \frac{2t}{\lambda_j} + \frac{2}{\lambda_j^2} \left(1 - e^{\lambda_j t} \right) \right) \right)^{\frac{1}{2}}$$

- *if* $\lambda_j = 0$:

$$\delta_j(\rho, t) = \left(\rho^2 e^t + C_j^2 (-t^2 - 2t + 2(e^t - 1)) \right)^{\frac{1}{2}}$$

- *if* $\lambda_j > 0$:

$$\delta_j(\rho, t) = \left(\rho^2 e^{3\lambda_j t} + \frac{C_j^2}{3\lambda_j^2} \left(-t^2 - \frac{2t}{3\lambda_j} + \frac{2}{9\lambda_j^2} \left(e^{3\lambda_j t} - 1 \right) \right) \right)^{\frac{1}{2}}$$

Note that $\delta_j(\rho, t) = \rho$ for $t = 0$.

Theorem 1. *Given a sampled switched system satisfying (H0–H1), consider a point* $\tilde{x}_0$ *and a positive real* ρ. *We have, for all* $x_0 \in B(\tilde{x}_0, \delta)$, $t \in [0, \tau]$ *and* $j \in U$:

$\phi_j(t; x_0) \in B(\tilde{\phi}_j(t; \tilde{x}_0), \delta_j(\rho, t))$.

See proof in [20].

Remark 1. In Theorem 1, we have supposed that the step size h used in Euler's method was equal to the sampling period τ of the switching system. Actually, in order to have better approximations, it is sometimes convenient to consider a uniform subdivision of $[0, \tau]$ and apply the Euler's method for a time step h equal to e.g. $h = \frac{\tau}{k}$, where $k \in \mathbb{N}$ is the number of sub-steps used in the interval $[0, \tau]$.

Corollary 1. *Given a sampled switched system satisfying (H0–H1), consider a point $\tilde{x}_0 \in S$, a real $\rho > 0$ and a mode $j \in U$ such that:*

1. *$B(\tilde{x}_0, \rho) \subseteq S$,*
2. *$B(\tilde{\phi}_j(\tau; \tilde{x}_0), \delta_j(\rho, \tau)) \subseteq S$, and*
3. *$\frac{\partial^2 \delta_j(\rho, t)}{\partial t^2} > 0$ for all $t \in [0, \tau]$.*

Then we have, for all $x_0 \in B(\tilde{x}_0, \rho)$ and $t \in [0, \tau]$: $\phi_j(t; x_0) \in S$.

Proof. By items 1 and 2, $B(\tilde{\phi}_j(t; \tilde{x}_0), \delta_j(\rho, t)) \subseteq S$ for $t = 0$ and $t = \tau$. Since $\delta_j(\rho, \cdot)$ is convex on $[0, \tau]$ by item 3, and S is convex, we have $B(\tilde{\phi}_j(t; \tilde{x}_0), \delta_j(\rho, t)) \subseteq S$ for all $t \in [0, \tau]$. It follows from Theorem 1 that $\phi_j(t; x_0) \in B(\tilde{\phi}_j(t; \tilde{x}_0), \delta_j(\rho, t)) \subseteq S$ for all $0 \le t \le \tau$.

Note that condition 3 of Corollary 1 on the convexity of $\delta_j(\rho, \cdot)$ on $[0, \tau]$ can be established again using an optimisation function. Since we have an exact expression for $\delta_j(\cdot)$, its second derivative (w.r.t. time) can be computed using a computer algebra software. Using an optimisation algorithm then allows to verify that its minimum is positive. Nevertheless, we believe that the convexity of $\delta_j(\rho, \cdot)$ with respect to time could be shown analytically. For the remainder of this paper, we state this condition as a hypothesis:

$$(H2) \quad \text{For all } j \in U, \rho > 0, \quad \frac{\partial^2 \delta_j(\rho, t)}{\partial t^2} > 0 \text{ for all } t \in [0, \tau].$$

4   Guaranteed Synthesis Using the Euler Method

Before stating the main result of this section, let us extend the definitions of the floor and ceiling functions to the n-dimensional setting as follows:

Definition 4. *Let $x = (x_1, \ldots, x_n)^\top \in \mathbb{R}^n$. The floor function maps a vector $x \in \mathbb{R}^n$ to a vector of $\mathbb{Z}^n$, denoted by $\lfloor x \rfloor$, with the following coefficients:*

$$\lfloor x \rfloor = (\max\{m \in \mathbb{Z} \mid m \le x_1\}, \ldots, \max\{m \in \mathbb{Z} \mid m \le x_n\})^\top \quad (10)$$

Similarly, the ceiling function maps a vector $x \in \mathbb{R}^n$ to a vector of $\mathbb{Z}^n$, denoted by $\lceil x \rceil$, with the following coefficients:

$$\lceil x \rceil = (\min\{m \in \mathbb{Z} \mid m \ge x_1\}, \ldots, \min\{m \in \mathbb{Z} \mid x_n \le m\})^\top \quad (11)$$

In the following, we denote by $\mathbb{1}$ the vector of $\mathbb{R}^n$ which coefficients are all one. We also consider the ordering of $\mathbb{R}^n$ with the relation $\leq$ defined as follows, for two vectors $x = (x_1, \ldots, x_n)^\top \in \mathbb{R}^n$ and $y = (y_1, \ldots, y_n)^\top \in \mathbb{R}^n$:

$$x \leq y \quad \text{if and only if} \quad x_i \leq y_i \ \forall i = 1, \ldots, n. \tag{12}$$

We now introduce the main functions allowing to compute safe approximations of the state of the continuous system using integers:

Definition 5. *Let $j \in U$ be the active mode for the time interval $[t, t + \tau]$. Consider a given initial condition $x_0 \in S$ and initial radius $\rho_0 > 0$, let $h = \tau/k$ be the step size of the Euler method, k thus being the number of time steps used for the interval. For $i \in \{0, \ldots, k\}$, we define the sequence of radiuses of the Euler method as follows:*

$$\rho_0^j = \rho_0 \tag{13}$$
$$\rho_{i+1}^j = \delta_j(\rho_i^j, h) \tag{14}$$

Similarly, we define the sequence of points computed by the Euler method as:

$$x_0^j = x_0 \tag{15}$$

$$x_{i+1}^j = \tilde{\phi}_j(h; x_i^j) = x_i^j + h f_j(x_i^j) \tag{16}$$

We define the integer under-approximation function $H_j^k(x_0, \rho_0)$ over time time interval $[t, t + \tau]$ as follows:

$$H_j^k(x_0, \rho_0) = \min_{i \in \{0, \ldots, k+1\}} \lfloor x_i^j - \rho_i^j \mathbb{1} \rfloor \tag{17}$$

We define the low integer successor state function $h_j^k(x_0, \rho_0)$ as follows:

$$h_j^k(x_0, \rho_0) = \lfloor x_{k+1}^j - \rho_{k+1}^j \mathbb{1} \rfloor \tag{18}$$

Similarly, we define the integer over-approximation function $G_j^k(x_0, \rho_0)$ over time time interval $[t, t + \tau]$ as follows:

$$G_j^k(x_0, \rho_0) = \max_{i \in \{0, \ldots, k+1\}} \lceil x_i^j + \rho_i^j \mathbb{1} \rceil \tag{19}$$

We define the high integer successor state function $g_j^k(x_0, \rho_0)$ as follows:

$$g_j^k(x_0, \rho_0) = \lceil x_{k+1}^j + \rho_{k+1}^j \mathbb{1} \rceil \tag{20}$$

Theorem 2. *Suppose that system (1) satisfies (H0), (H1), (H2). Consider a given initial condition $x_0 \in S$ and initial radius $\rho_0 > 0$, let $h = \tau/k$ be the step size of the Euler method, k thus being the number of time steps used for the interval. Functions H and G return safe integer under and over-approximations of* the continuous state of system (1) on the time interval $[t, t+\tau]$, for initial conditions in ball $B(x_0, \rho_0)$ at time t. I.e., for any initial condition $x \in B(x_0, \rho_0) \subseteq S$ at initial time t, for all mode $j \in U$ and any $k \in \mathbb{N}_{>0}$, we have:

$$H_j^k(x_0, \rho_0) \in S \wedge G_j^k(x_0, \rho_0) \in S \Rightarrow \phi_j(t'; x) \in S \quad \forall t' \in [t, t+\tau]. \quad (21)$$

If $H_j^k(x_0, \rho_0) \in S \wedge G_j^k(x_0, \rho_0) \in S$ holds, we furthermore have:

$$H_j^k(x_0, \rho_0) \leq \phi_j(t'; x) \leq G_j^k(x_0, \rho_0), \quad \forall t' \in [t, t+\tau]. \quad (22)$$

Proof. The proof relies on Corollary 1. Because of the convexity with respect to time of function $\delta(\cdot, \cdot)$, it is sufficient to verify that a reachability tube stays inside safety set S only by verifying that balls $B(x_0^i, \rho_0^i)$ belong to S at each discrete instant $t + \frac{i\tau}{k}$ with $i = 0, \ldots, k+1$. Functions H and G return integer vectors which bound the Euler tubes on the whole time interval $[t, t+\tau]$, thus containing all the possible trajectories issued from $B(x_0, \rho_0)$.

Theorem 2 allows to compute under and over-approximations of the minimum and maximum integer visited by the system on a given time-interval. If it allows to ensure safety properties, one also needs an accurate way of computing the successor state. The following corollary gives a general way to compute this successor state:

Corollary 2. *Suppose that system (1) satisfies (H0), (H1) and (H2). Consider a given initial condition $x_0 \in S$ and initial radius $\rho_0 > 0$, let $h = \tau/k$ be the step size of the Euler method, k thus being the number of time steps used for the interval. We have, for any initial condition $x \in B(x_0, \rho_0) \subseteq S$ at initial time t, for all mode $j \in U$ and any $k \in \mathbb{N}_{>0}$:*

$$H_j^k(x_0, \rho_0) \in S \wedge G_j^k(x_0, \rho_0) \in S \Rightarrow h_j^k(x_0, \rho_0) \leq \phi_j(t+\tau; x) \leq g_j^k(x_0, \rho_0) (23)$$

The main result allowing to compute safety controllers is the following:

Theorem 3. *Consider system (1) satisfying (H0), (H1) and (H2), and an initial condition $x_0 \in S$ at time 0.*

- *If x_0 is an integer, let $x_0' = x_0$*
- *Ohterwise, let $x_0' = \frac{\lfloor x_0 \rfloor + \lceil x_0 \rceil}{2}$*

Let $h = \tau/k$ be the step size of the Euler method with $k \in \mathbb{N}_{>0}$. Given a controller C, let us compute iteratively two sequences of integer states as follows:

$$y_0^{min} = \lfloor x_0' \rfloor \quad at\ t = 0$$
$$y_0^{max} = \lceil x_0' \rceil \quad at\ t = 0$$

and

$$y_{i+1}^{min} = h_{C(i\tau)}^k \left(\frac{y_i^{max} + y_i^{min}}{2}, \left\| \frac{y_i^{max} - y_i^{min}}{2} \right\| \right) \quad at\ t = (i+1)\tau$$

$$y_{i+1}^{max} = g_{C(i\tau)}^k \left(\frac{y_i^{max} + y_i^{min}}{2}, \left\| \frac{y_i^{max} - y_i^{min}}{2} \right\| \right) \quad at\ t = (i+1)\tau$$

If controller C verifies, for all $t = i\tau$ with $i \in \mathbb{N}$:

$$H_{C(t)}^k(\frac{y_i^{max} + y_i^{min}}{2}, \left\|\left\|\frac{y_i^{max} - y_i^{min}}{2}\right\|\right\|) \in S \wedge G_{C(t)}^k(\frac{y_i^{max} + y_i^{min}}{2}, \left\|\left\|\frac{y_i^{max} - y_i^{min}}{2}\right\|\right\|) \in S, \quad (24)$$

then system (1) is safe with respect to S.

Proof. The main idea of Theorem 3 is that we compute two sequences of integers which bound the continuous trajectory at discrete times, and functions H and G guarantee the correctness between discrete times. Corollary 1 guarantees that the sequences y_i^{min} and y_i^{max} do bound the continuous trajectory, since they are built as the bounds of the Euler tubes, but made wider using only integers. Theorem 2 then ensures that H and G bound the continuous trajectory between the time steps. If, for a controller C, they return values always belonging to S, we know that the controlled continuous trajectory stays inside S.

Note that functions H and G take integers as inputs (the sequences y_i^{min} and y_i^{max}), and return integers. Thus, functions H and G can be implemented in UPPAAL and used for computing guards in the time automata models, and the decidability results still hold, which ensures the termination of the computations. Due to the lack of space, we do not present how the strategy synthesis engine of UPPAAL TIGA works, and we refer the reader to [2]. In a nutshell, one has to exhaustively explore all the possible transitions, and eliminate the controllable actions leading to unsafe states. With the above theorem, we eliminate a transition as soon as (24) does not hold. Theorem 3 thus gives a general way of computing safety controllers for any system satisfying (H0)–(H1)–(H2), which are weak hypotheses. However, the accuracy of the Euler method can lack on some systems, particularly when looking far in the future, which leads us to the development of the refinement technique presented in the following section.

5   Refinement for Monotone Systems

The monotonicity property has been widely used in symbolic methods and control synthesis [1,25]. The monotonicity property can be expressed using an ordering of the state, of the input, or of a perturbation. In our case, we only need to consider the state ordering, or, more precisely, that each mode of the switched system is monotone with respect to the state. The monotonicity property is then expressed as follows:

Definition 6 (Monotonicity). *System (1) is monotone with respect to ordering $\leq$ if the following implication holds for all $j \in U$:*

$$x_0 \leq x_0' \Rightarrow \forall t > 0, \phi_j(t; x_0) \leq \phi_j(t; x_0') \quad (25)$$

We refer the reader to [16,24,25] for more information on monotone control systems and applications of the monotonicity property. If system (1) is monotone, we can refine Theorem 3 by computing more accurate sequences of integer points as follows:

Corollary 3. *Consider system (1) satisfying (H0), (H1), (H2) and the monotonicity property. Consider an initial condition $x_0 \in S$ at time 0.*

- *If x_0 is an integer, let $x_0' = x_0$*
- *Ohterwise, let $x_0' = \frac{\lfloor x_0 \rfloor + \lceil x_0 \rceil}{2}$*

Let $h = \tau/k$ be the step size of the Euler method with $k \in \mathbb{N}_{>0}$. Given a controller C, let us compute iteratively two sequences of integer states as follows:

$$y_0^{min} = \lfloor x_0' \rfloor \quad at \ t = 0$$
$$y_0^{max} = \lceil x_0' \rceil \quad at \ t = 0$$

and

$$y_{i+1}^{min} = \lfloor \phi_{C(i\tau)}(\tau; y_i^{min}) \rfloor \quad at \ t = (i+1)\tau$$
$$y_{i+1}^{max} = \lceil \phi_{C(i\tau)}(\tau; y_i^{max}) \rceil \quad at \ t = (i+1)\tau$$

If controller C verifies, for all $t = i\tau$ with $i \in \mathbb{N}$:

$$H_{C(t)}^k(\frac{y_i^{max} + y_i^{min}}{2}, \left\| \frac{y_i^{max} - y_i^{min}}{2} \right\|) \in S \wedge G_{C(t)}^k(\frac{y_i^{max} + y_i^{min}}{2}, \left\| \frac{y_i^{max} - y_i^{min}}{2} \right\|) \in S, \quad (26)$$

then system (1) is safe with respect to S.

Proof. Let us consider a controller C. We first show by induction on $i \in \mathbb{N}$ that for any initial condition $x_0 \in S$ we have: $y_i^{min} \le \phi_C(i\tau; x_0) \le y_i^{max}$. This is trivially true for $i = 0$ ($\lfloor x_0' \rfloor \le x_0 \le \lceil x_0' \rceil$). If this is true for $i \in \mathbb{N}$, then, from the monotonicity hypothesis with respect to ordering $\le$, we have:

$$\phi_{C(i\tau)}(\tau; y_i^{min}) \le \phi_{C(i\tau)}(\tau; \phi_C(i\tau; x_0)) \le \phi_{C(i\tau)}(\tau; y_i^{max})$$

i.e.:

$$\lfloor \phi_{C(i\tau)}(\tau; y_i^{min}) \rfloor \le \phi_C((i+1)\tau; x_0) \le \lceil \phi_{C(i\tau)}(\tau; y_i^{max}) \rceil$$
$$y_{i+1}^{min} \le \phi_C((i+1)\tau; x_0) \le y_{i+1}^{max}$$

which proves the induction. Thus, at every discrete time $t = i\tau$, we have:

$$\phi_C(i\tau; x_0) \in B(\frac{y_i^{max} + y_i^{min}}{2}, \left\| \frac{y_i^{max} - y_i^{min}}{2} \right\|).$$

This allows us to apply Theorem 2 on each interval $[i\tau, (i+1)\tau]$: under hypotheses (H0), (H1), (H2), for any step size $h = \tau/k$ of the Euler method, if controller C verifies, for all $t = i\tau$ with $i \in \mathbb{N}$:

$$H_{C(t)}^k(\frac{y_i^{max} + y_i^{min}}{2}, \left\| \frac{y_i^{max} - y_i^{min}}{2} \right\|) \in S \wedge G_{C(t)}^k(\frac{y_i^{max} + y_i^{min}}{2}, \left\| \frac{y_i^{max} - y_i^{min}}{2} \right\|) \in S, \quad (27)$$

then any (continuous) trajectory issued from $B(\frac{y_i^{max} + y_i^{min}}{2}, \left\| \frac{y_i^{max} - y_i^{min}}{2} \right\|)$ is safe with respect to S in the time interval $[i\tau, (i+1)\tau]$. Since $\phi_C(i\tau; x_0)$ does belong to $B(\frac{y_i^{max} + y_i^{min}}{2}, \left\| \frac{y_i^{max} - y_i^{min}}{2} \right\|)$, we conclude that $\phi_C(t; x_0) \in S$ for all $t \in [i\tau, (i+1)\tau]$, which is true for all $i \in \mathbb{N}$.

Corollary 3 uses the fact that we can use tighter integer bounds than those used in Theorem 3 when computing the integer sequences. Indeed, in Theorem 3, the sequences y_i^{min} and y_i^{max} are computed from the Euler tubes, which are quite pessimistic approximations of the trajectories. The sequences computed here do bound the trajectories of the continuous system at discrete instants because of the monotonicity property, but are this time computed from the exact solution.

Note that Corollary 3 requires the computation of the exact solution $\phi_C(\cdot\,;\cdot)$. If the system considered is subject to a linear dynamics, such as the cruise control example, the exact solution can be computed analytically. In other cases, an accurate numerical method can be used, such as a Runge–Kutta integration scheme with appropriate (fine) time-stepping. One could think about computing functions H and G using a similar fine-stepped numerical method, but it would require much more tests for each simulation step, or some numerically expensive optimisation methods, making it irrelevant in terms of computation times.

A simulation of a safe strategy computed with the refinement method[2] is given in Fig. 6. We observe a good accuracy of the integer bounds, the induced controller is thus not overly conservative. It illustrates that the refinement method keeps the approximations very close to the exact solution. Note that without the refinement method, it is be possible to obtain such accurate results if the OSL constants are negative. Indeed, when an OSL constant is negative, it is possible to choose a time step small enough to make the radius of the approximations decrease. This is due to the fact that a system with negative OSL constant presents trajectories getting exponentially closer together within time, and this behaviour can be captured with a time step small enough [19].

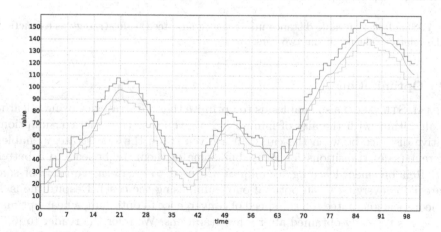

Fig. 6. Simulation of the real distance (red) and the guaranteed lower and integer distance (green and blue respectively) within time, using the refinement procedure. (Color figure online)

---

[2] In order to obtain a monotone system from the cruise control model, simply right (3) as $-\dot{v}_e = -a_e$ in order to have an addition in (4) which will indeed verify the monotonicity hypothesis.

6   Exploration of the Guaranteed Safe Strategy

We showed above how we can compute a guaranteed safe strategy for our system. We can now use UPPAAL STRATEGO to explore this new strategy and compare it with the discrete strategy computed in [18].

6.1   Model Checking Under the New Guaranteed Strategy

Using UPPAAL's model checker [5] we can explore which distances are possible at different relative velocities between the two cars, in Fig. 7 we see a plot of the different minimum possible distances of the two cars at different relative velocities, one for the strategy computed in [18] and one for the guaranteed safe strategy. We see that the two strategies are very similar, but the guaranteed safe strategy is slightly more conservative than the old non-safe strategy.

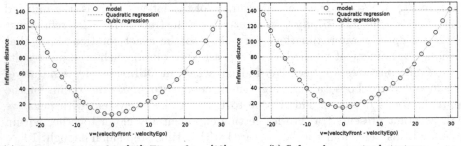

(a) Strategy computed in [18]. Figure from [18].   (b) Safe and guaranteed strategy.

Fig. 7. Smallest achievable distance under the (guaranteed) safe strategy as a function of the relative velocity of the two cars.

6.2   Optimisation

UPPAAL STRATEGO also enables us to optimise the safe strategies using a learning algorithm, with the aim of minimising a given cost (*e.g.* fuel consumption, relative distance between the cars). In a given state, the safe strategy enables different (safe) transitions for *Egos*, but some of them might lead to a better cost. Reinforcement-learning techniques are used to create a sequence of safe strategies converging to an optimal one (minimising the cost). Despite the lack of theoretical guarantees on the speed of convergence to optimum, a near-optimal strategy is typically obtained after a few iterations. We refer the reader to [6,7] for more information on the tool and the learning techniques used. This learning algorithm supports the use of continuous information. To use this algorithm we annotate the model with the continuous information using differential equations as seen in Fig. 8.

The learning algorithm also requires us to annotate the choices of *Front* with probabilities, in this case we assume that *Front* always chooses the acceleration and any other choice from a uniform distribution.

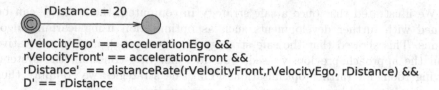

rDistance = 20

rVelocityEgo' == accelerationEgo &&
rVelocityFront' == accelerationFront &&
rDistance' == distanceRate(rVelocityFront,rVelocityEgo, rDistance) &&
D' == rDistance

Fig. 8. The monitor component defines a set of differential equation over real variables, these variables can then be used by the learning algorithm.

The measure we wish to optimise is the accumulated distance, we use the continuous variable D defined using the differential equation $D' == rDistance$, as seen Fig. 8. Our goal is to minimize this measure, which means to minimize the distance between the two cars. Clearly, just minimising the distance between the cars would lead to the cars crashing, so what we do is to constrain *Egos* allowed actions to only those which are safe according to the strategy computed above. In Fig. 9 we see ten simulations under respectively the optimised strategy from [18] and the optimised guaranteed safe strategy. Again, we see that the guaranteed strategy is slightly more conservative as it was not possible for the learning algorithm to optimise as well as it did in [18].

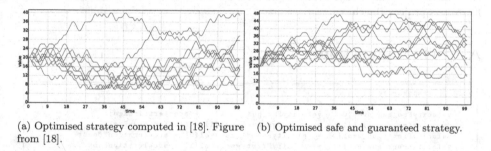

(a) Optimised strategy computed in [18]. Figure   (b) Optimised safe and guaranteed strategy.
from [18].

Fig. 9. Distance over time for 10 simulations under the two different optimised strategies.

7   Conclusion

In this paper, we presented a guaranteed approach for the synthesis of control strategies for continuous-time sampled switched systems. Our approach relies on the tool UPPAAL TIGA, which field of application can be extended with the use of guaranteed numerical schemes. This approach is made effective by enforcing the numerical scheme to bound the continuous trajectory using integers. We developed a refinement method for monotonic systems which allows to use a guaranteed Euler scheme even when the error grows rapidly.

We illustrated that once a safe strategy in computed, the strategy can be refined with further developments such as optimisation using learning algorithms. This showed that the safe strategy is, as expected, more conservative than the approach previously used, but does not over-constrain the system, leaving room for further optimisations. The safe strategies we compute thus constitute a sound basis for more specific computations.

We plan on testing this approach on more case studies, and implementing all the presented methods in the core of UPPAAL's analytical methods, which does not currently support continuous dynamical systems. In this work, we did not explore time dependent specifications, for example with a moving safety set, or an obstacle to avoid, but this approach could handle this kind of specifications thanks to the timed game framework. This is a noticeable improvement from standard symbolic control synthesis methods which should be explored.

Another issue which could be raised is the synchronisation of the players. In a real cruise control application, we cannot guarantee that the two players choose their acceleration at the same time. We plan on developing a time robust Euler scheme, which would guarantee that if the switch does not occur simultaneously, safety is still ensured. Note that this issue has already been studied in the literature in different frameworks, an interested reader might refer to [14,15].

Acknowledgements. This work is supported by the LASSO project financed by an ERC adv. grant; the DiCyPS project funded by Innovation Fund Denmark; and the Eurostars project Reachi.

A   UPPAAL Functions

```
void updateDiscrete(){

    velocityEgo_gua_evol[0] = velocityEgo_gua_evol[0] + accelerationEgo;
    velocityEgo_gua_evol[1] = velocityEgo_gua_evol[1] + accelerationEgo;
    velocityFront_gua_evol[0] = velocityFront_gua_evol[0] + accelerationFront;
    velocityFront_gua_evol[1] = velocityFront_gua_evol[1] + accelerationFront;

    if (distance_gua_evol[0] > maxSensorDistance) {
        distance_gua_evol[0] = maxSensorDistance + 1;
        distance_gua_evol[1] = maxSensorDistance + 1;
    } else {
        eulerDiscrete();
        distance_gua_evol[0] = distance_gua_evol[0] + (velocityFront_gua_evol[0]-
        accelerationFront) - (velocityEgo_gua_evol[0]-accelerationEgo) + (
        accelerationFront - accelerationEgo)/2;
        distance_gua_evol[1] = distance_gua_evol[1] + (velocityFront_gua_evol[0]-
        accelerationFront) - (velocityEgo_gua_evol[0]-accelerationEgo) + (
        accelerationFront - accelerationEgo)/2;

        if (distance_gua_evol[1] > maxSensorDistance) {
            distance_gua_evol[1] = maxSensorDistance + 1;
        }
    }
}
```

Listing 1.1. The function updating the discrete variables.

```
void eulerDiscrete(){
    //double velEgo, velFront,
    double dist, velEgo, velFront, delta;
    double memdist_min, memdist_max, memVF_min, memVF_max, memVE_min, memVE_max;

    int i;

    dist = (distance_gua_evol[0]+distance_gua_evol[1])/2;
    velFront = (velocityFront_gua_evol[0]+velocityFront_gua_evol[1])/2;
    velEgo = (velocityEgo_gua_evol[0]+velocityEgo_gua_evol[1])/2;

    delta = sqrt((distance_gua_evol[1]-distance_gua_evol[0])*(distance_gua_evol[1]-
      distance_gua_evol[0])/4 + (velocityFront_gua_evol[1]-velocityFront_gua_evol[0])*(
      velocityFront_gua_evol[1]-velocityFront_gua_evol[0])/4 + (velocityEgo_gua_evol[1]-
      velocityEgo_gua_evol[0])*(velocityEgo_gua_evol[1]-velocityEgo_gua_evol[0])/4);

    memdist_min = dist - delta;
    memdist_max = dist + delta;
    memVF_min = velFront - delta;
    memVF_max = velFront + delta;
    memVE_min = velEgo - delta;
    memVE_max = velEgo + delta;

    for (i=0;i<=euler_sub_step;i++){
        dist = dist + tau*(velFront - velEgo);
        velEgo = velEgo + tau*accelerationEgo;
        velFront = velFront + tau*accelerationFront;
        delta = delta_mode(delta,find_mode(accelerationFront,accelerationEgo));
        memdist_min = mini(memdist_min,dist-delta);
        memdist_max = maxi(memdist_max,dist+delta);
        memVF_min = mini(memVF_min,velFront-delta);
        memVF_max = maxi(memVF_max,velFront+delta);
        memVE_min = mini(memVE_min,velEgo-delta);
        memVE_max = maxi(memVE_max,velEgo+delta);

    }

    distance_gua_evol[0] = floor(dist-delta);
    distance_gua_evol[1] = ceil(dist+delta);
    velocityFront_gua_evol[0] = floor(velFront-delta);
    velocityFront_gua_evol[1] = ceil(velFront+delta);
    velocityEgo_gua_evol[0] = floor(velEgo-delta);
    velocityEgo_gua_evol[1] = ceil(velEgo+delta);

    distance_gua[0] = floor(memdist_min);
    distance_gua[1] = ceil(memdist_max);
    velocityFront_gua[0] = floor(memVF_min);
    velocityFront_gua[1] = ceil(memVF_max);
    velocityEgo_gua[0] = floor(memVE_min);
    velocityEgo_gua[1] = ceil(memVE_max);

}
```

Listing 1.2. The function using the Euler method and returning the lowest integer part visited by the continuous system.

References

1. Angeli, D., Sontag, E.D.: Monotone control systems. IEEE Trans. Autom. Control **48**(10), 1684–1698 (2003)
2. Behrmann, G., Cougnard, A., David, A., Fleury, E., Larsen, K.G., Lime, D.: UPPAAL-Tiga: time for playing games!. In: Damm, W., Hermanns, H. (eds.) CAV 2007. LNCS, vol. 4590, pp. 121–125. Springer, Heidelberg (2007). https://doi.org/10.1007/978-3-540-73368-3_14
3. Bouissou, O., Chapoutot, A., Djoudi, A.: Enclosing temporal evolution of dynamical systems using numerical methods. In: Brat, G., Rungta, N., Venet, A. (eds.) NFM 2013. LNCS, vol. 7871, pp. 108–123. Springer, Heidelberg (2013). https://doi.org/10.1007/978-3-642-38088-4_8
4. Bouissou, O., Martel, M.: GRKLib: a guaranteed Runge Kutta library. In: Scientific Computing, Computer Arithmetic and Validated Numerics (2006)
5. David, A., Fang, H., Larsen, K.G., Zhang, Z.: Verification and performance evaluation of timed game strategies. In: Legay, A., Bozga, M. (eds.) FORMATS 2014. LNCS, vol. 8711, pp. 100–114. Springer, Cham (2014). https://doi.org/10.1007/978-3-319-10512-3_8
6. David, A., et al.: On time with minimal expected cost!. In: Cassez, F., Raskin, J.-F. (eds.) ATVA 2014. LNCS, vol. 8837, pp. 129–145. Springer, Cham (2014). https://doi.org/10.1007/978-3-319-11936-6_10
7. David, A., Jensen, P.G., Larsen, K.G., Mikučionis, M., Taankvist, J.H.: Uppaal stratego. In: Baier, C., Tinelli, C. (eds.) Tools and Algorithms for the Construction and Analysis of Systems, pp. 206–211. Springer, Heidelberg (2015)
8. Donchev, T., Farkhi, E.: Stability and Euler approximation of one-sided Lipschitz differential inclusions. SIAM J. Control Optim. **36**(2), 780–796 (1998)
9. Fribourg, L., Soulat, R.: Control of Switching Systems by Invariance Analysis: Applcation to Power Electronics. Wiley, New York (2013)
10. Gajda, K., Jankowska, M., Marciniak, A., Szyszka, B.: A survey of interval Runge–Kutta and multistep methods for solving the initial value problem. In: Wyrzykowski, R., Dongarra, J., Karczewski, K., Wasniewski, J. (eds.) PPAM 2007. LNCS, vol. 4967, pp. 1361–1371. Springer, Heidelberg (2008). https://doi.org/10.1007/978-3-540-68111-3_144
11. Girard, A.: Controller synthesis for safety and reachability via approximate bisimulation. Automatica **48**(5), 947–953 (2012)
12. Girard, A., Martin, S.: Synthesis for constrained nonlinear systems using hybridization and robust controllers on simplices. IEEE Trans. Autom. Control **57**(4), 1046–1051 (2012)
13. Girard, A., Pola, G., Tabuada, P.: Approximately bisimilar symbolic models for incrementally stable switched systems. IEEE Trans. Autom. Control **55**(1), 116–126 (2010)
14. Kader, Z., Girard, A., Saoud, A.: Symbolic models for incrementally stable switched systems with aperiodic time sampling? IFAC-PapersOnLine **51**, 253–258 (2018)
15. Kido, K., Sedwards, S., Hasuo, I.: Bounding errors due to switching delays in incrementally stable switched systems. IFAC PapersOnLine **51**(16), 247–252 (2018)
16. Kim, E.S., Arcak, M., Seshia, S.A.: Symbolic control design for monotone systems with directed specifications. Automatica **83**, 10–19 (2017)
17. Larsen, K.G., Mikučionis, M., Muñiz, M., Srba, J., Taankvist, J.H.: Online and compositional learning of controllers with application to floor heating. In: Chechik, M., Raskin, J.-F. (eds.) TACAS 2016. LNCS, vol. 9636, pp. 244–259. Springer, Heidelberg (2016). https://doi.org/10.1007/978-3-662-49674-9_14

18. Larsen, K.G., Mikučionis, M., Taankvist, J.H.: Safe and optimal adaptive cruise control. In: Meyer, R., Platzer, A., Wehrheim, H. (eds.) Correct System Design. LNCS, vol. 9360, pp. 260–277. Springer, Cham (2015). https://doi.org/10.1007/978-3-319-23506-6_17
19. Le Coënt, A.: Guaranteed control synthesis for switched space-time dynamical systems. Theses, Université Paris Saclay, October 2017
20. Coënt, A.L., De Vuyst, F., Chamoin, L., Fribourg, L.: Control synthesis of nonlinear sampled switched systems using Euler's method. In: Ábrahám, E., Bogomolov, S. (eds.) Proceedings 3rd International Workshop on Symbolic and Numerical Methods for Reachability Analysis, Uppsala, Sweden, 22nd April 2017. Electronic Proceedings in Theoretical Computer Science, vol. 247, pp. 18–33. Open Publishing Association (2017)
21. Le Coënt, A., Chapoutot, A., Fribourg, L., Alexandre dit Sandretto, J.A.: An improved algorithm for the control synthesis of nonlinear sampled switched systems. Formal Methods Syst. Des. **53**(3), 1–21 (2017)
22. Le Coënt, A., Fribourg, L., Markey, N., De Vuyst, F., Chamoin, L.: Compositional synthesis of state-dependent switching control. Theor. Comput. Sci. **750**, 53–68 (2018)
23. Lin, H., Antsaklis, P.J.: Stability and stabilizability of switched linear systems: a survey of recent results. IEEE Trans. Autom. control **54**(2), 308–322 (2009)
24. Meyer, P.-J., Girard, A., Witrant, E.: Safety control with performance guarantees of cooperative systems using compositional abstractions. IFAC PapersOnLine **48**(27), 317–322 (2015)
25. Meyer, P.-J., Girard, A., Witrant, E.: Robust controlled invariance for monotone systems: application to ventilation regulation in buildings. Automatica **70**, 14–20 (2016)
26. Moore, R.: Interval Analysis. Prentice Hall, Upper Saddle River (1966)
27. Nedialko, N.S., Jackson, K.R., Corliss, G.F.: Validated solutions of initial value problems for ordinary differential equations. Appl. Math. Comput. **105**(1), 21–68 (1999)
28. Pintér, J.D.: Global Optimization in Action: Continuous and Lipschitz Optimization: Algorithms, Implementations and Applications. Springer, Heidelberg (2013)
29. Rungger, M., Zamani, M.: SCOTS: a tool for the synthesis of symbolic controllers. In: Proceedings of the 19th International Conference on Hybrid Systems: Computation and Control, pp. 99–104. ACM, New York (2016)
30. Saoud, A., Girard, A., Fribourg, L.: Contract based design of symbolic controllers for vehicle platooning. In: Proceedings of the 21st International Conference on Hybrid Systems: Computation and Control (part of CPS Week), pp. 277–278. ACM, New York (2018)
31. Saoud, A., Girard, A., Fribourg, L.: On the composition of discrete and continuous-time assume-guarantee contracts for invariance (2018)
32. Söderlind, G.: On nonlinear difference and differential equations. BIT Numer. Math. **24**(4), 667–680 (1984)

CPS Dependability Framework
Based on Inhomogeneous Stochastic
Hybrid Systems

Manuela L. Bujorianu[✉]

Maritime Safety Research Centre, University of Strathclyde, Glasgow, Scotland, UK
Luminita.Bujorianu@strath.ac.uk

Abstract. In this paper, we propose a time-inhomogeneous stochastic hybrid system, as the appropriate modelling framework for the performance of complex engineering systems. One important hypothesis for this hybrid system is the ergodicity that ensures the existence of some sort of invariant measures. The invariant measures constitute an important tool for defining performance measures for dependability. First, we define an appropriate model of time-inhomogeneous stochastic hybrid systems. Then, we adapt the concept of invariant measure for the non-homogeneous case. Under the assumption of geometric (or exponential) ergodicity of the underlying hybrid process, we prove the existence and uniqueness of this kind of invariant measure. The paper ends with some sort of sensitivity analysis of this invariant measure under appropriate perturbations of the infinitesimal generators associated to the stochastic process.

Keywords: Time-inhomogeneous Markov processes ·
Stochastic hybrid systems · Dependability ·
Kantorovich-Wasserstein metric · Wasserstein contraction ·
Exponential ergodicity

1 Introduction

In the safety engineering literature, different modelling techniques for reliability analysis have been developed. The most known quantitative ones are "Event - fault tree analysis" and "Markov Models". Markov models give the means of describing the dynamic behaviour of a system through the time-space specification. The system is specified by its states and the possible transitions between the states depicted by a matrix or a graph if the state space is finite. Other Markovian dynamics are represented by stochastic differential equations or by some evolution operators, when the state space is continuous. Moreover, in some cases, the state is hybrid including a discrete state, which is a label for a system component or for a system operating mode, and a continuous state, which is a variable or a collection of variables that evolves in time and describes the mode/component

R. Chamberlain et al. (Eds.): CyPhy 2018/WESE 2018, LNCS 11615, pp. 134–153, 2019.
https://doi.org/10.1007/978-3-030-23703-5_7

behaviour. The discrete states may be functioning, failed, standby, waiting to be repaired, or under maintenance. The continuous parameters that describe all these modes may evolve over the time and could be specified by algebraic or differential equations. The transitions among the discrete states are produced by different activities such as failures, operation switching, repairs, and so on. The most used discrete-space Markov model is the time-homogeneous Markov chain (see [21,24]), which is characterized by constant rates for its transitions among the states. Another more complex discrete model, for which the transition rates depend on time is the time-inhomogeneous Markov chain. Recently, hybrid-state Markov models have been applied for reliability purposes (see [15,31]).

In this paper, we propose a time-inhomogeneous stochastic hybrid system, as the appropriate framework for dependability (i.e. safety, reliability, maintainability, performance, availability) analysis of complex engineering systems. This model and its instantiations will be used in the follow-up papers to study safety and reliability issues for the shipboard power management system[1]. Time-inhomogeneity is justified by the fact that most of the continuous behaviours that we encounter in our system are non-autonomous (deterministic or random) dynamical systems (no periodicity or stationarity with respect to the time has been recorded).

When studying quantitative dependability tools using Markov models, one important tool is the invariant measure. When such a measure exists, it is used to define different safety and performance measures [25]. The existence of the invariant measure is usually ensured by the ergodicity of the underlying process. The general meaning of ergodicity is a sort of convergence, in a large time limit, of a probability distribution, associated to a stochastic process, to some limiting distribution that is stationary and independent of the initial setting. For time-inhomogeneous stochastic processes, the concept of ergodicity has to be redefined to consider the non-stationarity of the transition probabilities.

Here, we study some ergodicity conditions for a class of time-inhomogeneous stochastic hybrid systems without the assumption that the subordinated continuous time-space stochastic processes satisfy the Harris ergodicity condition [26]. Our definition of ergodicity is connected with a specific continuity property of the transition operator semigroups, called Wassertein contraction property. This sort of approach was employed in a more complex setting, namely for the existence and uniqueness of interacting stochastic systems with given probability transitions [14]. To describe it, we use the Kantorovich-Wasserstein metric defined on the space of probability measures, which is coarser than the total variance distance. Given a metric d on the space of values of random variables, the Kantorovich-Wasserstein metric or the transportation metric, between two probability distribution μ and ν, is defined as $\inf\{\mathbf{E}d(X,Y)\}$ where the infimum is taken with respect to all random variables X, Y with distribution μ, ν. This metric can be described, as well, by its dual formulation using Lipschitz functions (see Appendix, Subsect. A.1). The main advantage of the Kantorovich-

---

[1] This is a project under development in our Maritime Safety Research Centre at University of Strathclyde.

Wasserstein metric is the fact that it is compatible with the metric d defined on the underlying state space.

The novelty of this work is twofold: (i) We set up a simple model for inhomogeneous stochastic hybrid systems, which has no discontinuities, but switchings. (ii) We define an elegant type of exponential ergodicity, which is formalized using an appropriate space of signed bounded measures.

We are using a quite simple model of inhomogeneous stochastic hybrid systems, which has no proper jumps (discontinuities) associated to the discrete transition. This simplification is required in order to avoid extra assumptions for the ergodicity of embedded jump process (related mostly to the stochastic kernel that would describe the post-jump locations). If we allow discontinuities of the whole hybrid system, then we need a sort of compatibility integration of the ergodic conditions for continuous and discrete parts. This will constitute the subject of a further investigation for a follow-up paper.

The main objective of this paper is to give a nice simple sufficient condition for the existence and uniqueness of an "invariant measure" for the realization of an inhomogeneous stochastic hybrid system. Mainly, in the context of dependability analysis, the invariant measure is used to simplify the computation of the dependability indicators. Since the transition probabilities of such a system depend on two time parameters, the invariant measure is, in fact, a family of natural distributions depending on one time parameter, which satisfies the forward equation. For a time-inhomogeneous Markov process, it is possible to associate, in a standard way, an evolution system (of two parameters linear operators), i.e. a family of operators that satisfies a chain condition (evolution property derived from the Markovianity of the process). Augmenting the state space of the Markovian process with the time dimension, we can associate to the evolution system a semigroup of transition operators. Then, the family of invariant measures corresponding to the initial inhomogeneous process is nothing else but the invariant measure of the latest semigroup of operators. Usually, the evolution system of invariant measures for an inhomogeneous Markov process is not unique. A simple condition that will ensure the uniqueness of the evolution system of invariant measures is the Wasserstein contraction, which requires that the each operator of the evolution system is nonexpansive (i.e. it is exponentially Lipschitz with respect to the Kantorovich-Wasserstein metric). We rewrite the Wasserstein contraction, in terms of operator norms using the Kantorovich-Rubinstein norm defined on a suitable Banach space of measures. This will ensure the uniform exponential stability of the evolution system (and, consequently, of the corresponding operator semigroup) [5].

The paper is structured as follows. Next section briefly presents the concept of dependability for cyber-physical systems and the standard definitions for time-inhomogeneous Markov models. Section 3 gives the definition of the inhomogeneous stochastic hybrid system and its infinitesimal generator. Section 4 presents the definitions of ergodicity and the main results of the paper. The paper ends with some final remarks, Sect. 5. Here, we include a subsection, which explains the practical application of the results of this paper in the context of a large project on dependability of the shipboard power system. To improve the readability of the paper, we moved the measure theory background (the definitions of the Kantorovich-Wasserstein type metrics and norms) and the proofs of the theorems in the Appendix.

2   Background

The first part of this section is dedicated to a brief introduction on the topic of CPS dependability, in order to motivate the contribution of this work. Then, the second part provides a mathematical background on nonstationary Markov models. To improve readability of this paper, the definitions of the Kantorovich-Wasserstein type metrics and their corresponding norms have been moved in the appendix. The reason is that, these metrics/norms represent just a tool used to prove some of the paper results and their understanding depends on the reader mathematical background in measure theory. The use of the Wasserstein metric is motivated by its "naturalness", i.e. its compatibility of the distance of the underlying state space. This means that the distance between two points in the state space coincides with the Wasserstein distance between their associated Dirac distributions.

2.1   Highlights on CPS Dependability

Dependability concepts are critical for the avant-garde progress in an expanding comprehensive world that is more and more counting on interconnected technologies such as the Cyber-Physical Systems and the Internet of Things.

"A cyber-physical system (CPS) integrates computing, communication and storage capabilities with monitoring and/or control of entities in the physical world, and must do so dependably, safety, securely, efficiently and real-time" (according to Shankar Sastry from University of California, Berkeley in 2008). The actual definition of dependability of an item is "the ability to perform as and when required". "Dependability includes availability, reliability, recoverability, maintainability, and maintenance support performance, and, in some cases, other characteristics such as durability, safety and security" (see the IEC Electropedia IEV 192 for exact definitions)[2]. Existing standards define formally these attributes, and their probability measures. Most of the current standards do not consider safety as a component of dependability. Safety is the capability of a system to circumvent the appearance of critical or disastrous events that may affect machines and humans. Measures of the safety may be defined also in a probability context. The main objective of safety is to assess it with respect to the consequence of the occurrence of the critical or fatal events. Many researchers prefer the RAMS acronym for reliability, availability, maintainability and safety instead of dependability. Nonetheless, RAMS has a wider extension, covering all the attributes of dependability and safety: hazards/threats analysis, achievement

---

[2] http://tc56.iec.ch/index-tc56.html.

means, validation and verification methods, and quantitative/qualitative measures. The concept of dependability, included in the definition of CPSs as their attribute, has to be considered in the life cycle (evolution) of a system. This is the reason why most of the approaches on dependability of CPS are model based approaches like: [13] (based on UML/SysML), [30] (Modelica), [7,15] (based on stochastic hybrid automata).

This work propose a hybrid modelling framework where problems related to dependability can be formally defined and, then rigorous abstractions can be further developed for checking the reliability and safety by model checking or control techniques. The hybrid models we propose are nonstationary with respect to the time. In the engineering practice, the study of reliability (or, more general, dependability) starts with some data analysis. For dynamic reliability analysis, these data are initially modeled as time-series. It is generally accepted that these time series are regime changing or switching are they are nonstationary with respect to time [16]. In order to apply formal methods tools, these time series have to be transformed in equivalent state based models like finite state machines or hybrid automata [1]. Therefore, we have identified the need to study CPS dependability using time-inhomogenous Markov models with regime changes.

In the context of dependability, for example, the evolution of transition probabilities (i.e. the Chapman-Kolmogorov equations) provide the relation between the system output probabilities of reaching different states provided that the transition rates between states are known (i.e. inputs can be failures/repairs of the system components).

The global CPS model has to comprise two parts: (i) a set of continuous functional models that describe the physical behaviours (real deterministic/stochastic parameters governed by differential/difference equations); (ii) a discrete event functional model that describes the computational or control "events" which appear at random times (modeled, usually, as a Markov chain). Both parts are tightly integrated, and the whole system is seen, usually, as a hybrid automaton.

In a standard way, dependability indicators will include: (i) reliability measures (failure probabilities, mean time to failure, etc.); (ii) maintainability measures (repair rate, mean time to repair, etc.); (iii) availability measures (the probability to perform a requested function under given conditions at a specific time instant). Formal definitions of these measures can be found in [1]. When we consider safety under the umbrella of dependability, we need to add extra indicators like risk measures.

The computation of the dependability performance relies on the management of these indicators. When a formalism is available, the scalability of these indicators depends on the stability (long time/asymptotic behaviour) of the underlying model. Therefore, the existence of the invariant measure, even for a time-inhomogeneous model, is essential. The importance of this has been proven for inhomogeneous Markov chains in [6].

2.2 Inhomogeneous Markov Processes

In the following, standard definitions regarding inhomogeneous Markov processes and their standard characterizations are given.

Let us consider a filtration $(\mathcal{F}_t)_{t\geq0}$ and, further, a measurable and adapted process $X = (X_t)_{t\geq0}$ defined on $(\Omega, \mathcal{F}, \mathcal{F}_t, \mathbf{P})$ with values in a Polish or Borel space $(\mathbf{S}, \mathcal{B}(\mathbf{S}))$. The process X is Markov with respect to the filtration $(\mathcal{F}_t)$ if for all $s \leq t$ there exists a stochastic kernel $p_{st}(\cdot,\cdot)$ on $\mathbf{S}$, called transition probability from time s to time t, such that

$$\mathbf{P}(X_t \in A|\mathcal{F}_s) = p_{st}(X_s, A), \text{ for all } A \in \mathcal{B}(\mathbf{S}).$$

If, in addition, the stochastic kernels $p_{st}(\cdot,\cdot)$ are *stationary*, i.e. they depend only on the difference $t - s$, $p_{st}(\cdot,\cdot) = p_{0(t-s)}(\cdot,\cdot)$, then the process X is a *time-homogeneous* Markov process.

The transition probabilities satisfy the Chapman-Kolmogorov equations, i.e. $p_{su}(x, A) = \int p_{st}(x, dy)p_{tu}(y, A)$, for all $0 \leq s \leq t \leq u$, $x \in \mathbf{S}$, $A \in \mathcal{B}(\mathbf{S})$.

The transition probabilities for a non-homogeneous Markov define a two-parameter semigroup of operators on the Banach space $\mathbf{B}(\mathbf{S})$ by

$$P_{st}f(x) := \int_{\mathbf{S}} f(y)p_{st}(x, dy), \ s \leq t.$$

The Chapman-Kolmogorov equations will ensure the semigroup property, i.e.

$$P_{su} = P_{st}P_{tu}, \ P_{tt} = I \tag{1}$$

for all $0 \leq s \leq t \leq u$ with I the identity operator.

When the time is allowed to be also negative, these operators define an *evolution system* [8]

$$\begin{aligned} U(s,t)f(x) &:= P_{st}f(x) \\ &= \mathbf{E}(f(X_t)|X_s = x), \ s \leq t, \ s, t \in \mathbb{R} \end{aligned} \tag{2}$$

The linear operators are positivity preserving and satisfy $U(s,t)\mathbf{1} = 1$, $U(s,s) = I$ and the evolution property

$$U(s,u) = U(s,t)U(t,u)$$

for $s \leq t \leq u$. The evolution system is strongly continuous, if for each $v, w \in \mathbb{R}$ with $v \leq w$

$$\lim_{\substack{(s,t)\to(v,w) \\ s\leq t}} \|U(s,t)f - U(v,w)f\|_\infty = 0.$$

In the following, we will consider the real time two-parameter semigroup (P_{st}) (which coincides with the evolution system). (P_{st}) is acting also on the space of probability measures $\mathcal{M}_1(\mathbf{S})$ via

$$\mu P_{st}(\cdot) := \int p_{st}(x, \cdot)\mu(dx)$$

$$(\mu P_{st})f := \int P_{st}f d\mu.$$

Obviously, the evolution semigroup can be extended to all finite signed measures from $\mathcal{M}(\mathbf{S})$.

A family of right *infinitesimal generators* can be associated with a strongly continuous evolution semigroup

$$L_s^+ f := \lim_{h \searrow 0} \frac{P_{s,s+h}f - f}{h}, \ \forall s \in \mathbb{R}_+$$

defined on $\mathcal{D}(L_s^+)$, i.e. for all $f \in \mathbf{B}(\mathbf{S})$ such that the limit exists in the strong sense.

If the evolution semigroup is strongly continuous (which is true for Markov processes), then the following backward/forward equations can be verified:

$$\frac{d^+}{dt}P_{st}f = -L_s^+ P_{st}f \tag{3}$$

$$\frac{d^+}{dt}P_{st}f = P_{st}L_t^+ f \tag{4}$$

for all $f \in \mathcal{D}(L_s^+)$, $s, t \in \mathbb{R}_+$, $s \leq t$.

The nonhomogeneous counterpart of the concept of invariant measure is the so-called *evolution system of invariant measures* (entrance laws), i.e. a family (μ_s) of probability measures such that

$$(\mu_s P_{st})f = \mu_t f, \ s < t, \ f \in B(\mathbf{S}). \tag{5}$$

Let $L_\infty(\mathbb{R}, \mathcal{M}(\mathbf{S}))$ be the space of measure valued functions $\widehat{\mu} : \mathbb{R} \to \mathcal{M}(\mathbf{S})$. We use also the notation $\widehat{\mu} := (\mu_t)_t$. This space is equipped with the norm

$$||\widehat{\mu}||_\infty = \sup_t ||\mu_t|| < \infty$$

where the $|| \cdot ||$ will be chosen later on according to the appropriate state of measures. Similarly, we consider the space $L_\infty(\mathbb{R}, \mathbf{B}(\mathbf{S}))$ and denote its elements by $\widehat{f} : \mathbb{R} \to \mathbf{B}(\mathbf{S})$ or $\widehat{f} := (f_t)_t$.

The evolution semigroup $\mathcal{T} = \{T_t\}_{t \geq 0}$ of operators is defined as follows:

– on $L_\infty(\mathbb{R}, \mathbf{B}(\mathbf{S}))$

$$(T_t \widehat{f})(s) := P_{s-t,s}f_{s-t}, \ s \in \mathbb{R}, \ t \geq 0.$$

– on $L_\infty(\mathbb{R}, \mathcal{M}(\mathbf{S}))$

$$(\widehat{\mu}T_t)(s) := \mu_{s-t}P_{s-t,s}, \ s \in \mathbb{R}, \ t \geq 0. \tag{6}$$

Remark 1. Obviously, if (μ_s) is an evolution system of invariant measures satisfying (5) then (μ_s) is invariant for the semigroup $\mathcal{T} = \{T_t\}_{t \geq 0}$.

The generator $\mathcal{L}$ of the evolution semigroup $\mathcal{T}$ is given by

$$(\mathcal{L}\widehat{f})(\tau) := \frac{d\widehat{f}}{d\tau} + L_\tau^+ \widehat{f}(\tau), \ \tau \in \mathbb{R}_+ \tag{7}$$

with domain the set of differentiable functions $\widehat{f}$ such that $\mathcal{L}\widehat{f} \in L_\infty(\mathbb{R}, \mathbf{B}(\mathbf{S}))$ (see [8]).

3   Inhomogeneous Stochastic Hybrid Systems

Different models of time-homogeneous stochastic hybrid systems exist in the literature. Their nonhomgeneous versions are quite easy to define with respect to both continuous and discrete behaviours. However, even if it is possible to enlarge their state space with the time dimension, the analysis of such systems is not straightforward.

In this section, we give a succinct presentation of the model of inhomogeneous stochastic hybrid system used in this paper. As in the homogeneous case, the main tool for the analysis of such a system is the infinitesimal generator. Then Dynkin or differential formulas can be easily adapted from the homogeneous case. The main challenge in the nonhomogeneous case is the understanding of the different types of ergodicity.

3.1   Inhomogeneous Switching Markov Processes

We define an inhomogeneous stochastic hybrid system (ISHS) whose realization is a switching inhomogeneous Markov process. We need the following ingredients:

- a Borel space $(\mathbf{S}, \mathcal{B}(\mathbf{S}))$ and a finite set Q;
- a family of inhomogeneous Markov processes $(X^q)_{q \in Q}$ with values in $\mathbf{S}$, which are characterized by their two parameter transition semigroup $(P^q)_{q \in Q}$;
- a family of intensity rates $(\lambda(q, l, \cdot))_{q,l \in Q}$ of non-negative functions on $\mathbf{S}$.

We will consider the inhomogeneous hybrid process $(\mathbf{X}_t) := (q_t, X^{q_t})$ defined on $Q \times \mathbf{S}$, which switches between the component process trajectories. In plain words, the process $\mathbf{X}_t$ behaves like X^q as long as $q_t = q$ (i.e. q_t does not jump). The discrete process (q_t) has jumps triggered by the intensity rate λ.

Formally, the realization of $(\mathbf{X}_t)$ can be described by the following algorithm:

1. Set $i := 0$.
2. Start with an initial state $(q_i, x_i) \in Q \times \mathbf{S}$. Then, the process X^{q_i} is enabled with initial condition $X_0^{q_i} := x_i$. Note that the initial time can be chosen in a flexible way on the real line.
3. The discrete component q_t remains constant equal to q_i until the first switching jump T_{i+1} occurs. The stopping time $T_{i+1} = \min_{q \in Q} T^{q_i \to q}$, where $(T^{q_i \to q})$ is a family of random variables that are conditionally independent given X^{q_i} with the probability distributions defined using the survivor function

$$\mathbf{P}(T^{q_i \to q} > t | \mathcal{F}_t^{q_i})$$

$$= \exp(-\int_0^t \lambda(q_0, q, X_s^{q_i}) ds), \forall q \in Q$$

where $\mathcal{F}_t^{q_i}$ is the filtration generated by the process (X^{q_i}).
4. At time T_{i+1}, there exists a unique $q_{i+1} \in Q$ such that $T_{i+1} = T^{q_i \to q_{i+1}}$. Then the discrete component becomes $q_{i+1} := q_{T_{i+1}}$ and the continuous state becomes $x_{i+1} := X_{(T_{i+1})-}^{q_i}$ and the new initial state (q_{i+1}, x_{i+1}).
5. Set $i := i + 1$ and repeat from 2.

Assumption 1 (Boundedness of the jumping rates). *We suppose that the following inequality holds:* $\sup_{q \in Q} \sup_{x \in \mathbf{S}} \sum_{l \in Q} \lambda(q, l, x) < \infty$.

3.2   Infinitesimal Generators

Considering the time-space transformation of the inhomogeneous hybrid process $(\mathbf{X}_t)_{t \geq 0}$, the family of right infinitesimal generators associated to this are given by

$$
\begin{aligned}
L_s^+ f(q, x) &:= L^+ f(s, q, x) \\
&= \frac{\partial}{\partial t} f(s, q, x) + L^{+q} f(s, q, x) \\
&\quad + \sum_{l \in Q} \lambda(q, l, x)[f(s, l, x) - f(s, q, x)].
\end{aligned}
$$

for any bounded function f such that $f(q, \cdot)$ belongs to the domain of generator associated to the process (X_t^q). We will denote by $(\mathbf{P}_{st})$ the evolution system associated to the process $(\mathbf{X}_t)$.

4   Geometric Ergodicity

The concept of geometric (exponential) ergodicity for inhomogeneous Markov chains has been defined using different mathematical techniques (e.g. see [18, 22]). For continuous space Markov processes, a specific exponentially mixing condition (based on Harris recurrence) has been studies by Tweedie and Meyn in a series of papers (see, e.g., [26]).

The generalization to inhomogeneous Markov processes (with continuous space) is not straightforward. The main difficulty is the fact the evolution systems of invariant measures (if they exist) may not be unique. Then, the ergodicity condition has to be strong enough to ensure both the existence and uniqueness of the system of invariant measures. It is easy to remark that any evolution system of invariant measures defines an "invariant measure" for the one-parameter semigroup defined by (6) associated to the evolution family. Therefore, we are looking for an exponential ergodicity condition defined first for the evolution system, which will imply automatically the exponential ergodicity for the evolution semigroup (6). Since we do not have standard hypotheses regarding the system of invariant measures, we will consider a stronger condition related to Wasserstein curvature [11] that will provide a necessary condition for the existence and uniqueness.

4.1   Wasserstein Curvature

For the two parameter semigroup (P_{st}), we define the *Wasserstein curvature* as the best (maximal) constant Δ for which the following inequality holds:

$$
||(\mu_1 - \mu_2) P_{st}||_{\mathcal{F}} \leq \exp[(-\Delta)(t - s)]||(\mu_1 - \mu_2)||_{\mathcal{F}}, \tag{8}
$$

for all $s, t \in \mathbb{R}$, $s < t$; where $\mu_1, \mu_2 \in \mathcal{M}^d(\mathbf{S})$. It is enough to check the Wasserstein contraction (8) only for probability measures.

We say that the evolution system (P_{st}) is *exponentially Lipschitz* if there exists a constant K such that

$$|P_{st}f|_L \leq \exp[(-K)(t-s)]|f|_L,$$

for all $s, t \in \mathbb{R}$, $s < t$, $f \in Lip(\mathbf{S})$. The case of interest for the exponential ergodicity will be when $K > 0$.

In this paper, we say that an inhomogeneous Markov process is *uniformly exponentially ergodic* if the Wasserstein curvature of its semigroup is strictly positive, i.e. $\Delta > 0$. From the uniform exponential ergodicity, we can also prove that the evolution system is exponentially Lipschitz (i.e. it maps Lipschitz functions into Lipschitz ones).

In practice, the Wasserstein contraction (8) might be difficult to be checked. Then, we consider the simplex of probability measures embedded in the space of zero charge measures $\mathcal{M}_0(\mathbf{S})$ equipped with the Kantorovich-Rubinstein $|| \cdot ||_\mathcal{K}$. Note that $(\mathcal{M}_0(\mathbf{S}), || \cdot ||_\mathcal{K})$ is not a Banach space, but we can work with its completion in an appropriate Banach space, which is the dual space of $BL(\mathbf{S})$. This space is also known as the Arens-Eells space and the characterization of its completion can be found in [12].

In this way, we will consider the two parameter semigroup (P_{st}) of operators defined on the completion of $(\mathcal{M}_0(\mathbf{S}), || \cdot ||_\mathcal{K})$ and rewrite the Wasserstein contraction as follows

$$||P_{st}|| \leq C \exp[(-\Delta)(t-s)], \forall s, t \in \mathbb{R}_+, \ s < t \tag{9}$$

where $||P_{st}||$ is the operator norm defined with respect to $|| \cdot ||_\mathcal{K}$, and $C > 0$ and $\Delta > 0$ are two constants. The condition (9) ensures that the evolution system (P_{st}) is *uniformly exponentially stable*, when P_{st} is thought of as an operator defined on $\mathcal{M}_0(\mathbf{S})$.

4.2 Existence and Uniqueness of Invariant Measures

In the following, we make the assumption that the given ISHS satisfies the uniform exponential ergodicity.

Assumption 2. *We suppose that the inhomogeneous Markov process* $\mathbf{X}_t^q = (q, X_t^q)$ *is uniformly geometrically ergodic (or, exponentially mixing), i.e., for all* $q \in Q$, *there exists the constants* $\Delta > 0$, $C > 0$ *such that (9) holds for each* $(P^q{}_{st})$.

Assumption 3. *We suppose that for each* $x \in \mathbf{S}$, *the Markov kernels* $p_{s,t}^q(x, \cdot)$ *belong to* $\mathcal{M}_1^d(\mathbf{S})$, *for all* $q \in Q$.

The previous assumption ensures that the evolution system $(P_{s,t}^q)$ is well defined for all $f \in Lip(\mathbf{S})$.

Theorem 1. *For each $q \in Q$, the evolution system $(P^q_{s,t})$ is exponentially Lipschitz with positive exponent if and only if (X^q_t) is uniformly exponentially ergodic.*

Remark 2. Theorem 1 ensures that the evolution system (P_{st}) is *uniformly exponentially stable*, when P_{st} is thought of as an operator defined on $Lip_0(\mathbf{S})$. Considering the fact that our ergodicity condition is expressed using the Wasserstein-Kantorovich metric, the uniform exponential stability of the evolution system (P_{st}) holds only for the Lipschitz functions.

Then the *kernel operator* G, associated to the semigroup $\{T_t\}_{t\geq 0}$ on $L_\infty(\mathbb{R}, Lip_0(\mathbf{S}))$, is defined as: $G\widehat{f}(s) := \int_0^\infty (T_t\widehat{f})(s)dt$. It is known that G is equal to $(-\mathcal{L})^{-1}$ provided that the semigroup $\mathcal{T}$ or the evolution family is uniformly exponentially stable [5].

The following result has been proved by different authors for homogeneous Markov processes [11]. Mainly, it says that the exponential ergodicity assures the existence and uniqueness of the invariant measure. For inhomogeneous Markov processes, under the condition (9), we have the existence and uniqueness of the evolution system of invariant measures.

Proposition 1. *For each $q \in Q$, under the Assumptions 2, 3, there exists a unique evolution system of invariant measures $\widehat{\pi}^q := (\pi^q_t)$ such that*

$$||\widehat{\mu}T^q_t - \widehat{\pi}^q||_\infty \leq ||\widehat{\mu} - \widehat{\pi}^q||_\infty$$

for every sequence of probability measures $\widehat{\mu} := (\mu_t)_{t\geq 0}$ on $\mathbf{S}$. Here, T^q_t is defined via (6) on $L_\infty(\mathbb{R}, \mathcal{M}_0(\mathbf{S}))$ corresponding to the process (X^q_t).

On the discrete space Q, we consider also the space of probability distributions $\mathcal{M}^d_1(Q)$ and its corresponding Kantorovich-Wasserstein metric.

Assumption 4. *Suppose that the switching rates $\lambda(q, l, x)$ do not depend on x and define an irreducible and positive recurrent Markov chain (q_t) on Q. Moreover, we suppose that (q_t) is uniformly exponentially ergodic with the invariant measure $\nu = (\nu_i)_{i\in Q}$, i.e. there exist constants $K_d, M > 0$ such that*

$$||\delta_q P_t - \nu||_{\mathcal{KW}} \leq M \exp(-K_d t)$$

for all $q \in Q$.

The following theorem states that if the continuous part and the discrete part of stochastic hybrid process are ergodic then the whole process (their integration) is ergodic.

Theorem 2. *If Assumptions 2, 3 and 4 are satisfied, then the hybrid process $(\mathbf{X}_t)$ is uniformly geometrically ergodic.*

The exponential ergodicity of the hybrid process will ensure the existence and uniqueness of the system of invariant measures. Note that exponential ergodicity is just a sufficient conditions for the uniqueness of the system of invariant measures. Other types of ergodicity could be defined by using different metrics on the probability distribution space or the existence of Lyapunov type functions (see [18] and the references therein). We have chosen the Wasserstein space since this is the natural framework to study also optimal control problems or fault tolerant control [17], which are also relevant in the context of CPS dependability. As well, Kantorovich-Wasserstein metric can be used for abstraction/bisimulation purposes [9].

4.3   Robustness of Invariant Measures

In the following, we study the robustness of these invariant measures. For discrete time processes like Markov chains, robustness analysis of the invariant measure is done by perturbing the transition probabilities at one instant of time (one time perturbation), or at each time instant. Then, we are interested in bounds of these perturbations such that the system still has an invariant measure.

For time inhomogeneous processes, the perturbations have to be applied the time dependent infinitesimal generators, not to the transition probabilities that depend on two time parameters. Of course, the generalization from time-homogeneous to time-inhomogeneous processes can follow some intermediate steps considering, for example, periodic inhomogeneous processes. This is not the purpose of this paper. In the following, we show that exponential ergodicity offers us, for free, a bound for the stability of the invariant measures.

Let us consider forward equation associated to the ISHS corresponding to the forward Eq. (4) and to the evolution system of invariant measures. The perturbed version of

$$\frac{d^+}{dt}\pi_t = \pi_t(L_t^+ + \Delta_t) \tag{10}$$

where L_t^+ is the family of right infinitesimal generators associated to the ISHS. Here, $\overline{\Delta} = (\Delta_t)$ is a family of bounded operators on $\mathbf{B}(\mathbf{S})$.

Then the stability of the perturbed equation is determined by whether or not the perturbed generator $\mathcal{L} + \overline{\Delta}$ is invertible (where $\mathcal{L}$ is given by (7)). The stability of a linear system such as the one given by (10) is usually measured using the concept of *stability radius*. This concept was introduced by Hinrichsen and Pritchard for studying robustness of linear (autonomous and non-autonomous) systems [19,20].

Therefore, the stability radius $\rho_{stab}(\mathcal{U})$ (where $\mathcal{U}$ is the evolution system associated to the ISHS) with respect to a operator perturbation is the largest $\|\Delta_{(*)}\|_\infty$ such that $\mathcal{L} + \overline{\Delta}$ is invertible.

Proposition 2. *If the ISHS* $(\mathbf{X}_t)$ *is exponentially mixing, we have:*

$$\frac{1}{\|G\|} \le \rho_{stab}(\mathcal{U}) \le \frac{1}{r(G)}$$

where $r(G)$ *denotes the spectral radius of the kernel operator.*

Recall that the *spectral radius* of an operator G is defined as

$$r(G) := \sup\{|\alpha| : \alpha \in \sigma(G)\},$$

where $\sigma(G)$ is the spectrum of G (i.e., the set of all scalars α for which $\alpha I - G$ is not invertible). The spectral radius is given the following known Beurling formula [10]:

$$r(G) = \lim_{n \to \infty} ||G^n||^{1/n}.$$

In the dependability analysis, we use abstract models for the real systems. Then it is important to have some flexibility degree (related to the approximation error) for the existence of the invariant measures. Therefore, the existence of stability radius is essential for the robustness of the results.

Using the system of the invariant measures, one could define long-run average rewards for the time-space Markov model associated to an inhomogeneous stochastic hybrid system. Then there exists a time instant after which the computation of this reward can be done along only trajectory of the complex model. Infinitesimal perturbation analysis can be performed in a similar way like in the reference [6].

5   Final Remarks

5.1   Towards a Case Study

Here, we sketch a case study in reliability and safety of the shipboard power system. This is under development within a project undertaken at the Maritime Safety Research Centre at University of Strathclyde and funded by DNV-GL.

The cyber-physical system we are considering is the Medium Voltage Direct-Current (MVDC) shipboard power system (SPS). The SPS is vital to assuring continuity for ship equipment service. Failures of SPS may provoke blackouts, or makes powerless components of the vital equipment, which may cause serious threats to the crew and to the ship. An initial hybrid automaton model for such a system has been proposed recently in [2,32] for reliability and control purposes. The general architecture of the model for an MVDC shipboard power system includes: four turbine generators, two electrical propellers, four zonal loads one energy storage and one isolated pulse load [32]. The general model of this power system can be described as a network of hybrid automata, connected by a single communication bus. The connections to the bus are realized using a variety of linear and nonlinear components, which include DC disconnect switches and power conversion modules. The entire system has no more than 37 continuous variables [32]. The general continuous dynamics is described by a set of parameter-dependent differential algebraic equations [2].

The state space of above hybrid CPS is usually too large for analysing properties and behaviours using formal verification or dynamic reliability methods (in the context of dependability). We propose an alternative method that aims to provide safety and reliability control strategies. The aim is to use formal methods for the System-Theoretic Analysis (STPA) applied to different marine cyber-physical systems, including the shipboard power system. STPA [29] is a hazard identification method, where the system is described by an hierarchical control structure and the hazardous premises are induced by the lack of control actions, or their application at the wrong times. STPA is a top-down approach:

- it starts with an undesired event for the whole system, and then
- it goes down, in a deductive way, to the lower levels, in order to identify the local interactions that conduct to the top event.

There is no need for a detailed description of the system and it can be implemented very early in the system design. The STPA objective is to identify scenarios that lead to hazards and, based on this, define safety requirements that should be satisfied by the system. STPA provides circumstances that are in conflict with safety and reliability requirements.

When applying the STPA hazard analysis to the shipboard power system, we can identify the hazards that lead to a blackout event [4]. Examples of such hazards are: unbalanced power generation, transients in network, electrical disturbances like short circuits, fire in the engine room, and so on. The second step of the STPA analysis is the identification of the unsafe control actions. These are, more or less, described as control actions associated to each module of the power system applied at the wrong time. More details can be found in [4].

Our approach is developing an integration of hybrid automata analysis with STPA to show how this modelling framework can support the safety/reliability analysis methods performed with STPA. The combined methodology can boost dependability analysis during STPA to identify those control strategies that lead to dangerous states. The integration of stochastic hybrid automata with the STPA analysis can be done for each component of the SPS. We consider the SPS components that are dynamic. The main SPS dynamic components are: generator, exciter, governor. To exemplify, let us take a generator. A generator is one of the most complicated component of SPS. It includes electrical and mechanical subsystems. It has continuous behaviour (generator exciter system, prime mover, speed governor, rotor dynamics) and discrete behaviour (corresponding to the tripping of generator). The continuous behaviour of generator is governed by differential equations associated to the electromechanical dynamics. On the other hand, we can apply the STPA analysis to the generator in order to identify the unsafe control actions and causal events/factors. Then driven by the STPA outcome, we map these results into a transition system, most likely a Markov chain. Then we combine the continuous dynamics of the SPS generator with the transition system/Markov chain, and we obtain a stochastic hybrid system. It is expected that the whole integrated system will not be stationary due to the heterogeneity of the component dynamics. In this step, the theoretical results of dependability developed in this paper for inhomogeneous stochastic hybrid systems can be applied.

5.2   Conclusions

Dependability concepts as safety/security, availability, maintainability, performance, failure rates, invariance are very important in the life-cycle management of complex engineering systems. From a mathematical (complexity) perspective, the analysis related to dependability is mostly involving reachability/viability problem, first passage problem (hitting time, mean time), stability and invariance. In this context, complexity is understood in the sense of complexity science [23]. The concept of "complex" systems should not be confused with "large-scale" or "complicated" systems. For example, a recurrent transition system has an infinity of states making the real life system very large or complicated. Similar examples are situations of the combinatorial explosion of states. The nice characteristic of such examples is that they are compact. For complex engineering systems we have a physical structure, which is usually large/complicated, of interacting components. The resulting behaviours may no longer be described in a compact manner. This is why, a case study will be treated in a follow-up paper.

This paper is the first step towards setting up a framework for the study of dependability of complex engineering systems based on time-inhomogeneous stochastic hybrid systems. Our study is motivated by the use of inhomogeneous Markov models and stochastic hybrid systems for phased-mission reliability analysis [15, 28].

Our first development is concerned with the existence and uniqueness of the family of invariant measures for the underlying stochastic process. We impose a variant of geometric ergodicity that ensures the desired existence and uniqueness result. The novelty of our approach is the use of Wasserstein contraction for inhomogeneous stochastic processes, which is defined in terms of Kantorovich-Rubinstein metric on the space of probability measures. This provides the main hypothesis for proving of the uniqueness of the evolution system of invariant measures and of the uniform exponential stability of the associated semigroup of operators. The main challenge of this piece of research was to translate the exponential ergodicity condition in terms of Kantorovich-Rubinstein norm on an appropriate space of measures, and then to derive nice properties related to nonexpansitivity and stability under perturbations of the transition semigroup. This work will be developed further for general inhomogeneous stochastic hybrid systems and their reliability analysis.

A   Appendix

A.1   Metrics and Norms on Measure Spaces

In this section, Wasserstein metrics and Kantorovich-Rubinstein type norms on the space of finite signed Borel measures are briefly presented. We suppose that $\mathbf{S}$ is a Polish space (i.e. complete, separable, metric space), such that any finite signed Borel measure is a Radon measure (i.e. $\mathbf{S}$ is a Radon space). Recall that a measure μ defined on the Borel σ-algebra $\mathcal{B}(\mathbf{S})$ is called *Radon measure* if it is locally finite (i.e. for any point $x \in \mathbf{S}$ there is a neighborhood that has finite measure) and the following (inner regularity) property is satisfied:

$$\mu(B) = \sup\{\mu(K)|K \subset B, \, K \text{ compact}\}.$$

Let $\mathcal{M}(\mathbf{S})$ be the Banach space of finite signed Borel measures with the norm $||\mu|| := |\mu|(\mathbf{S})$, which is called the *variation norm* of the measure. Let $\mathcal{M}^+(\mathbf{S})$ denote the subset of $\mathcal{M}(\mathbf{S})$ consisting in all nonnegative Borel measures. By $\mathcal{M}_1(\mathbf{S})$ we denote the set of $\mathcal{M}^+(\mathbf{S})$ that are probability measures (i.e. $\mu(\mathbf{S}) = 1$ for $\mu \in \mathcal{M}_1(\mathbf{S})$).

If d is a metric on $\mathbf{S}$, the space of Lipschitz functions is defined as follows

$$Lip(\mathbf{S}) := \{f : \mathbf{S} \to \mathbb{R} | \exists L \geq 0 \text{ s.t. } |f(x) - f(y)| \leq Ld(x,y), \forall x,y \in \mathbf{S}\}.$$

For $f \in Lip(\mathbf{S})$, the quantity

$$|f|_L := \sup_{\substack{x,y \in \mathbf{S} \\ x \neq y}} \frac{|f(x) - f(y)|}{d(x,y)}$$

is called *Lipschitz constant* and this is a seminorm on $Lip(\mathbf{S})$ ($|f|_L = 0$ if and only if f is constant). The quotient space with respect to the constant functions is denoted by $Lip_0(\mathbf{S})$ and it is a Banach space. We will need also the set of Lipschitz contraction, which is

$$Lip_1(\mathbf{S}) := \{f : \mathbf{S} \to \mathbb{R} | |f|_L \leq 1\}.$$

As usual, $\mathbf{B}(\mathbf{S})$ is the space of bounded measurable functions $f : \mathbf{S} \to \mathbb{R}$ and $C(\mathbf{S})$ is the space of all bounded continuous functions. Both spaces are equipped with the supremum norm: $||f||_\infty := \sup_{x \in \mathbf{S}} |f(x)|$.

For a function $f : \mathbf{S} \to \mathbb{R}$ which is integrable with respect to $\mu \in \mathcal{M}(\mathbf{S})$ we write

$$<f, \mu> := \int_\mathbf{S} f(x) d\mu(x).$$

The space of signed measures $\mathcal{M}(\mathbf{S})$ is complete (Banach space) with respect to the Radon norm: $||\mu||_\mathcal{R} := \sup\{|<f, \mu>| : ||f||_\infty \leq 1\}$.

We denote by $\mathcal{M}^d(\mathbf{S})$ the space of signed measures ν such that

$$\int_\mathbf{S} d(x,y)|\nu|(dx) < \infty \tag{11}$$

for some (or, equivalently for all) $y \in \mathbf{S}$. Similarly, one can define the space $\mathcal{M}_1^d(\mathbf{S})$. The condition (11) ensures that the Lipschitz functions are integrable with respect to the measures from $\mathcal{M}^d(\mathbf{S})$.

In the following, we will introduce some well-known metrics.

On the space $\mathcal{M}^d(\mathbf{S})$, the *Fortet-Mourier metric* is given by the formula

$$||\mu_1 - \mu_2||_\mathcal{F} := \sup_{\substack{||f||_\infty \leq 1 \\ |f|_L \leq 1}} |<f, \mu_1 - \mu_2>|$$

The space of probability measures $\mathcal{M}_1^d(\mathbf{S})$ with respect to the Fortet-Mourier metric is a complete metric space [3]. Since the state space $\mathbf{S}$ is supposed to be a Polish space, then the weak convergence in $\mathcal{M}_1(\mathbf{S})$ is generated by this metric [27].

In the space $\mathcal{M}_1^d(\mathbf{S})$, we also can introduce the *Kantorovich-Wasserstein* (called also Hutchinson) *metric* by the formula

$$||\mu_1 - \mu_2||_{\mathcal{KW}} := \sup\{|<f, \mu_1 - \mu_2>|: |f|_L \leq 1\}.$$

The norms associated to the above metrics can be defined in a standard way, as follows:

– the Kantorovich-Rubinstein norm (or dual Lipschitz norm); which is defined on the closed subspace $\mathcal{M}_0(\mathbf{S})$ of zero-charge measures (i.e. measures with total mass equal to zero)

$$||\mu||_{\mathcal{K}} := ||\mu^+ - \mu^-||_{\mathcal{KW}}$$

– the Fortet-Mourier (Wasserstein) norm

$$||\mu||_{\mathcal{F}} := \sup\{|\int_{\mathbf{S}} f d\mu|: |f|_L \leq 1; ||f||_\infty \leq 1\}.$$

We can employ the equivalent norm

$$||\mu||_{BL}^* := \sup\{|\int_{\mathbf{S}} f d\mu|: f \in BL(\mathbf{S}), ||f||_{BL} \leq 1\},$$

where $BL(\mathbf{S})$ is the space of all bounded Lipschitz functions on $\mathbf{S}$ with the norm: $||f||_{BL} := ||f||_\infty + |f|_L$.

Theorem 3 (Kantorovich-Rubinstein Maximum Principle). *[27] For any μ_1, $\mu_2 \in \mathcal{M}_1^d(\mathbf{S})$, $\mu_1 \neq \mu_2$, there exists $f \in Lip_1(\mathbf{S})$ such that*

$$<f, \mu_1 - \mu_2> = ||\mu_1 - \mu_2||_{\mathcal{KW}}.$$

Moreover, every such a function f satisfies the condition: $|f(x) - f(y)| = d(x, y)$, $\forall x, y \in \mathbf{S}$, $x \neq y$.

A.2   Proofs

Proof of Theorem 1

Proof. $\Longrightarrow$: Suppose that the evolution system $(P_{s,t}^q)$ is exponentially Lipschitz with positive exponent $K > 0$. For μ_1, $\mu_2 \in \mathcal{M}_1^d(\mathbf{S})$, we have, using the Kantorovich-Rubinstein Maximum Principle, the following computations:

$$||(\mu_1 - \mu_2)P_{st}^q||_{\mathcal{KW}} = \sup_{f \in Lip_1(\mathbf{S})} |<f, (\mu_1 - \mu_2)P_{st}^q>|$$

$$= \sup_{f \in Lip_1(\mathbf{S})} |<P_{st}^q f, \mu_1 - \mu_2>| \leq e^{(-K)(t-s)}||(\mu_1 - \mu_2)||_{\mathcal{KW}}.$$

$\Longleftarrow$: Suppose that the evolution system $(P_{s,t}^q)$ is uniformly geometrically ergodic. It is known that the dual of $\mathcal{M}_0(\mathbf{S})$ is the quotient of space of Lipschitz functions by constant functions $Lip_0(\mathbf{S})$ with norm $|\cdot|_L$. Then the dual space of $Lip_0(\mathbf{S})$ is the completion of $\mathcal{M}_0(\mathbf{S})$ with respect to the Kantorovich-Rubinstein norm. Then the semi-norm $|P_{s,t}^q f|_L$, for any $f \in Lip(\mathbf{S})$ can be calculated as the norm of a linear functional on $\overline{\mathcal{M}_0(\mathbf{S})}$, i.e.

$$|P_{s,t}^q f|_L = \sup_{\|\mu\|_\mathcal{K} \leq 1} \|\mu P_{s,t}^q f\|_\mathcal{K}$$

$$= \sup_{\|\mu_1 - \mu_2\|_{\mathcal{KW}} \leq 1} |<f, (\mu_1 - \mu_2) P_{s,t}^q>| \leq |f|_L \cdot C e^{(-\Delta)(t-s)}.$$

Proof of Proposition 1

Proof. Fix $q \in Q$ and define the semigroup of operators associated the evolution system $P_{s,t}^q$ via

$$(\widehat{\mu} T_t^q)(s) := \mu_{s-t} P_{s-t,s}^q, \ s \in \mathbb{R}, \ t \geq 0.$$

Let $\widehat{\mu} := (\mu_l)_l$ be an $\mathcal{M}_1^d(\mathbf{S})$-valued sequence. Then

$$\|\widehat{\mu} T_{t+s}^q - \widehat{\mu} T_t^q\|_\infty$$

$$= \sup_l \|(\widehat{\mu} T_{t+s}^q)(l) - (\widehat{\mu} T_t^q)(l)\|_{\mathcal{KW}}$$

$$= \sup_l \|\mu_{l-(t+s)} P_{l-(t+s),l}^q - \mu_{l-t} P_{l-t,l}^q\|_{\mathcal{KW}}$$

$$\stackrel{(1)}{=} \sup_l \|[\mu_{l-(t+s)} P_{l-(t+s),l-t}^q - \mu_{l-t}] P_{l-t,l}^q\|_{\mathcal{KW}}$$

$$\leq \sup_l \|P_{l-t,l}^q\| \cdot \|\mu_{l-(t+s)} P_{l-(t+s),l-t}^q - \mu_{l-t}\|_{\mathcal{KW}}$$

$$\leq C' e^{(-\Delta t)}$$

with $C' = C \cdot K$, where K is a bound for $\|\mu_{l-(t+s)} P_{l-(t+s),l-t}^q - \mu_{l-t}\|_{\mathcal{KW}}$ (this bound exists due to the fact that $(P_{s,t}^q)$ is uniformly exponentially Lipschitz).

Therefore, the sequence $(\widehat{\mu} T_t^q)$ is a Cauchy sequence in the complete space $L^\infty(\mathbb{R}, \mathcal{M}_1^d(\mathbf{S}))$, thus it converges to a sequence of probability measures $\widehat{\pi}^q = (\pi_t^q)$, which is trivially the unique evolution system of invariant measures.

References

1. Aubry, J.-F., Brinzei, N.: Systems Dependability Assessment: Modelling with Graphs and Finite State Automata. Willey, Hoboken (2015)
2. Babaei, M., Shi, J., Zohrabi, N., Abdelwahed, S.: Development of a hybrid model for shiboard power systems. In: IEEE Electric Ship Technology Symposium (2015)
3. Basso, G.: A Hitchhiker's guide to Wasserstein distances. Report (2015)
4. Bolbot, V., et al.: A novel method for safety assessment of cyber-physical systems - application to cruise ship diesel-electric propulsion plant blackout probability prediction. J. Saf. Reliab. (submitted)

5. Buse, C., Niculescu, C.P.: An ergodic characterization of uniformly exponentially stable evolution families. Bull. Math. Soc. Roumanie **52**(100) (1), 33–40 (2009)
6. Cao, X.-R.: Optimization of average rewards of time nonhomogeneous Markov chains. IEEE Trans. Autom. Control **60**(7), 1841–1856 (2015)
7. Perez Castaneda, G.A., Aubry, J.-F., Brinzei, N.: Stochastic hybrid automata for dynamic reliability assessment. Proc. Inst. Mech. Eng. Part O: J. Risk Reliab. **225**(1), 28–41 (2011)
8. Chicone, C., Latushkin, Y.: Evolution Semigroups in Dynamical Systems and Differential Equations. Mathematical Surveys and Monographs, vol. 70. AMS (1999)
9. Chatzikokolakis, K., Gebler, D., Palamidessi, C., Xu, L.: Generalized bisimulation metrics. In: Baldan, P., Gorla, D. (eds.) CONCUR 2014. LNCS, vol. 8704, pp. 32–46. Springer, Heidelberg (2014). https://doi.org/10.1007/978-3-662-44584-6_4
10. Clark, S., Latushkin, Y., Montgomery-Smith, S., Randolph, T.: Stability radius and internal versus external stability in Banach spaces: an evolution semigroup approach. Siam J. Control Optim. **38**(6), 1757–1793 (2000)
11. Cloez, B., Hairer, M.: Exponential ergodicity for Markov processes with random switchings. Bernoulli **21**(1), 505–536 (2015)
12. Cuth, M., Doucha, M., Wojtaszczyk, P.: On the structure of Lipschitz-free spaces. Proc. Amer. Math. Soc. **144**, 3833–3846 (2016)
13. Cressent, R., Idasiak, V., Kratz, F., David, P.: Mastering safety and reliability in a model based process. In: Proceedings Annual Reliability and Maintainability Symposium (2011)
14. Dobrushin, R.L.: Prescribing a system of random variables by conditional distributions. Theory Probab. Appl. **XV**(3), 458–486 (1970)
15. Fan, M., Zeng, Z., Zio, E., Kang, R., Chen, Y.: A stochastic hybrid systems based framework for modeling dependent failure processes. PLoS ONE **12**(2), e0172680 (2017). Public Library of Science
16. Hamilton, J.D.: Analysis of time series subject to changes in regime. J. Econom. **45**(1–2), 39–70 (1990)
17. Heirung, A.N., Mesbah, A.: Stochastic nonlinear model predictive control with active model discrimination: a closed-loop fault diagnosis application. In: 20th IFAC World Congress (2017, preprint)
18. Heidergott, B., Leahu, H., Lopker, A., Pflug, G.: Perturbation analysis of inhomogeneous Markov processes. Working Paper (2012)
19. Hinrichsen, D., Pritchard, A.J.: Stability radii of linear systems. Syst. Control Lett. **7**, 1–10 (1986)
20. Hinrichsen, D., Ilchmann, A., Pritchard, A.J.: Robustness of stability of time-varying linear systems. J. Differ. Equ. **82**, 219–250 (1989)
21. Hsu, Y., Wu, W.F., Huang, T.W.: Reliability analysis based on nonhomogeneous continuous-time Markov modelling with application to repairable pumps of a power plant. Int. J. Reliab. Qual. Saf. Eng. **24**(1), 1750004 (2017). 14 p
22. Iosifescu, M.: Finite Markov Processes and their Applications. Wiley, Hoboken (1980)
23. Johnson, N.F.: Simply Complexity: A Clear Guide to Complexity Theory. Oneworld Oxford, London (2009)
24. Lewis, E.E., Zhuguo, T.: Monte Carlo reliability modeling by inhomogeneous Markov processes. Reliab. Eng. **16**(4), 277–296 (1986)
25. Limnios, N.: Reliability measures of semi-Markov systems with general state space. Method. Comput. Appl. Probab. **14**(14), 895–917 (2012)
26. Meyn, S., Tweedie, R.L.: Markov Chains and Stochastic Stability. Springer, Heidelberg (1993). https://doi.org/10.1007/978-1-4471-3267-7

27. Rachev, S.T.: Probability Metrics and the Stability of Stochastic Models. Wiley, New York (1991)
28. Smotherman, M., Zemoudeh, K.: A non-homogeneous Markov model for phased-mission reliability analysis. IEEE Trans. Reliab. **38**(5), 585–590 (1989)
29. Thomas, J.: Extending and automating a systems-theoretic hazard analysis for requirements generation and analysis. MIT (2013)
30. Tundis, A., Buffoni, L., Fritzson, P., Garro, A.: Model-based dependability analysis of physical systems with modelica. Model. Simul. Eng., 15 p. (2017)
31. Zhang, H., Dufour, F., Dutuit, Y., Gonzalez, K.: Piecewise deterministic Markov processes and dynamic reliability. J. Risk Reliab. **222**(4), 545–551 (2008)
32. Zohrabi, N., Abdelwahed, S.: On the application of distributed control structure for medium-voltage DC shipboard power system. In: IEEE Conference on Control Technology and Applications (2017)

Controlled Recurrence of a Biped
with Torso

Adrien Le Coënt[1][(✉)] and Laurent Fribourg[2]

[1] Department of Computer Science, Aalborg University,
Selma Largerløfs Vej 300, 9220 Aalborg, Denmark
adrien@cs.aau.dk
[2] LSV - ENS Paris-Saclay and CNRS and INRIA, University Paris-Saclay,
91 Avenue du Président Wilson, 94230 Cachan, France
fribourg@lsv.ens-paris-saclay.fr

Abstract. We have recently used a symbolic reachability method for controlling the stability of special hybrid systems called "sampled switched systems". We show here how the method can be extended in order to control the stability of more general hybrid systems with guard conditions and state resets. We illustrate the method through the example of a biped robot with 6 state variables, using a proportional-derivative (PD) controller. More specifically, we isolate a state region R such that, starting from a state located in R just after a footstep, the PD-control makes the robot state return to R at the end of the following footstep.

Keywords: Nonlinear systems · Verification · Hybrid systems

1 Introduction

The study of bipedal robot control has been pioneered by McGeer [14]. The original model considered in [14] had 4 state variables. Today the experimental implementations of bipedal robots may have 12 state variables [1]. In order to synthesize controllers which are *correct-by-construction* for such sophisticated robots, we need to obtain *reduced-order dynamics*. This is done by designing outputs and classical controllers driving these outputs to zero. The resulting controlled system evolves on a lower dimensional manifold and is described by the hybrid zero dynamics (HZD) governing the remaining degrees of freedom [1]. In a second step, a symbolic method constructs a *finite-state abstraction* (see [15]) of the HZD, then synthesizes a controller enforcing the desired specifications to be satisfied on the full order model. The interest in itself for constructing such finite-state abstractions has been illustrated in [11] where a control correct-by-construction is synthesized, without need for a preliminary step of order reduction, in the case of a bipedal model with 4 state variables.

In this paper, we show that an alternative symbolic method can be used in order to synthesize *directly* (i.e., without constructing a finite-state abstraction) a controller for a bipedal model with 6 state variables. Our symbolic method

R. Chamberlain et al. (Eds.): CyPhy 2018/WESE 2018, LNCS 11615, pp. 154–169, 2019.
https://doi.org/10.1007/978-3-030-23703-5_8

consists in isolating a zone R of the 6-dimensional state space, and proving R to be a basin of (recurrent) attraction.

The plan of the paper is as follows: in Sect. 2, we present our symbolic direct method for proving controlled recurrence; in Sect. 3, we apply the method to a bipedal model with 6 state variables; we conclude in Sect. 4.

2   Controlled Recurrence Method

In the context of the biped robot with torso [5], the state x is a vector of dimension 6 of the form $(\dot{\theta}_1, \dot{\theta}_2, \dot{\theta}_3, \theta_1, \theta_2, \theta_3)$, where θ_1 (resp. θ_2, θ_3) is the angle between the stance leg (resp. swing leg, torso) with the vertical. See Fig. 1. The robot is controlled by a proportional-derivative (PD) controller depending on the angle between the torso and the stance leg (viz., $(\theta_1 - \theta_3)$) while the swing leg remains free. We suppose that there is a finite set values $U = \{\theta_{SP}^1, \ldots, \theta_{SP}^p\}$ for the possible setpoints (objective values) assigned to the PD-controller. For each value θ_{SP}^i $(1 \leq i \leq p)$, the dynamics of the robot is governed by a differential equation of the form $\dot{x} = f_i(x)$. The footstep of the robot terminates when there is "collision" of the swing leg with the level ground, which corresponds to the equation

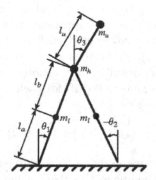

Fig. 1. Schematic of the robot (taken from [5])

$$\theta_1 + \theta_2 = 0. \tag{1}$$

At this point, a *reset* of the robot state is performed instantaneously, and a new footstep starts. This footstep is governed by an equation of the form $\dot{x} = f_j(x)$, where j is the new selected control index; and so on iteratively.

The control problem consists in selecting at each collision, an appropriate control index $i \in \{1, \ldots, p\}$ which makes the robot perform a new footstep (i.e., reach a state with $\theta_1 + \theta_2 = 0$). Such a problem can be solved using a *controlled recurrence* procedure (see, e.g., [8]):

1. *isolation*: isolate a rectangular zone R (corresponding to the "recurrent zone").

2. *bisection*: divide the zone R into 2^{nD} rectangular tiles (or "boxes") of the same size,[1] where n is the dimension of the state space, and D the depth of bisection of R.
3. *controlled recurrence*: for each tile T, try to find $i \in \{1, \ldots, p\}$ such that, for *any* starting point in T, the trajectory governed by $\dot{x} = f_i(x)$, reaches a collision hyperplane (here: $\theta_1 + \theta_2 = 0$), which, after reset, belongs to R.

If, for some tile T, the search for an appropriate index $i \in \{1, \ldots, p\}$ fails, one can restart the procedure with an incremented value of D or an augmented set of setpoint values θ_{SP}^i.

The controlled recurrence (item 3) is guaranteed using the method of *reachability with zonotopes* [2,9]. The initial tile T is seen as a "zonotope" [12]. We then compute an approximative form of successive discrete-time integrations of T for $\dot{x} = f_i(x)$, under the form of zonotopes. Let h be the step size of the discrete-time integration sequence. Let us first suppose that f_i is *linear* of the form $f_i(x) = Ax + \theta_{SP}^i b$. Each k-th integration of T can be computed efficiently in an exact manner, using the structure of *zonotopes* (see [9,10]). The computation then stops at first step k, say N^-, for which the k-th image of T intersects with (1) (see Sect. 3.1). As explained in [9], it is easy to compute a lower bound $\tau^- = N^-h$ of the first time (resp. upper bound $\tau^+ = N^+h$ of the last time) for which the intersection of the k-th image of T with hyperplane (1) is non-empty. It is also possible to compute an overapproximation of the *continuous* image of T during time $t \in [\tau^-, \tau^+]$ intersected with (1) (see, e.g., [10]); this image is denoted by $Post_i^N(T) \cap (1)$. The reset mapping due to the collision with the floor is then applied, and the resulting set denoted by $Reset(Post_i^N(T) \cap (1))$. The controlled recurrence is guaranteed if, for each tile T of R, one can find an index $i \in \{1, \ldots, p\}$ satisfying:

$$Reset(Post_i^N(T) \cap (1)) \subseteq R. \tag{2}$$

When f_i is a *non-linear* mapping, it is explained, e.g. in [2,9,10], how to extend the computation of the image $Post_i^N(T)$ using zonotopes. The basic idea is, in our context, to replace the nonlinear equation $\dot{x} = f_i(x)$ with an equation of the form

$$\dot{x} = Ax + \theta_{SP}^i\, b + Hd \tag{3}$$

where $Ax + \theta_{SP}^i\, b$ is the linearized form of $f_i(x)$, H a constant matrix, and d a "perturbation" term corresponding to the linearization error. It is supposed furthermore that an upper bound δ of $\|d\|$ is known or can be evaluated (see Sect. 3.2 for details).

In Figs. 2 and 3, the recurrence box R is represented in color cyan, the initial tile T as well as the successive discrete-time integration images are in blue, and the zone obtained after the reset operation, is represented in red. One can see

---

[1] Actually, the boxes are not *all* of the same size, but are generated according to an *adaptive* tiling procedure (see Sect. 3.3).

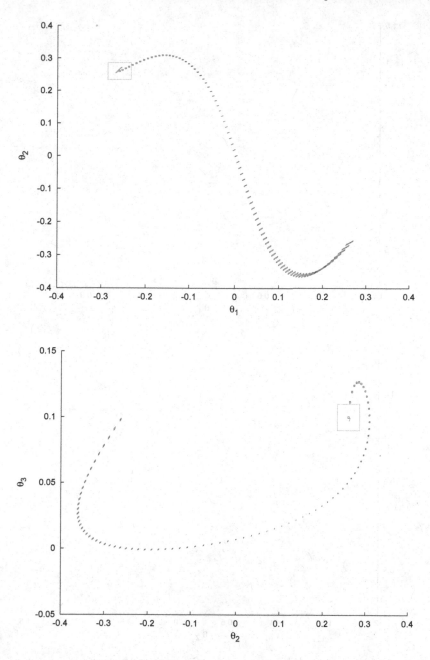

Fig. 2. $Post_i^k(T)$ in the planes (θ_1, θ_2) and (θ_2, θ_3) for $K_p = 124.675$, $K_d = 19.25$ and $\theta_{SP}^i = -0.075$. The cyan boxes correspond to the projections of box R. The blue zones are the successive (projections of the) images $Post_i^k(T)$ at discrete times, starting from $T = [0.58263, 0.59737] \times [0.273, 0.287] \times [1.36144, 1.37856] \times [-0.26162, -0.258375] \times [0.258375, 0.26162] \times [0.099375, 0.10063]$ located inside R. The red zones correspond to the final zonotopes, after the reset has been applied. (Color figure online)

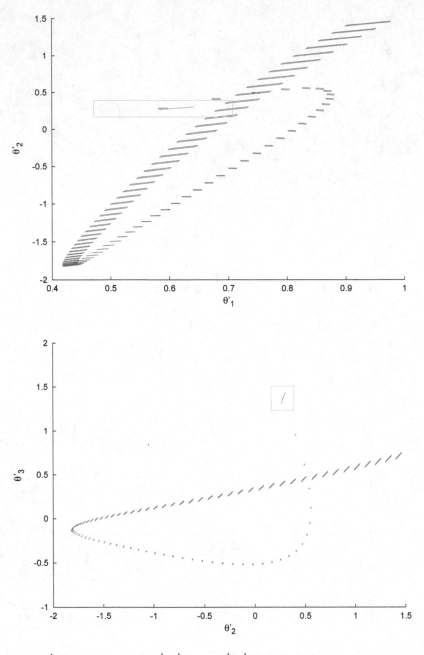

Fig. 3. $Post_i^k(T)$ in the planes $(\dot{\theta}_1, \dot{\theta}_2)$ and $(\dot{\theta}_2, \dot{\theta}_3)$ for $K_p = 124.675$, $K_d = 19.25$ and $\theta_{SP}^i = -0.075$. The cyan boxes correspond to the projections of box R. The blue zones are the successive (projections of the) images $Post_i^k(T)$ at discrete times, starting from $T = [0.58263, 0.59737] \times [0.273, 0.287] \times [1.36144, 1.37856] \times [-0.26162, -0.258375] \times [0.258375, 0.26162] \times [0.099375, 0.10063]$ located inside R. The red zones correspond to the final zonotopes, after the reset has been applied. (Color figure online)

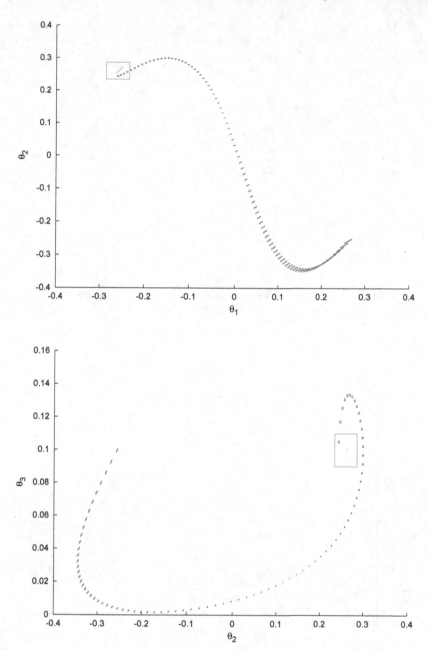

Fig. 4. $Post_i^k(T')$ in the planes (θ_1, θ_2) and (θ_2, θ_3) for $K_p = 124.675$, $K_d = 19.25$ and $\theta_{SP}^i = -0.075$. The cyan boxes correspond to the projections of box R. The blue zones are the successive (projections of the) images $Post_i^k(T')$ at discrete times, starting from $T' = [0.55300, 0.56700] \times [0.2535, 0.26650] \times [1.45087, 1.46913] \times [-0.24452, -0.24148] \times [0.24218, 0.24452] \times [0.10434, 0.10566]$ located inside R. The red zones correspond to the final zonotopes, after the reset has been applied. (Color figure online)

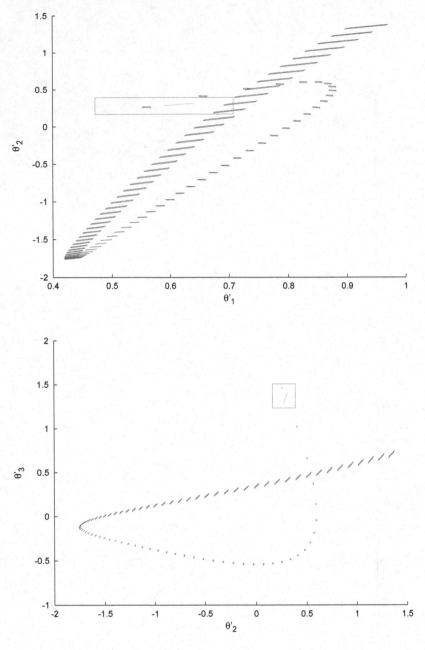

Fig. 5. $Post_i^k(T')$ in the planes $(\dot{\theta}_1, \dot{\theta}_2)$ and $(\dot{\theta}_2, \dot{\theta}_3)$ for $K_p = 124.675$, $K_d = 19.25$ and $\theta_{SP}^i = -0.075$. The cyan boxes correspond to the projections of box R. The blue zones are the successive (projections of the) images $Post_i^k(T')$ at discrete times, starting from $T' = [0.55300, 0.56700] \times [0.2535, 0.26650] \times [1.45087, 1.46913] \times [-0.24452, -0.24148] \times [0.24218, 0.24452] \times [0.10434, 0.10566]$ located inside R. The red zones correspond to the final zonotopes, after the reset has been applied. (Color figure online)

that the final red zone is located inside R (recurrence property). Figures 4 and 5 depict an analogous behavior, but starting from another initial tile T' of R. We explain in further details in Sect. 3 how such figures are generated.

3 Application to the Biped with Torso

3.1 Model

The model is taken from [5], to which the following text is mainly borrowed. The dynamics of the robot consists of a swing phase starting with both feet touching the ground. A torque is applied between the stance leg and the torso, so the swing leg moves forward. It is followed by a collision when both legs touch the ground again, meaning the end of a step. Due to inherent symmetries in the robot, one can consider that once a step is finished, the previous stance leg becomes the new swing leg. This requires the application of a reset in the model ("collision"). A collision happens when both feet touch the ground. The condition to be met for the collision is (1): $\theta_1 + \theta_2 = 0^2$.

Once the collision happens, conservation of the momentum and considering of symmetries in the system leads to a *reset* to apply, leading to a new set of initial conditions. The equations of the reset are the following:

$$\begin{pmatrix} I & 0 \\ 0 & L^n(\theta^+) \end{pmatrix} \begin{pmatrix} \theta^+ \\ \dot{\theta}^+ \end{pmatrix} = \begin{pmatrix} Q & 0 \\ 0 & L^o(\theta^-) \end{pmatrix} \begin{pmatrix} \theta^- \\ \dot{\theta}^- \end{pmatrix}$$

where I is the identity matrix, and

$$Q = \begin{pmatrix} 0 & 1 & 0 \\ 1 & 0 & 0 \\ 0 & 0 & 1 \end{pmatrix}$$

$$L^n(\theta) = \begin{pmatrix} L_{11}^n & L_{12}^n & L_{13}^n \\ L_{21}^n & L_{22}^n & L_{23}^n \\ L_{31}^n & L_{32}^n & L_{33}^n \end{pmatrix}$$

$$L^o(\theta) = \begin{pmatrix} L_{11}^o & L_{12}^o & L_{13}^o \\ L_{21}^o & L_{22}^o & L_{23}^o \\ L_{31}^o & L_{32}^o & L_{33}^o \end{pmatrix}$$

with

$L_{11}^n = -(m_h + m_l + m_u)(l_a + l_b)^2 - m_l l_a^2 - + m_l(l_a + l_b)l_b cos(\theta_1^+ - \theta_2^+) - m_u(l_a + l_b)l_u cos(\theta_1^+ - \theta_3^+)$, $L_{12}^n = m_l l_b(l_a cos(\theta_1^+ - \theta_2^+) - l_b + l_b cos(\theta_1^+ - \theta_2^+))$, $L_{13}^n = -m_l l_u(l_u + l_a cos(\theta_1^+ - \theta_3^+) + l_b cos(\theta_1^+ - \theta_3^+))$, $L_{21}^n = -m_u(l_a + l_b)l_u cos(\theta_1^+ - \theta_3^+)$, $L_{22}^n = 0$, $L_{23}^n = -m_u l_u^2$, $L_{31}^n = m_l(l_a + l_b)l_b cos(\theta_1^+ - \theta_2^+)$, $L_{32}^n = -m_l l_b^2$, $L_{33}^n = 0$, $L_{11}^o = m_l l_a l_b - (m_h + m_u)(l_a + l_b)^2 cos(\theta_1^- - \theta_2^-) - 2m_l(l_a + l_b)l_b cos(\theta_1^- - \theta_2^-) - m_u(l_a + l_b)l_u cos(\theta_1^- - \theta_3^-)$, $L_{12}^o = m_l l_a l_b$, $L_{13}^n = -m_u l_u(l_u + l_a cos(\theta_2^- - \theta_3^+) +$

---

[2] Condition (1) is true a first time when the legs are parallel, but we ignore such a "scuffing" and assume the swing leg to continue without collision.

$l_b cos(\theta_2^+ - \theta_3^+))$, $L_{21}^n = -m_u(l_a + l_b)l_u cos(\theta_1^+ - \theta_3^+)$, $L_{22}^n = 0$, $L_{23}^n = -m_u l_u^2$, $L_{31}^n = m_l l_a l_b$, $L_{32}^n = 0$, $L_{33}^n = 0$.

A PD-controller controls the torque during the swing phase. During a step, the dynamics of the robot is given by the nonlinear equation

$$M(\theta)\ddot{\theta} + N(\theta, \dot{\theta}) + G(\theta) = c\,u \tag{4}$$

with $\theta = (\theta_1, \theta_2, \theta_3)^\top$. The vector u is the control input corresponding to a PD-controller defined by:

$$u = K_p(\theta_{SP} - (\theta_3 - \theta_1)) - K_d(\dot{\theta}_3 - \dot{\theta}_1) \tag{5}$$

where θ_{SP} is the "setpoint". In our context, θ_{SP} belongs to a finite set U of values. The value of θ_{SP} in U is chosen after each collision for the whole duration of the forthcoming footstep (i.e., till the next collision) in order to make the robot return in the recurrence zone R (see Sect. 2). The matrices M, N, G and b are of the form

$$M(\theta) = \begin{pmatrix} M_{11} M_{12} M_{13} \\ M_{21} M_{22} M_{23} \\ M_{31} M_{32} M_{33} \end{pmatrix}$$

$$N(\theta, \dot{\theta}) = \begin{pmatrix} N_1 \\ N_2 \\ N_3 \end{pmatrix}$$

$$G(\theta) = \begin{pmatrix} G_1 \\ G_2 \\ G_3 \end{pmatrix}$$

$$c = \begin{pmatrix} -1 \\ 0 \\ 1 \end{pmatrix}$$

with:

$M_{11} = (m_u + m_h + m_l)(l_a + l_b)^2 + m_l l_a^2$,
$M_{12} = M_{21} = M_{12}^* cos(\theta_1 - \theta_2)$, with $M_{12}^* = -m_l(l_a + l_b)l_b$,
$M_{13} = M_{31} = M_{13}^* cos(\theta_1 - \theta_3)$ with $M_{13}^* = m_u(l_a + l_b)l_u$,
$M_{22} = m_l l_b^2$, $M_{23} = M_{32} = 0$, $M_{33} = m_u l_u^2$;
$N_1 = N_{12}^* sin(\theta_1 - \theta_2)\dot{\theta}_2^2 + N_{13}^* sin(\theta_1 - \theta_3)\dot{\theta}_3^2$,
$N_{12}^* = -m_l(l_a + l_b)l_b$ and $N_{13}^* = m_u(l_a + l_b)l_u$.
$N_2 = N_2^* sin(\theta_1 - \theta_2)\dot{\theta}_1^2$ with $N_2^* = m_l(l_a + l_b)l_b$,
$N_3 = N_3^* sin(\theta_1 - \theta_3)\dot{\theta}_1^2$ with $N_3^* = -m_u(l_a + l_b)l_u$;
$G_1 = G_1^* sin(\theta_1)$ with $G_1^* = -((m_h + m_l + m_u)(l_a + l_b) + m_l l_a)g$,
$G_2 = G_2^* sin(\theta_2)$ with $G_2^* = m_l l_b g$,
$G_3 = G_3^* sin(\theta_3)$ with $G_3^* = -m_u l_u g$.

The linear form of $M(\theta)$ is $M^*\theta$ with:

$$M^* = \begin{pmatrix} M_{11} M_{12}^* M_{13}^* \\ M_{12}^* M_{22} M_{23} \\ M_{13}^* M_{32} M_{33} \end{pmatrix}$$

Likewise, the linear form of $G(\theta)$ is $G^*\theta$ with $G^* = (G_1^*, G_2^*, G_3^*)^\top$, and the linear form of N is null.

A simulation of the PD-controller over two steps with $K_p = 124.675$ and $K_d = 19.25$, $\theta_{SP} = -0.075$ (for both steps) is given in Fig. 6.

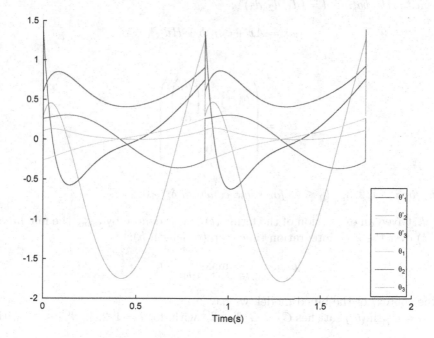

Fig. 6. Simulation of two robot footsteps for $K_p = 124.675$, $K_d = 19.25$ and $\theta_{SP} = -0.075$.

3.2   Linearization with Perturbation

From a general point of view, we are interested in the control synthesis problem for a continuous-time dynamical system subject to disturbances, described by the set of nonlinear ordinary differential equation:

$$\dot{x} = f(x, d), \tag{6}$$

where $x \in \mathbb{R}^n$ is the state of the system, and $d \in \mathbb{R}^m$ is a bounded perturbation. The functions $f : \mathbb{R}^n \times \mathbb{R}^m \to \mathbb{R}^n$, is the vector field describing the dynamics of the system. There exist today several efficient symbolic tools which perform reachability analysis of nonlinear systems, and control them in a provably safe manner: e.g., SpaceEx [6], Flow* [3] or DynIBEX [4]. Rather than using such tools, we propose here for the biped case study, to follow a *specific linearization* approach in order to take advantage of our tool MINIMATOR [7,8,13] (cf. Sect. 3.3). We first explain how to reformulate system (4–5) under the linearized form (3). As mentioned in Sect. 2, when the system is under form (3), one can easily construct (overapproximations of) reachable sets $Post_i^k(T)$ using zonotopes (see, e.g., [9]).

Proposition 1. *System (4–5) can be written under the linearized form with bounded perturbation* $d = (d_1, d_2, d_3)^\top$:

$$\dot{x} = Ax + \theta_{SP}\, b + Hd$$

where

$$Hd = \begin{pmatrix} (M^*)^{-1} \begin{pmatrix} d_1 \\ d_2 \\ d_3 \end{pmatrix} \\ 0 \\ 0 \\ 0 \end{pmatrix}$$

with, for $i = 1, 2, 3$, $|d_i| \leq \delta_i$ *for some constant* $\delta_i > 0$.

Proof. Given an expression of the form $e(t)$, let us denote by $e_{\max}$ the maximum of $e(t)$ over the k-th integration time step (of length h):[3]

$$e_{\max} := \max_{t \in [kh,(k+1)h]} e(t).$$

In the context of the biped model, we have:

$G_i = G_i^* \sin(\theta_i)$ satisfies $G_i = G_i^* \theta_i + d_i^G$ with, for $i = 1, 2, 3$: $|d_i^G| \leq \delta_i^G$ with

$$\delta_i^G := \frac{|G_i^*|}{6} |\theta_i|_{\max}^3.$$

$N_1 = d_1^N = N_{12}^* \sin(\theta_1 - \theta_2)\dot{\theta}_2^{\,2} + N_{13}^* \sin(\theta_1 - \theta_3)\dot{\theta}_3^{\,2}$ satisfies $|d_1^N| \leq \delta_1^N$ with

$$\delta_1^N := |N_{12}^*||\dot{\theta}_2|_{\max}^2 |\theta_1 - \theta_2|_{\max} + |N_{13}^*||\dot{\theta}_3|_{\max}^2 |\theta_1 - \theta_3|_{\max}.$$

$N_2 = d_2^N = N_2^* \sin(\theta_1 - \theta_2)\dot{\theta}_1^{\,2}$ satisfies $|d_2^N| \leq \delta_2^N$ with

$$\delta_2^N := |N_2^*||\dot{\theta}_1|_{\max}^2 |\theta_1 - \theta_2|_{\max}.$$

$N_3 = d_3^N = N_3^* \sin(\theta_1 - \theta_3)\dot{\theta}_1^{\,2}$ satisfies $|d_3^N| \leq \delta_3^N$ with

$$\delta_3^N := |N_3^*||\dot{\theta}_1|_{\max}^2 |\theta_1 - \theta_3|_{\max}.$$

$M_{12} = M_{21} = M_{12}^* \cos(\theta_1 - \theta_2) = M_{12}^* + d_{12}^M$ with: $|d_{12}^M| \leq \delta_{12}^M$ with

$$\delta_{12}^M := \frac{1}{2}|M_{12}^*|(\theta_1 - \theta_2)_{\max}^2.$$

---

[3] The expression $e_{\max}$ differs for each k, and the notation should be $e_{\max}^k$, but the upper index k is dropped for the sake of simplicity.

$M_{13} = M_{31} = M_{13}^* \cos(\theta_1 - \theta_3) = M_{13}^* + d_{13}^M$ with: $|d_{13}^N| \leq \delta_{13}^M$ with

$$\delta_{13}^M := \frac{1}{2}|M_{13}^*|(\theta_1 - \theta_3)_{\max}^2.$$

Let us write

$$B^p = \begin{pmatrix} -K_p & 0 & K_p \\ 0 & 0 & 0 \\ -K_p & 0 & K_p \end{pmatrix}$$

and

$$B^d = \begin{pmatrix} -K_d & 0 & K_d \\ 0 & 0 & 0 \\ -K_d & 0 & K_d \end{pmatrix}$$

Let us write

$$A = \begin{pmatrix} ((M^*)^{-1}B^d) & ((M^*)^{-1}(-G^* + B^p)) \\ \begin{pmatrix} 1 & 0 & 0 \\ 0 & 1 & 0 \\ 0 & 0 & 1 \end{pmatrix} & \begin{pmatrix} 0 & 0 & 0 \\ 0 & 0 & 0 \\ 0 & 0 & 0 \end{pmatrix} \end{pmatrix}$$

and

$$\theta_{SP}\, b = \begin{pmatrix} (M^*)^{-1}\begin{pmatrix} -K_p\theta_{SP} \\ 0 \\ K_p\theta_{SP} \end{pmatrix} \\ 0 \\ 0 \\ 0 \end{pmatrix}$$

System (4–5) can thus be reformulated as the following linearized system with bounded perturbation $d = (d_1, d_2, d_3)^\top$ as follows:

$$\dot{x} = Ax + \theta_{SP}\, b + Hd$$

where

$$Hd = \begin{pmatrix} (M^*)^{-1}\begin{pmatrix} d_1 \\ d_2 \\ d_3 \end{pmatrix} \\ 0 \\ 0 \\ 0 \end{pmatrix}$$

with, for $i = 1, 2, 3$, $|d_i| \leq \delta_i$ with:

$$\delta_1 := \delta_1^G + \delta_1^N + \delta_{12}^M|\ddot{\theta}_2|_{\max} + \delta_{13}^M|\ddot{\theta}_3|_{\max}$$
$$\delta_2 := \delta_2^G + \delta_2^N + \delta_{12}^M|\ddot{\theta}_1|_{\max}$$
$$\delta_3 := \delta_3^G + \delta_3^N + \delta_{13}^M|\ddot{\theta}_1|_{\max}$$

We have thus obtained a system of the form (3) with $d = (d_1, d_2, d_3, 0, 0, 0)^T$. Furthermore, we have: $|d_i| \leq \delta_i$ for $i = 1, 2, 3$. $\square$

When we perform discrete-time integration, we will now check that, at each time step (of length h), the norm of the perturbation $(M^*)^{-1}d$ is always less than or equal to $\frac{1}{10}\|\theta^i_{SP}b\|$. More precisely, at each k-th step, we check that the upper bound of the linearization error $\delta := \max\{\delta_1, \delta_2, \delta_3\}$ satisfies:

$$\delta \leq \frac{K_p}{10}|\theta^i_{SP}|. \tag{7}$$

This guarantees that the linearization error (seen as a perturbation) is always "small" with respect to the constant term $\theta^i_{SP}b$ of (3). Given an initial tile T, we then construct an overapproximation of $Post^k_i(T)$ for $1 \leq k \leq N^+$, by

1. computing the images of T through successive discrete-time *linear* integrations, and
2. extending these images to account for error δ.

Both operations are efficiently performed using zonotopes. A similar approach (linearization with addition of a disturbance term) can be done for the collision phase. The sets $Post^N_i(T)$ (corresponding to the *continuous-time* reachable set $Post^t_i(T)$ for $t \in [N^-h, N^+h]$) and $Reset(Post^N_i(T))$ (due to the collision phase) are then computed along the lines of the method sketched out in Sect. 2.

3.3 MINIMATOR Procedure

In order to prove the recurrence property (2), we adapt the MINIMATOR algorithm defined in [7]: given the input box R and a positive integer D, the algorithm provides, when it succeeds, a decomposition (by bisection) Δ of R of the form $\{(T_i, \theta^i_{SP})\}_{i \in I}$, with the properties:

- $\bigcup_{i \in I} T_i = R$,
- $\forall i \in I$, $Reset(Post^N_i(T_i)) \subseteq R$ and, for all $k = 1, \ldots, N^+$, $\delta \leq \frac{K_p}{10}|\theta^i_{SP}|$.

Here R is a "box" (i.e., a cartesian product of real intervals), which is seen here as a special form of zonotope. The tiles $\{T_i\}_{i \in I}$ are sub-boxes obtained by repeated bisection. At first, function *Decomposition* calls sub-function *Find_Control* which looks for a value $\theta^i_{SP} \in U$ such that $Reset(Post^N_i(R)) \subseteq R$. If such a value θ^i_{SP} is found, then a uniform control over R is found. Otherwise, R is divided into two sub-boxes T_1, T_2, by bisecting R w.r.t. its longest dimension. Values of θ_{SP} are then searched to control these sub-boxes. If for each T_i, function *Find_Control* manages to get a value for θ^i_{SP} verifying $Reset(Post^N_i(T_i)) \subseteq R$, then it is a success and algorithm stops. If, for some T_j, no such mode is found, the procedure is recursively applied to T_j. It ends with success when every sub-box T_i of R has a value of θ^i_{SP} verifying the latter conditions, or fails when the maximal degree of decomposition D is reached. The algorithmic form of functions *Decomposition* and *Find_Control*, adapted from [8], are given in Algorithms 1 and 2 respectively. The procedure is called initially with *Decomposition*(R, R, D), i.e. $T := R$.

Algorithm 1. Algorithmic form of Function *Decomposition*.

Function: *Decomposition*(T, R, D)

Input: A box T, a box R, a degree D of bisection
Output: $\langle \{(T_i, \theta_{SP}^i)\}_i, True\rangle$ or $\langle \_, False\rangle$

$(\theta_{SP}, bool) := Find\_Control(T, R)$
if $bool = True$ **then**
    return $\langle \{(T, \theta_{SP})\}, True\rangle$
else
    if $D = 0$ **then**
        return $\langle \_, False\rangle$
    else
        Divide equally T into (T_1, T_2)
        for $i = 1, 2$ **do**
            $(\Delta_i, bool_i) := Decomposition(T_i, R, D - 1)$
        end for
        return $(\bigcup_{i=1,2} \Delta_i, \bigwedge_{i=1,2} bool_i)$
    end if
end if

3.4   Experimentation

The verification procedure is implemented in an adaptation of the tool MINI-MATOR [13], using the interpreted language Octave, and the experiments are performed on a 2.80 GHz Intel Core i7-4810MQ CPU with 8 GB of memory.

The physical constants of the biped robot are the same as those given in [5]: $m_u = m_h = 10$, $m_l = 5$, $l_u = l_b = l_a = 0.5$, $g = 9.81$. The PD-constants used here are: $K_p = 124.675$, $K_d = 19.25$. The set of possible values for the setpoint θ_{SP} is $U = \{-0.07 + 0.001\, i\}_{i=0,\pm 1,\pm 2,...,\pm 9}$.

The verification procedure requires 3 h computation time. We use an integration time step of length $h = 10^{-2}$ s. We manage to control entirely the zone $R = [0.48, 0.72] \times [0.18, 0.42] \times [1.26, 1.54] \times [-0.286, -0.234] \times [0.234, 0.286] \times [0.09, 0.11]$ with a bisection depth $D = 4$: for each tile T of R there is some $\theta_{SP} \in U$ which makes T return to R. For example, as illustrated in Figs. 2 and 3, the value $\theta_{SP} = -0.075$ makes the initial tile $T = [0.58263, 0.59737] \times [0.273, 0.287] \times [1.36144, 1.37856] \times [-0.26162, -0.258375] \times [0.258375, 0.26162] \times [0.099375, 0.10063]$ return to R. Figures 4 and 5 show that the same value $\theta_{SP} = -0.075$ achieves also the recurrence property for tile $T' = [0.55300, 0.56700] \times [0.2535, 0.26650] \times [1.45087, 1.46913] \times [-0.24452, -0.24148] \times [0.24218, 0.24452] \times [0.10434, 0.10566]^4$.

---

[4] In Figs. 2, 3, 4 and 5, we did not plot *all* the images $Post^k(T)$, and $Post^k(T')$, for $1 \le k \le N^+$, but only some of them for the sake of readability of the pictures.

Algorithm 2. Algorithmic form of Function *Find_Control*.

Function: *Find_Control*(T, R)

Input: A box T, a box R
Output: $\langle \theta_{SP}, True \rangle$ or $\langle \_, False \rangle$

$U :=$ finite set of values of θ_{SP}^i
while U is non empty **do**
  Select θ_{SP}^i in U
  $U := U \setminus \{\theta_{SP}^i\}$
  if $Reset(Post_i^N(T) \cap (1)) \subseteq R$ with, for all $1 \leq k \leq N^+$, $\delta \leq \frac{K_p}{10} |\theta_{SP}^i|$ **then**
    return $\langle \theta_{SP}^i, True \rangle$
  end if
end while
return $\langle \_, False \rangle$

---

4   Final Remarks

We have shown how a direct symbolic method for proving controlled recurrence successfully applies to the robot model of [5]. Up to our knowledge, this is the first time that a symbolic method has synthesized a control correct-by-construction for a bipedal robot of dimension 6.

It would be interesting to try this method to higher dimensional robots or other hybrid systems with impact, possibly using a preliminary step of order reduction along the lines of [1]. This would probably require to use, not a specific linearization technique as here, but a general procedure designed for nonlinear reachability analysis, as in SpaceEx [6], Flow* [3] or DynIBEX [4].

References

1. Agrawal, A., et al.: First steps towards translating HZD control of bipedal robots to decentralized control of exoskeletons. IEEE Access **5**, 9919–9934 (2017)
2. Althoff, M., Stursberg, O., Buss, M.: Reachability analysis of nonlinear systems with uncertain parameters using conservative linearization. In: Proceedings of the 47th IEEE Conference on Decision and Control, CDC 2008, Cancún, Mexico, pp. 4042–4048 (2008)
3. Chen, X., Ábrahám, E., Sankaranarayanan, S.: Flow*: an analyzer for non-linear hybrid systems. In: Sharygina, N., Veith, H. (eds.) CAV 2013. LNCS, vol. 8044, pp. 258–263. Springer, Heidelberg (2013). https://doi.org/10.1007/978-3-642-39799-8_18
4. Alexandre dit Sandretto, J.A., Chapoutot, A., Mullier, O.: Tuning PI controller in non-linear uncertain closed-loop systems with interval analysis. In: 2nd International Workshop on Synthesis of Complex Parameters (SynCoP 2015). OpenAccess Series in Informatics (OASIcs), Dagstuhl, Germany, vol. 44, pp. 91–102 (2015)
5. Feng, S., Amur, S.A.Y., Sun, Z.: Biped walking on level ground with torso using only one actuator. Sci. China Inf. Sci. **56**(11), 1–9 (2013)

6. Frehse, G., et al.: SpaceEx: scalable verification of hybrid systems. In: Gopalakrishnan, G., Qadeer, S. (eds.) CAV 2011. LNCS, vol. 6806, pp. 379–395. Springer, Heidelberg (2011). https://doi.org/10.1007/978-3-642-22110-1_30
7. Fribourg, L., Kühne, U., Soulat, R.: Finite controlled invariants for sampled switched systems. Formal Methods Syst. Des. **45**(3), 303–329 (2014)
8. Fribourg, L., Soulat, R.: Control of Switching Systems by Invariance Analysis: Application to Power Electronics, 144 p. Wiley-ISTE (2013)
9. Girard, A.: Reachability of uncertain linear systems using zonotopes. In: Morari, M., Thiele, L. (eds.) HSCC 2005. LNCS, vol. 3414, pp. 291–305. Springer, Heidelberg (2005). https://doi.org/10.1007/978-3-540-31954-2_19
10. Girard, A., Le Guernic, C.: Zonotope/hyperplane intersection for hybrid systems reachability analysis. In: Egerstedt, M., Mishra, B. (eds.) HSCC 2008. LNCS, vol. 4981, pp. 215–228. Springer, Heidelberg (2008). https://doi.org/10.1007/978-3-540-78929-1_16
11. Hussien, O., Ames, A.D., Tabuada, P.: Abstracting partially feedback linearizable systems compositionally. IEEE Control Syst. Lett. **1**(2), 227–232 (2017)
12. Kühn, W.: Zonotope dynamics in numerical quality control. In: Hege, H.C., Polthier, K. (eds.) Mathematical Visualization, pp. 125–134. Springer, Heidelberg (1998). https://doi.org/10.1007/978-3-662-03567-2_10
13. Kühne, U., Soulat, R.: MINIMATOR 1.0 (2015). https://bitbucket.org/ukuehne/minimator/overview
14. McGeer, T.: Passive dynamic walking. Int. J. Rob. Res. **9**(2), 62–82 (1990)
15. Tabuada, P.: Verification and Control of Hybrid Systems: A Symbolic Approach, 1st edn. Springer, New York (2009). https://doi.org/10.1007/978-1-4419-0224-5

A Quantitative Metric Temporal Logic for Execution-Time Constrained Verification

Sascha Lehmann[1]([✉]), Sven-Thomas Antoni[2], Alexander Schlaefer[2], and Sibylle Schupp[1]

[1] Institute for Software Systems, Hamburg University of Technology, Hamburg, Germany
{s.lehmann,schupp}@tuhh.de
[2] Institute of Medical Technology, Hamburg University of Technology, Hamburg, Germany
{antoni,schlaefer}@tuhh.de

Abstract. In the context of run-time model checking, it could be desirable to prioritize and schedule the verification of system properties, so that the verification process, too, meets the time constraints of the underlying online experiment. In this paper, we introduce the *Quantitative Metric Temporal Logic for Verification Time* (QMTL-VT) to formally describe these constraints on verification time for properties formulated in a given temporal logic. Using QMTL-VT, we can query for satisfaction of time constraints ($\mathcal{V}$), the bounds of execution times ($\mathcal{V}_I$), and the probability of being checkable within these bounds ($\mathcal{V}_P$). Building up on that, we can execute queries under temporal conditions ($\mathcal{V}_C$), express their order ($\mathcal{V}_S$), and provide alternatives ($\mathcal{V}_A$) for the case of constraint violations. We apply a tool implementation of QMTL-VT to a set of *UPPAAL* sample models to demonstrate how to perform verification of given properties under real-time constraints, and discuss syntax and semantics in a medical case study on heart-motion tracking as an online real-time scenario.

Keywords: Online model checking · QMTL-VT · Verification time · Run-time verification · Medical cyber-physical systems · Heart-motion tracking

Partially funded by fmthh - Forschungszentrum Medizintechnik Hamburg

1 Introduction

Medical devices, robotics, autonomous vehicles, energy supply systems - In a real-time context, we usually encounter complex systems of which we require to meet strict timing constraints and exhibit only specified behaviour. To ensure safety, it is often beneficial to verify the desired properties via model checking

© Springer Nature Switzerland AG 2019
R. Chamberlain et al. (Eds.): CyPhy 2018/WESE 2018, LNCS 11615, pp. 170–189, 2019.
https://doi.org/10.1007/978-3-030-23703-5_9

performed on a formal model of such systems. Some of these properties can be verified statically and offline without continuously updated information on the system environment and its concrete state. However, other types of properties exist which highly depend on the system state and model parameters, and thus can only be verified for limited temporal scopes.

Online model checking [1] aims towards such bounded verification at run time, but introduces new timing-related difficulties, since in real-time systems the time frame for each verification step is generally restricted. Thus, we have to ensure that we select the most suitable property prioritization, model-traversal order, and checking technique in terms of the remaining verification time. Similar to the actual model properties, verification-time requirements can be verified either statically or dynamically, and are formally expressible.

In this paper, we target the necessity of such expression of timing constraints in the verification process itself. In particular, we introduce the *Quantitative Metric Temporal Logic for Verification Time* (QMTL-VT) as a logic to formally describe verification-time properties. The logic allows expressing both qualified and quantified timing requirements for the verification process, and queries for time constraints given by the model topology and state. This paper is structured as follows: First, we provide a short introductory example in Sect. 2, and describe the context and related work of model checking techniques and timing-related terms in Sect. 3. Afterwards, we formally introduce the syntax and semantics of our QMTL-VT logic in Sect. 4, and cover requirements and possible constructs for its use. Finally, we demonstrate and discuss the application of QMTL-VT for online verification using both a set of sample models, and a medical case study on heart-motion tracking in Sect. 5, followed by an outlook towards future work and the conclusion in Sect. 6.

2   Introductory Example

As initially stated, verification-time constraints become relevant as soon as the verification shifts from offline to run-time approaches. First, we need to point out that a notable difference exists in the literature between *real-time* model checking and *run-time* model checking:

Definition 1 (Real-Time Model Checking). *Real-time model checking* describes a category of model checking techniques that verify temporal properties of models exhibiting explicit timing behaviour.

Definition 2 (Run-Time Model Checking). *Run-time model checking* describes the process of model checking performed under time constraints for continuous verification of a system at run time.

We can see that these two concepts especially differ in the context of their time evaluation. The former uses timed models, but does not necessarily require the verification process to be performed in real time. The latter is performed

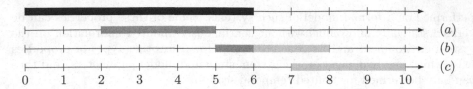

Fig. 1. Verification-time intervals for three possible scenarios: the verification will either *always* (a), *possibly* (b), or *never* (c) finish within the available time frame (black bar).

during run time, but is not necessarily applied to a system with real-time requirements or properties.

Our considerations focus on run-time model checking, and distinguish between three cases as shown in Fig. 1. In case (a), the maximum verification-time duration $t_{v,max} = 5$ lies below or at the time bound of available verification time $t_a = 6$. Therefore, we can safely check the property, and consider any further, yet unchecked properties for the remaining time interval $[5,6]$. A different situation is given with case (b). Here, the minimum verification-time duration $t_{v,min} = 5$ lies below the time bound t_a, while the maximum duration $t_{v,max} = 8$ clearly exceeds it. A probability value can express how likely it is for the actual verification duration t_v to undercut t_a. This probability value depends on the probability and duration of the individual model paths, paired with the time costs of checking the property on these paths. As third possibility, case (c) has both $t_{v,min} = 7$ and $t_{v,max} = 10$ exceeding the available time t_a. In that situation, the query of that property can either be cancelled (bearing the risk of malicious system behavior), or still be executed using parts of the next or previous time frames.

For an exemplary system consisting of two propositions Nrm and Er (indicating normal and erroneous behavior) and some physical variable v, we might now want to check two properties: The value of v invariantly needs to lie between the threshold values $v_{th,min}$ and $v_{th,max}$ ($\phi_1 = AG(v \geq v_{th,min}$ && $v \leq v_{th,max})$), and an erroneous state should eventually lead back to normal behavior ($\phi_2 = AG(Er => AF\ Nrm)$). Unfortunately, checking the invariant property ϕ_1 might be quite computationally intensive. As we still want to ensure safety as far as practicable, we might consider to use a weakened property instead, expressing that the erroneous state Er is never reached ($\phi_3 = AG(not\ Er)$). Furthermore, verifying that v lies within expected bounds (or that the erroneous state is never reached) might have more importance than checking that Er finally leads back to Nrm. This is especially the case when reaching Er causes an external intervention into the system under consideration, which involves non-determinism. Combining the requirements, we thus want to express that ϕ_1 is checked first, and if not possible in time, ϕ_3 is checked instead, all followed by checking ϕ_2 if possible. QMTL-VT provides the required constructs for this purpose. Using this logic, we can express the complete property as $\phi_{vt} = \mathcal{V}_S(\mathcal{V}_A(\phi_1, \phi_3), \phi_2)$, where $\mathcal{V}_S$ stands for sequencing, and $\mathcal{V}_A$ for alternatives.

3   Related Work

In the literature, both the fields of real-time and run-time model checking are widely studied. Contributions to the analysis of underlying time constraints, enforced on either the model level or the verification level, have a long history dating back to the 1980s [2] with active research since then (e.g., [3] and [4]). Nowadays, these time constraint analyses also find application in a broad range of industry [5]. There, new logics are introduced to express the temporal inter-dependency of actions and events (e.g., with TiCL in the automotive domain [6]). Regardless of all advancements in model checking, performance issues still exist, and are considered the major bottleneck of these techniques. In the past, this problem was addressed mostly in either of three ways: The first aims for a state space reduction by altering the model, including relaxation, reduction, and abstraction [7]. The second reduces the considered portion of the state space, applying sample based techniques such as Monte-Carlo Model Checking [8], or limiting the temporal scope with Bounded Model Checking [9]. Finally, the third targets a performance increase by distributing and parallelizing the verification procedure [10]. What all three approaches have in common, is, that they do not cover the prioritization and scheduling of the verifiable properties per se. In contrast, QMTL-VT allows for a declarative specification of scheduling to handle the performance issue. Furthermore, related work is concerned with the analysis of the worst-case execution time (WCET) and best-case execution time (BCET) of processes. The field of WCET analysis includes both static [11] and dynamic program analyses, and covers exhaustive as well as statistical approaches to WCET-based scheduling [12]. Furthermore, WCET analysis was elaborately combined with different model checking techniques [13]. And again, as in the original model-checking problem, the performance bottleneck brings about further research on acceleration, e.g., by exploiting structural properties [14]. For QMTL-VT, we can utilize WCET and BCET results both at the modeling level and for the actual verification process.

QMTL-VT as a logical layer expresses timing constraints for run-time verification, and the model checking techniques and execution time analyses mentioned above can put these constraints into practice. A recent work by Li et al. [15] already covers different scenarios that target the run-time aspect of model checking for cyber-physical systems. The authors apply online finite-horizon reachability model checking to hybrid medical systems, and for that, design the verification task based on the available time frame. Using an upper bound for time costs, model checking is performed either as hard or soft real-time task, depending on whether the duration undercuts ($t_{v,max} < t_a$) or exceeds ($t_{v,max} > t_a$) the verification horizon. With our paper, we contribute to this work by providing a formal representation of exactly that time-constrained verification process in the context of online experiments.

In the literature, we also find approaches that focus on the structure of model properties to improve verification performance. Filieri et al. [16] aim to improve the performance of run-time verification by including a *pre-computation* step to transform the model properties into a set of faster verifiable expressions for

Discrete Time Markov Chains (DTMCs). Using these expressions in place of the original properties, it is possible to check the probabilistic system online where timing behaviour is the critical factor. With QMTL-VT, we do not alter the model property structures, but provide a non-intrusive way to put these properties both into a mutual relation and into a context with the available time frame. Instead of applying optimizations on the implementation-level, we shift the consideration of timing behaviour to the model-level, where we use QMTL-VT properties to describe a suitable sequencing and alternation of underlying model properties. We perform this shift of focus as the system model and the set of property formulae can already provide valuable information about verification time, which can then be incorporated on the implementation-level in a run-time context. In summary, the three main objectives of the QMTL-VT logic are:

1. Quantified constructs to express verification-time constraints for run-time verification
2. Time-conditional verification of properties based on temporal queries
3. Independence from the concrete underlying base logic and duration analysis technique

In the following section, we will pursue these aims and provide a formal definition of QMTL-VT.

4   The Logic QMTL-VT

In the following, we provide a formal definition for the syntax and semantics of QMTL-VT, and cover necessary design decision for a practical application of the language.

4.1   Definition of QMTL-VT

As emphasized in the introducing example, the syntax of QMTL-VT requires constructs that express time constraints of single properties, as well as the relation between those properties. A definition of the complete QMTL-VT syntax is given in Definition 3.

Definition 3 (QMTL-VT Syntax). The following syntax is inductively defined for the *Quantitative Metric Temporal Logic for Verification Time* (QMTL-VT):

$$
\begin{aligned}
\phi &::= \quad \varPhi \quad | \quad (\neg\phi) \quad | \quad (\phi \wedge \phi) \quad | \\
&\qquad \mathcal{V}_{\lhd\tau}(\varPhi) \ | \ \mathcal{V}_{P,\lhd\tau,\rhd\lambda}(\varPhi) \\
\iota &::= \mathcal{V}_{P,\lhd\tau}(\varPhi) \ | \quad \mathcal{V}_I(\varPhi) \\
\alpha &::= \mathcal{V}_{C,\lhd\tau}(\varPhi) \ | \ \mathcal{V}_{A,\lhd\tau}(\alpha,\alpha) \ | \ \mathcal{V}_{S,\lhd\tau}(\alpha,\alpha)
\end{aligned}
\tag{1}
$$

where $\lhd \in \{<, \leq\}$, $\rhd \in \{\geq, >\}$, λ = prob. threshold, τ = time bound

Φ is an arbitrary property formulated in the underlying logic (e.g., CTL, PCTL, LTL). $\neg$ and $\wedge$ are defined as usual. With QMTL-VT, we provide a way to express that a formula ϕ, which is based on an expression of the underlying logic (Φ), is checkable in a certain amount of time. These formulae cover the timing cases (a) and (c) of Fig. 1. If this verifiability cannot be asserted with certainty within given time bounds, as in case (b) of Fig. 1, we furthermore want to express that a formula is provable in these bounds with some required probability. Therefore, we introduce $\mathcal{V}_{\lhd\tau}$ and $\mathcal{V}_{P,\lhd\tau,\rhd\lambda}$ to assert that the verification process meets time and probability conditions.

$\mathcal{V}_{\lhd\tau}(\Phi)$:   Is Φ always (dis-)provable in $t_v \lhd \tau$?

$\mathcal{V}_{P,\lhd\tau,\rhd\lambda}(\Phi)$:   Is Φ always (dis-)provable in $t_v \lhd \tau$ with prob. $p_v \rhd \lambda$?

In some cases, we do not want to check that requirements are met, but rather query for the timing or probability bounds of a formula. In our logic, this is expressed with $\mathcal{V}_{\mathcal{I}}$ and $\mathcal{V}_{\mathcal{P}}$ by omitting the time bound $\lhd\tau$ or probability bound $\rhd\lambda$ respectively.

$\mathcal{V}_{P,\lhd\tau}(\Phi)$:   Which probability p_v is Φ (dis-)provable with in $t_v \lhd \tau$?

$\mathcal{V}_{\mathcal{I}}(\Phi)$:   Which time interval $[t_{vl}, t_{vu}]$ is Φ always (dis-)provable in?

Besides expressing the satisfiability of constraints for the verification process only, we also want to use the results of such queries to trigger the verification on the underlying property ϕ afterwards. We use $\mathcal{V}_C$, $\mathcal{V}_A$, and $\mathcal{V}_S$ to express three such combining formulae.

$\mathcal{V}_{C,\lhd\tau}(\phi)$:   Is ϕ (dis-)provable in $t_v \lhd \tau$? If yes, verify it.

$\mathcal{V}_{A,\lhd\tau}(\alpha_1,\alpha_2)$: Is α_1 (dis-)provable in $t_v \lhd \tau$? If yes, verify it, otherwise verify α_2.

$\mathcal{V}_{S,\lhd\tau}(\alpha_1,\alpha_2)$: Is α_1 (dis-)provable in $t_v \lhd \tau$? If yes, verify it, then verify α_2.

As we see, $\mathcal{V}_{C,\lhd\tau}(\phi)$ is used to check ϕ under the condition (C) $t_v\lhd\tau$. It determines if ϕ is proved or disproved in $\lhd\tau$ time units, and if so, verifies the formula ϕ. $\mathcal{V}_C$ is the most basic combination of verification time and property check. $\mathcal{V}_{A,\lhd\tau}(\alpha_1,\alpha_2)$ decides between checks of α_1 and its alternative (A) α_2, based on the time condition $t_v \lhd \tau$. It determines if the first formula α_1 is checkable in $\lhd\tau$ time units, and if not, verifies the second formula α_2. Such expression becomes useful in situations where we can formulate the same general property with formulae of different complexities. We can then use the weaker formulae as a *fallback* alternative in case that the original formulae cannot be thoroughly checked due to time limitations. Finally, $\mathcal{V}_{S,\lhd\tau}(\alpha_1,\alpha_2)$ verifies α_1 and α_2 in sequence (S), based on the time condition $t_v\lhd\tau$. It checks if the first formula α_1 is checkable in $\lhd\tau$ time units, and if so, verifies it, followed by a verification of the second formula α_2. We use such expression in cases where we can put the set of requirements into a prioritized order. We then check the next formula with lower priority (α_{lp}) only if the formula with higher priority (α_{hp}) was checked and the remaining time is still sufficient for a subsequent verification of α_{lp}. For a nested use of the formulae $\mathcal{V}_A$ and $\mathcal{V}_S$, we omit $\lhd \tau$ for the inner formulae. In that case, either the original time constraint of the outer formula (for $\mathcal{V}_A$ or the left sub-formula of $\mathcal{V}_S$), or the new remaining time (for the right sub-formula of $\mathcal{V}_S$) is forwarded to the inner formulae.

Next, we define a measure for the verification process duration for state formulae Φ and path formulae ψ, applied to a state s or path π, respectively. A path π in a given model M is defined as a sequence of states $(s_0, s_1, ..., s_n)$, for which all pairs of subsequent states (s_i, s_{i+1}) are included in the transition relation $R \subseteq S \times S$ of M. Paths of both finite length (for non-cyclic model sections) and infinite length (in case of loops) can be considered for the verification time properties. Generally speaking, the verification time of Φ for a single state depends on the complexity of the state formula. Additionally, the verification time of a complete path is influenced by further computation and model traversion steps based on the underlying structure and model checking technique.

Definition 4 (Verification Duration Measure). Given a single state s and a state formula Φ in the underlying logic, we define $t_e(s, \Phi) > 0$ as the execution time needed to verify the formula Φ for s. For a path $\pi = (s_0, s_1, ..., s_n)$ and a given path formula ψ, we define the verification duration as the sum of the durations for the states s_i on that path.

$$\delta(\pi, \psi) = \sum_{i=0}^{n} t_e(s_i, \psi) \tag{2}$$

Given a function $init(M)$ that returns the initial state of a model M, and a set of paths $\Pi = (\pi_0, \pi_1, ..., \pi_n)$, we define $\pi_{i,j}$ as the jth state on the ith path of Π. Finally, we define the total verification duration of a path formula ψ on a model M for the set of all paths Π with $\pi_{i,0} = init(M)$ as the sum of the individual path verification durations.

$$\Delta_{Exh}(M, \psi) = \sum_{\pi_i \in paths} \delta(\pi_i, \psi) \tag{3}$$

The definition of the total verification duration is based on the *exhaustive* strategy that searches the complete state space - and thus all paths starting in s_0 - to check the property ψ. In case that a more optimized strategy is applied (e.g., sample-based verification), alternative definitions can be provided instead:

Definition 5 (Alternative Total Duration Measures).

$$\Delta_{Sim}(M, \psi) = \sum_{\pi \in S_{sim,\psi}} \delta(\pi, \psi) \text{ (simulation-based)}$$
$$\Delta_{Bnd}(M, \psi) = \sum_{\pi \in \Pi} \delta(\pi, \psi), \text{ with } \Pi = \{\pi = (s_0, ..., s_i) | |\pi| = B\} \text{ (bounded)} \tag{4}$$
$$\Delta_{Sym}(M, \psi) = \sum_{\pi \in S_{sym}} \delta(\pi, \psi), \text{ with } S_{sym} = unique(\Pi) \text{ (symmetric)}$$

The lower and upper bounds for the verification time based on the complexity of the underlying formula depend on the formula type (state formula or path formula), the number of atomic calculations for the (composed) formula, and the use of path quantifiers. For the case of exhaustive model checking of classical CTL formulae, we can derive the following bounds:

$$
\begin{aligned}
\psi = X\Phi: \quad & t_{v,min} = t_{v,max} = t_e(s_0, \Phi) \\
\psi = G\Phi: \quad & t_{v,min} = t_e(s_0, \Phi), & t_{v,max} = \delta(\pi, \psi) \\
\psi = F\Phi: \quad & t_{v,min} = t_e(s_0, \Phi), & t_{v,max} = \delta(\pi, \psi) \\
\psi = \Phi_1 U \Phi_2: \quad & t_{v,min} = t_e(s_0, \Phi_1) + t_e(s_0, \Phi_2), & t_{v,max} = \delta(\pi, \psi) \\
\sigma = A(\psi): \quad & t_{v,min} = t_e(s_0, \Phi), & t_{v,max} = \Delta_{Exh}(M, \psi) \\
\sigma = E(\psi): \quad & t_{v,min} = t_e(s_0, \Phi), & t_{v,max} = \Delta_{Exh}(M, \psi)
\end{aligned}
$$

The definition of the verification duration measure is applicable to all three timing scenarios of Fig. 1. But it does not incorporate the possibility yet that time exceeding or underrunning verification paths may only occur in some simulation runs, or may be traversed only with specific probabilities. To allow for the expressions $V_{P,\triangleleft\tau,\triangleright\lambda}(\Phi)$ and $V_{P,\triangleleft\tau}(\Phi)$, we need to define a time probability measure to quantify those probabilities. As foundation, we use the following probability measure as defined in [17], where it is used in PCTL.

Definition 6 (Probability Measure) [17]. Let $paths_{s_0}^M$ denote the set of paths of M starting in s_0, and T be a transition probability function, such that for all states s in S, $\sum_{s' \in S} T(s, s') = 1$. Furthermore, let $\pi \uparrow n$ denote the prefix $s_0 \ldots s_n$ of π. We define:

- For any sequence $s_0 \ldots s_n$ starting in s_0:
  $\mu_{s_0}^M(\{\pi \in paths_{s_0}^M | \pi \uparrow n = s_0 \ldots s_n\}) = T(s_0, s_1) \times \cdots \times T(s_{n-1}, s_n)$
- For $n = 0$:
  $\mu_{s_0}^M(\{\pi \in paths_{s_0}^M | \pi \uparrow 0 = s_0\}) = 1$
- For any countable set $\{X_i\}_{i \in I}$ of disjoint subsets of $paths_{s_0}^M$:
  $\mu_{s_0}^M(\bigcup_{i \in I} X_i) = \sum_{i \in I} \mu_{s_0}^M(X_i)$
- If $X \subseteq paths_{s_0}^M$, the measure of the complement set $paths_{s_0}^M \setminus X$ is defined as:
  $\mu_{s_0}^M(paths_{s_0}^M \setminus X) = 1 - \mu_{s_0}^M(X)$

We combine the probability measure $\mu_{s_0}^M$ with our timing data, which results in the time probability measure μ_{τ,s_0}^M:

Definition 7 (Time Probability Measure). For a path formula ψ, a model M, and a time bound τ, we define $\mu_{\tau,s_0}^M(\pi)$ as the summed probability of paths starting in s_0 for which ψ is (dis-)provable in at most τ time units:

$$
\mu_{\tau,s_0}^M(\psi) = \sum_{\pi \in \Pi} \mu_{s_0}^M(\pi) \times p_\tau(\pi, \psi)
$$

$$
\text{with } p_\tau(\pi, \psi) = \begin{cases} 1 & \delta(\pi, \psi) \leq \tau \\ 0 & \delta(\pi, \psi) > \tau \end{cases}
$$

Based on the Definitions 3, 4, and 7, and the intended behavior introduced in the beginning, we can now define the semantics of QMTL-VT. For that, we use the common notations of $M \models \phi$, if for a model structure M, the formula ϕ is satisfied.

Definition 8 (QMTL-VT Semantics). The following semantics are inductively defined in QMTL-VT with relation $\models$ on a model M:

$$
\begin{aligned}
M &\models \Phi && \text{iff } \Phi \text{ satisfied in the underlying logic} \\
M &\models \neg\phi && \text{iff not } (M \models \phi) \\
M &\models \phi_1 \wedge \phi_2 && \text{iff } (M \models \phi_1) \wedge (M \models \phi_2) \\
M &\models \mathcal{V}_{\vartriangleleft\tau}(\Phi) && \text{iff } \Delta(M,\Phi) \vartriangleleft \tau \quad \text{(as defined in Eq. 3)} \\
M &\models \mathcal{V}_{P,\vartriangleleft\tau,\vartriangleright\lambda}(\Phi) && \text{iff } \mu^{M}_{\tau,init(M)}(\Phi) \vartriangleright \lambda \\
M &\models \mathcal{V}_{C,\vartriangleleft\tau}(\Phi) && \text{iff } (\Delta(M,\Phi) \vartriangleleft \tau) \text{ and } (M \models \Phi) \\
M &\models \mathcal{V}_{A,\vartriangleleft\tau}(\alpha_1,\alpha_2) && \text{iff } (M \not\models \alpha_1) \implies (M \models \alpha_2) \\
M &\models \mathcal{V}_{S,\vartriangleleft\tau}(\alpha_1,\alpha_2) && \text{iff } (M \models \alpha_1) \text{ and } (M \models \alpha_{2,\tau_{rem}}) \\
& && \quad \text{with } \tau_{rem} = \tau - \Delta(M,\alpha_1)
\end{aligned}
$$

Finally, $\mathcal{V}_I(\Phi)$ and $\mathcal{V}_{P,\vartriangleleft\tau}(\Phi)$ can be defined via $\Delta(M,\Phi)$ and $\mu^{K}_{\tau,init(M)}$, respectively.

4.2   Practical Aspects

To put the defined logic for verification time into practice, four aspects should be taken into consideration: The choice of the *model* to be checked, the underlying temporal *logic* for QMTL-VT, the evaluation of *execution times*, and the decision on a preferable *verification technique*.

Model Choice. In terms of model choice, the general idea of QMTL-VT is not restricted to a specific class of automata. For the logic to be beneficial in a run-time verification context, it seems natural, though, to select a model type with an explicit representation of time. This allows us to express a bounded time scope for the set of states to verify, and to put this scope into direct relation to time constraints on the verification process level. In that regard, the model and the verification process share the common domain of time for that model type. Simply put, the underlying interpretation of time expressed via clocks in the model thus equals the concept of time on the verification level. Nevertheless, applying QMTL-VT is not limited to timed automata, as we can certainly reason about verification durations of systems that do not involve a continuous time model.

Logic Choice. QMTL-VT is defined on top of a given logic. Therefore, we have to choose a logic to define the underlying temporal properties Φ for our verification time logic. In applications, a common choice for the underlying logic is a temporal logic, following a motivation analogously to the model choice. But as checking a property formulated in any arbitrary logic necessarily involves a certain time cost, QMTL-VT can be applied to non-temporal logics as well. Depending on the concrete property to express, suitable temporal logics applied to cyber-physical systems include LTL for single paths (e.g., $F(x > 10)$), CTL for branching time (e.g., $AF(x > 10)$), PCTL for probabilistic properties (e.g., $P[< 0.1](F(x > 10))$, or MITL for properties on time intervals (e.g., $F[0, 10]$ $(x > 10)$).

Execution Time Evaluation. Two different approaches are conceivable to determine concrete execution times for property checking and model simulation: The first is a *numerical* solution based on a reduced set of simulation runs, and repeated evaluations of expressions and statements of the models and properties involved. The second is an *analytical* solution based on the analysis of atomic operations for property expressions, model invariants, guards, clock resets and value assignments.

For the numerical approach, we measure the execution time for m simulation runs ($m \ll n$ for a total of n simulation runs), and scale the measured time up to n. Alternatively, we might track execution times "on-the-fly" throughout the experiment, and predict the currently expected duration based on these previous measurements. The advantages of the numerical approach are obvious: The procedure is easy to implement and to perform, and it implicitly takes into account possibly varying execution times due to the operating system scheduler on non-RT systems. Its greatest disadvantage is that it does not consider the complete system, but only specific traces of it, so that the actual execution time might still exceed a determined bound. For our tool prototype, we implemented this first approach.

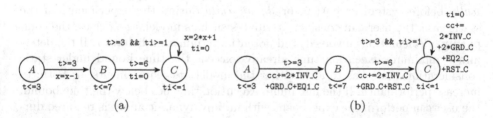

Fig. 2. The original model (a) and the corresponding execution time model (b)

As an alternative to the numerical approach, one may consider to analyze the model execution times analytically instead. For the analytical approach, one can target the determination of fixed computation/CPU cycle counts for formula evaluations and model simulations. On the model level, one then transforms a timed system model into an *execution time model* (ETM), which sums up the number of cycles required for all operations involved. An example of such a model transformation performed on a sample model is shown in Fig. 2. The original model (a) consists of three locations A, B, and C, two clocks t and ti, and guarded edges which either alter the variable x or reset the clock variable ti. In the derived ETM, we added a new variable cc as a computation cycle counter, which is incremented by a cost value on every transition between two locations. The execution time model retains invariants, guards, assignments, and resets of the original model. On the transition from A to B, the costs of two invariant checks (INV_C), one guard check (GRD_C), and the execution of equation $x = x - 1$ (named EQ1_C) are added to cc. Likewise, the costs for the transition from B to C are calculated, using the clock reset costs (RST_C) instead of equation costs. Finally, the self loop at C involves the costs of two invariant checks, two guard checks, equation $x = 2 * x + 1$ (named EQ2_C), and one clock reset. Based on this model, we can now query for the expected cycle counts on arbitrary paths, and check whether that value lies below a defined threshold.

The concrete implementation of the model may vary depending on the model trace generation strategy: If the model traversal is based on fixed time steps, the model must further contain self-loops triggered on each time step to count the CPU cycles for the ongoing invariant checks. If the triggerable state transitions are determined via region-based constructs such as difference bound matrices (DBMs), one has to include the computational cost of the DBM analysis into the model as well. A major advantage of this approach is that preparational steps can already be taken in advance (e.g., ETM creation, global WCET analysis, or simplifications for loops). Furthermore, the strictly monotonically increasing time costs may allows for further ETM simplifications. Nevertheless, in contrast to the first method, a more complex implementation is required. And after all, the determined cycles once again may not reliably correlate with the actually consumed time due to influences of the scheduler. For our tool prototype, this second approach is scheduled for a future implementation.

Both the numerical and the analytical approach are applicable either *statically* before system execution, or *dynamically* during the experiment. In the static case, the user can consider attributes such as model size, cycles, the complexity of calculations involved, and potential termination behavior. If the determined minimum execution time already exceeds the time bound under static considerations, one has to alter either the model, its requirements, or both, to increase performance. If the maximum execution time lies below the time bound, the user can perform the experiment without any dynamic analysis required during run time. In the remaining cases, dynamic analysis can help to determine the required verification time online and more precisely, based on the current system state. The dynamic analysis would then be performed on a per-query base, and can involve further scheduling steps such as time frame expansion or property skipping.

Verification Technique Selection. As a final consideration, one needs to decide which verification technique is suitable to fit the time constraints expressed via QMTL-VT, while making the best use of the time frame given. Several techniques are potentially applicable, including the exhaustive search through the complete state space, time-bounded verification, or sample-based checking. Although this decision is still an open task, it is possible to put the techniques in relation to the three timing cases identified in the introduction. If $t_{v,max} \leq t_a$, the verification process is certainly finished within the time frame. In that case, it is not necessary to sample the state space, taking risk to miss paths that do not satisfy the required properties. Therefore, one would select the exhaustive method to check our system properties. On the contrary, if $t_{v,min} > t_a$, an exhaustive approach would exceed the time bound by all means, making a statistically sampled approach more suitable here. Finally, in the intermediate case ($t_{v,min} < t_a \wedge t_{v,max} > t_a$), neither of the two techniques is an obvious better choice. In that case, a final decision needs to take into account additional factors like potentially available slack time, safety criticality, and the probability of $t_{v,max} > t_a$.

While the overall benefit of QMTL-VT is greatly influenced by the four aspects covered above, relations between individual properties allow for an even more effective application. We already introduced $\mathcal{V}_S$ as the logic component that puts the evaluation of properties into a defined sequence. Thus, we can use an order on the priority of properties to increase the performance of our approach. Several orders are sensible, e.g., checking safety properties first, and shifting reachability properties to the end of a verification frame. Anyway, the most beneficial order highly depends on the concrete application, and its focus on safety, liveness, fairness, or other properties. In the same manner, alternatives expressed via $\mathcal{V}_A$ can provide meaningful substitutions for main properties in case of time violations. For the alternative properties, we can either adapt the model step size, verification scope, and simulation sample count, or functionally reduce the formula to a property that is cheaper to verify.

5   Benchmark/Case Study

For a demonstration of the benefits and the work flow of QMTL-VT, we apply it to both a set of *UPPAAL* sample models, and an online, time-sensitive experiment on heart-motion analysis in the medical domain. For the experiments, we use a tool implementation of the QMTL-VT checker, which is accessible online [18]. A sample output of the tool is shown in Fig. 3.

5.1   Benchmark Setup

At first, we apply QMTL-VT to a set of models taken from the demo resources of the official tool distribution of the model checker *UPPAAL*. The frame data of the benchmark models is shown in Fig. 4. We selected the models based on their differing sizes (*2doors* and *bridge* are more extensive compared to *interrupt* and *lsc_example*), the amount of properties to check, and the temporal extent of each individual verification. Furthermore, we based our choice on the feature compatibility of each individual model to the current tool prototype implementation. For each property query, we provide the following alternatives:

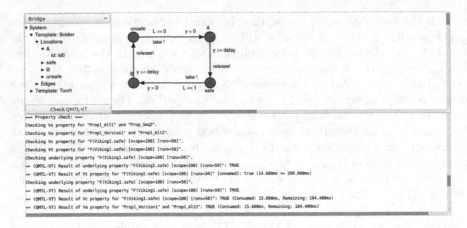

Fig. 3. An exemplary view of the QMTL-VT checker prototype, showing a tree view of the model data as well as the graphical model representation (top), and the verification data of the QMTL-VT properties and sub-formulae (bottom)

1. The formula with normal sim scope ($dt = 100$) and normal run count (50)
2. The formula with normal sim scope ($dt = 100$) and reduced run count (10)
3. The formula with reduced sim scope ($dt = 25$) and normal run count (50)

We further assume an available time frame of 200 ms for the verification of all properties P1–P4 together. Finally, we check the properties $A(\phi)$ and $E(\phi)$ for all experiments based on multiple simulation runs instead of an exhaustive state space search.

Model	2doors	interrupt	bridge	lsc_example
Automata	4	3	5	4
Locs/Edges	16 / 22	8 / 10	20 / 21	8 / 10
Grds/Invs	10 / 8	0 / 0	16 / 0	1 / 2
P1	A[] (not (Door1.open and Door2.open))	A[] not env1.ERROR	E<> Viking1.safe	A<> C1.loc5
P2	A[] ((Door1.opening imply User1.w<=31) and (Door2.opening imply User2.w<=31))		A[] not (Viking4.safe and time<slowest)	
P3	E<> (Door1.open)		E<> Viking4.safe imply time>=slowest	
P4	E<> (Door2.open)		E<> Viking1.safe and Viking2.safe and Viking3.safe and Viking4.safe	

Fig. 4. General data of the selected UPPAAL models (Locs = locations, Grds = guards, Invs = invariants, P = property)

		Prop	2doors	interrupt	bridge	lsc_example
Original		P1	E (235/200)	E (236/200)	T (14/200)	T (5/200)
		P2	S (xxx/-35)		T (77/186)	
		P3	S (xxx/-35)		T (9/109)	
		P4	S (xxx/-35)		E (639/100)	
QMTL-VT	P1	Alt1	E (235/200)	E (236/200)	T (14/200)	T (5/200)
		Alt2	T (47/200)	F (49/200)	S (xxx/200)	S (xxx/200)
		Alt3	S (xxx/200)	S (xxx/200)	S (xxx/200)	S (xxx/200)
	P2	Alt1	E (601/153)		T (77/186)	
		Alt2	T (127/153)		S (xxx/186)	
		Alt3	S (xxx/153)		S (xxx/186)	
	P3	Alt1	T (16/26)		T (9/109)	
		Alt2	S (xxx/26)		S (xxx/109)	
		Alt3	S (xxx/26)		S (xxx/109)	
	P4	Alt1	E (16/10)		E (639/100)	
		Alt2	T (3/10)		T (85/100)	
		Alt3	S (xxx/10)		S (xxx/100)	

Fig. 5. Experiment data for the UPPAAL models based on the *original* and *QMTL-VT* properties (E = exceed, S = skip, T = true, F = false). The pairs (Co/Av) represent the consumed (Co) and available (Av) time [ms] for each property

5.2 Benchmark Results

Figure 5 shows the time progression and execution order handling of the property (P) verification for the selected models. The first four rows present the execution data of the original queries (without the use of QMTL-VT formulae). Here, the properties P1–P4 are verified in order, and as soon as the verification of a property results in the exceedance (E) of the available time frame, the verification step is terminated. For *2doors* and *interrupt*, the time frame is exceeded after the first property check, so that the properties P2–P4 are skipped (S) for the former model. In contrast, we can check P1–P3 for the model *bridge* before reaching the time limit with P4, and for model *lsc_example*, we can check its single property P1 completely in time.

The remaining rows of Fig. 5 depict the behaviour when we perform verification based on a QMTL-VT property. The properties P1–P4 now consist of three different alternatives (Alt), whose verification is checked for time exceedance, and which - if no time constraint is violated - are executed, skipping all remaining alternatives. The verification for model *2doors* utilized these alternatives frequently, as we can see for the properties P1, P2, and P4. Here, the original queries with predicted verification times of 235 ms (P1), 601 ms (P2), and 16 ms (P4), exceed the available time frames of 200 ms, 153 ms, and 10 ms, respectively. Therefore, the second alternatives are chosen, which are checkable within the corresponding time frame in all three cases. Similarly, we can verify the properties for the models *interrupt*, *bridge*, and *lsc_example* in time using one of the alternatives. As a result, we thus obtain verification data for all proper-

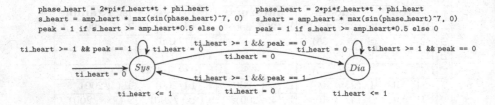

Fig. 6. The heart motion model

ties of our models based on either the original or alternative formulae, which is advantageous compared to the original, purely sequential approach.

5.3 Experiment Setup

In the literature, complex models of heart systems are used for model checking tasks, e.g., to verify the behavior of implantable cardiac pacemakers [19]. In [20], a simplified heart model is used to check the validity of selected heart parameters by comparing the simulated signal data against an observed heart motion trace. Validation requires that the distinct phases of heart motion based on the selected parameters are reachable within a set time scope. In this case study, we want to apply QMTL-VT to formulae that express such requirements, as well as to properties on the signal value bounds. We first introduce the model of the heart system and the required properties, and derive the QMTL-VT versions of these properties. Afterwards, we verify both sets of formulae during run time, and compare their performance in terms of verification-time behavior.

The heart system shown in Fig. 6 continually provides signal values based on selected *amplitude* (`amp_heart`), *phase shift* (`shift_heart`), and *frequency* (`freq_heart`) parameters. A simplified model of this system contains locations for the two main phases of a cardiac cycle, *systole* (ranging over the pumping period) and *diastole* (ranging over the filling period). Furthermore, switching between these phases is initiated on the base of the current heart signal value in relation to its maximum amplitude (`peak = 1 if s_heart >= amp_heart*0.5 else 0`). If the signal value rises above $amp_{heart}/2$ and thus to the proximity of the peak value, the `peak` variable is set to 1, initiating a change to the *Systole* location. Likewise, the model switches to the *Diastole* location as soon as the heart signal value falls below $amp_{heart}/2$. A more detailed explanation of the medical relevance of the parameters involved, and the choice of sinusoidal model equations, can be found in [20]. Several properties are required for this heart system, three of which we want to focus on during this experiment:

$$\text{Systole reach: } \Phi_{sys} = F(Sys) \text{ [checked via 100 sim runs]}$$
$$\text{Diastole reach: } \Phi_{dia} = F(Dia) \text{ [checked via 100 sim runs]}$$
$$\text{Amplitude bounds: } \Phi_{amp} = G(|s_{heart}| \leq amp_{heart}) \text{ [checked via 25 sim runs]}$$

The first two properties check whether the two heart phases are reachable or not, starting from the current state of the system. These properties are especially relevant as we want to validate the amplitude, shift, and frequency parameters via this model, which is only possible with distinct phases of both the high and low signal within a given time scope. The last property ensures that the simulated heart signal value always lies below the maximum amplitude value. Since the parameters and resulting motion data are continuous, it is not feasible to verify the complete model state space spanned by these continuous variables prior to the experiment. Therefore, we will only verify time-bounded parts of the state space for sampled paths of the model. As furthermore the system parameters may change during the experiment, the experiment requires ongoing, updated verification data of the mutable system. In consequence, for each verification step, only a limited time window can be used to ensure that actions on the heart are only performed when in a desired state. For the particular experiment, the properties are iteratively checked at a time distance of 1000 ms with a verification scope of 1000 ms.

As the verification intervals are time-bounded, all three properties can only be verified if sufficient time is left in the current verification step. We express this constraint with the conditional formula $\mathcal{V}_{C,\lhd\tau}(\psi)$, leading to:

$$\phi_{sys} = \mathcal{V}_{C,\lhd\tau}(\Phi_{sys}), \phi_{dia} = \mathcal{V}_{C,\lhd\tau}(\Phi_{dia}), \phi_{amp} = \mathcal{V}_{C,\lhd\tau}(\Phi_{amp}) \tag{5}$$

Based on the relevance of verification results obtained for each property, we introduce a *priority order* using the sequential formula $\mathcal{V}_{S,\lhd\tau}(\psi_1, \psi_2)$ to describe which properties to check first. In our case, ensuring that indeed both heart phases are reachable on every verification step is more important than checking the validity of the amplitude bounds. Again, it is only possible to validate the amplitude, shift and frequency parameters when we have both phases of the heartbeat cycle in scope, so we want to ensure that first. We connect the conditional formulae of Eq. 5 for sequential evaluation, and obtain:

$$\phi_{seq} = \mathcal{V}_{S,\lhd\tau}(\Phi_{sys}, \mathcal{V}_{S,\lhd\tau}(\Phi_{dia}, \Phi_{amp})) \tag{6}$$

Finally, we want to provide alternative *fallback properties* (alt) that are less computationally intensive and will be used if the corresponding main property is not checkable in time. For this experiment, we use the original properties Φ_{sys}, Φ_{dia}, and Φ_{amp}, with altered numbers of simulation runs, which we introduced as one possible fallback strategy in Sect. 4.2. Therefore, we use the alternative formula $\mathcal{V}_{A,\lhd\tau}(\psi_1, \psi_2)$ in include the following formulae:

$$\text{Systole reach: } \Phi_{sys,alt} = F(Sys) \text{ [checked via 10 sim runs]}$$
$$\text{Diastole reach: } \Phi_{dia,alt} = F(Dia) \text{ [checked via 10 sim runs]}$$
$$\text{Amplitude bounds: } \Phi_{amp,alt} = G(|s_{heart}| \leq amp_{heart}) \text{ [checked via 5 sim runs]}$$

Combining these alternative properties with the property sequence defined in Eq. 6 leads to the following final property equation for the experiment:

$$\phi_{exp} = \mathcal{V}_{S,\lhd\tau}(\mathcal{V}_{A,\lhd\tau}(\Phi_{sys}, \Phi_{sys,alt}), \mathcal{V}_{S,\lhd\tau}(\mathcal{V}_{A,\lhd\tau}(\Phi_{dia}, \Phi_{dia,alt}),$$
$$\mathcal{V}_{A,\lhd\tau}(\Phi_{amp}, \Phi_{amp,alt})))$$

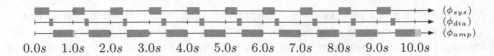

Fig. 7. Verification duration for properties of an original run

In the following, we use both this QMTL-VT formula and the original properties Φ_{sys}, Φ_{dia}, and Φ_{amp} over 100 experiment executions, and compare their timing behavior within the available time frame of each verification step.

5.4 Experiment Results

Figure 7 shows a sample experiment run performing the originally sequential, temporally unconditioned verification of the properties ϕ_{sys}, ϕ_{dia}, and ϕ_{amp}. Figure 8, in contrast, shows a sample experiment execution utilizing the timing information of the QMTL-VT formula. During the experiment, we verify the system properties every 1000 ms, which we call the *time frame* of the verification step. We can see that the original experiment run suffers from exceeded verification-time frames at several stages during its execution (e.g., the query of ϕ_{amp} at $t = 10\,\mathrm{s}$). Partly, this exceedance is influenced by the scheduling mechanisms of the operating system, which is not specifically designed for real-time purposes, and can hence delay computations. But we also notice a more systematic problem throughout the verification steps: Reading the figure column-wise, we see that the query of all three properties together generally requires more time than each available time frame permits. In the worst case, an experiment with such behavior may repeatedly sum up negative time balances, up to the point where a complete verification step needs to be skipped. The time data depicted in Fig. 8, however, sticks to the fixed deadlines, which is achieved by an initial ordering and potential weakening of the properties. In sections where checking ϕ_{amp} would exceed the available time frame, the experiment automatically switches to the less time-consuming alternative $\phi_{amp,alt}$. As a result, the verifier in the experiment reduces the workload in a controlled manner where required, selecting only properties checkable in the remaining time.

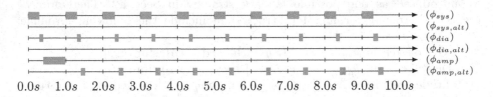

Fig. 8. Verification duration for properties of a QMTL-VT run

The experiment data provided in Fig. 9 gives an overview of the verification-time behavior across the experiment runs. It compares the experiments without

Experiment type	Runs	Verification time[ms]			Missed windows		
		min	*max*	*avg*	*min*	*max*	*avg*
Original	100	962	1255	1210	42/50	50/50	45/50
QMTL-VT	100	523	982	633	0/50	0/50	0/50

Fig. 9. Experiment data based on *original* and *QMTL-VT* properties

and with the usage of the QMTL-VT formula, and shows that the timing behavior can be improved using QMTL-VT properties. We executed the model for 50 s in each experiment run, which results in a total of 50 time windows, each ranging over 1000 ms of the experiment. The minimum, maximum, and average values for both the verification time and missed time windows are calculated over all 100 experiment runs. The experiments without further time constraints exceed the available time of 1000 ms by 210 ms on average, while for the QMTL-VT-based experiments, the maximum time value of 982 ms lies below. This difference in the timing results is also reflected by the numbers of missed time windows, where an average of 45/50 missed frames for the original experiments contrasts with 0/50 missed frames of the adapted ones. We see that in all cases using the QMTL-VT formula, choosing formulae from a set of alternatives allows for picking one which strictly complies with the time constraints. In this way, we ensure that the property checks are finished before the end of the verification-time frame is reached, and can start the next verification step in time. In future experiments, the remaining time in each frame may even be used to either extend the verification scope of the current step, or to start the next verification step prematurely.

6   Future Work and Conclusion

6.1   Future Work

Important for future considerations is the handling of QMTL-VT timing behavior itself. Currently, only the query time of the underlying sub-formula Φ is considered during the evaluation of a QMTL-VT formula. Neglected at this point is the additional time that the checking process of verification time might consume, in particular during dynamic analysis of verification time at run time. Expressing and enforcing these time constraints will require further changes of the syntax, semantics, and implementation of the QMTL-VT logic: For the semantics of $\mathcal{V}_A$ and $\mathcal{V}_S$, we cannot simply forward τ and $\tau - \Delta(M, \phi)$, respectively, as we currently do. The term for the remaining time would need to include the value τ_+ as additional time cost for the top-level verification process. For this purpose, we will need to provide a way to formulate queries for this time value τ_+ syntactically. A natural way to extend the current syntax might be to allow nesting for QMTL-VT formulae, so that QMTL-VT can express properties using itself as underlying logic. As an example, with ϕ as underlying property, and $\mathcal{V}_\phi$ as its verification-time property, $\mathcal{V}_{\mathcal{V}_\phi}$ then checks time constraints on $\mathcal{V}_\phi$. For the execution time model, we will then have to create another model based on the time costs of checking properties on the original execution time model. Research on that matter will also need to determine up to which depth this recursion is still reasonable, and how that depth bound can be determined and restricted.

In the experiment results, we have seen that the QMTL-VT sub-formulae are only verified if possible in the remaining time frame. Conversely, if no property alternatives are checkable in time, the verification process will only indicate the exceedance of the time limit, without verifying any intended system behavior. For safety-critical systems, this can become impractical. In fact, it might actually be favorable - and in the long term compensable - to prolong particular verification steps. The decision on whether to skip a property, use previously buffered time (if possible), or consume time from future verification frames, is still an open task. An extension of the underlying mechanisms of QMTL-VT that applies a suitable scheduling algorithm to handle properties in case of a time constraint violation may further improve the approach.

6.2 Conclusion

With this work, we address the timing behavior of property verification, a crucial factor to allow for more flexible run-time model checking. In particular, the goal is an increase in the degree of control we have over the verification process when strict time constraints require checking results within fixed time bounds. We defined a new logic, QMTL-VT, to express quantitative constraints on that time aspect, enabling us to schedule property queries with prioritized order and alternatives. As the benchmark and case study demonstrated, QMTL-VT in its current form is capable of ensuring real-time behavior of continuous verification in a real-world application. Still, as our discussion showed, future research might push the approach towards full control of verification timing behavior.

References

1. Rinast, J.: An online model-checking framework for timed automata. Ph.D. thesis, Technische Universität Hamburg (2015)
2. Dasarathy, B.: Timing constraints of real-time systems: constructs for expressing them, methods of validating them. IEEE Trans. Softw. Eng. **SE–11**(1), 80–86 (1985)
3. Wang, F.: Timing behavior analysis for real-time systems. In: Proceedings of Tenth Annual IEEE Symposium on Logic in Computer Science, pp. 112–122 (1995)
4. Xu, J., Parnas, D.L.: On satisfying timing constraints in hard-real-time systems. IEEE Trans. Softw. Eng. **19**, 70–84 (1993)
5. Buttazzo, G.C.: Hard Real-Time Computing Systems: Predictable Scheduling Algorithms and Applications, vol. 24. Springer, Heidelberg (2011). https://doi.org/10.1007/978-1-4614-0676-1
6. Lisper, B., Nordlander, J.: A simple and flexible timing constraint logic. In: Margaria, T., Steffen, B. (eds.) ISoLA 2012. LNCS, vol. 7610, pp. 80–95. Springer, Heidelberg (2012). https://doi.org/10.1007/978-3-642-34032-1_12

7. Pelánek, R.: Reduction and abstraction techniques for model checking. Ph.D. thesis, Masarykova univerzita, Fakulta informatiky (2006)
8. Grosu, R., Smolka, S.A.: Monte Carlo model checking. In: Halbwachs, N., Zuck, L.D. (eds.) TACAS 2005. LNCS, vol. 3440, pp. 271–286. Springer, Heidelberg (2005). https://doi.org/10.1007/978-3-540-31980-1_18
9. Dershowitz, N., Hanna, Z., Katz, J.: Bounded model checking with QBF. In: Bacchus, F., Walsh, T. (eds.) SAT 2005. LNCS, vol. 3569, pp. 408–414. Springer, Heidelberg (2005). https://doi.org/10.1007/11499107_32
10. Kumar, R., Mercer, E.G.: Load balancing parallel explicit state model checking. Electron. Notes Theor. Comput. Sci. **128**(3), 19–34 (2005)
11. Ferdinand, C., Heckmann, R.: aiT: worst-case execution time prediction by static program analysis. In: Jacquart, R. (ed.) Building the Information Society. IIFIP, vol. 156, pp. 377–383. Springer, Boston (2004). https://doi.org/10.1007/978-1-4020-8157-6_29
12. Edgar, S., Burns, A.: Statistical analysis of WCET for scheduling. In: Proceedings of 22nd IEEE Real-Time Systems Symposium (RTSS 2001), pp. 215–224 (2001)
13. Kim, S., Patel, H.D., Edwards, S.A.: Using a Model Checker to Determine Worst-Case Execution Time. Computer Science Technical Report CUCS-038-09. Columbia University, New York (2009)
14. Al-Bataineh, O., Reynolds, M., French, T.: Accelerating worst case execution time analysis of timed automata models with cyclic behaviour. Formal Aspects Comput. **27**, 917–949 (2015)
15. Li, T., Tan, F., Wang, Q., Bu, L., Cao, J.N., Liu, X.: From offline toward real time: a hybrid systems model checking and cps codesign approach for medical device plug-and-play collaborations. IEEE Trans. Parallel Distrib. Syst. **25**, 642–652 (2014)
16. Filieri, A., Ghezzi, C., Tamburrelli, G.: Run-time efficient probabilistic model checking. In: Proceedings of the 33rd International Conference on Software Engineering (ICSE), pp. 341–350 (2011)
17. Hansson, H., Jonsson, B.: A logic for reasoning about time and reliability. Formal Aspects Comput. **6**, 512–535 (1994)
18. STS Institute, Website of the QMTL-VT tool implementation (2018). https://www.tuhh.de/sts/research/model-checking-abstract-interpretation/qmtl-vt.html
19. Chen, T., Diciolla, M., Kwiatkowska, M., Mereacre, A.: Quantitative verification of implantable cardiac pacemakers. In: 2012 IEEE 33rd Real-Time Systems Symposium (RTSS), pp. 263–272. IEEE (2012)
20. Antoni, S.T., et al.: Model checking for trigger loss detection during Doppler ultrasound-guided fetal cardiovascular MRI. Int. J. Comput. Assist. Radiol. Surg. **13**, 1755–1766 (2018)

Workshop on Embedded and Cyber-Physical Systems Education

Introducing IoT Subjects to an Existing Curriculum. An Ongoing Experience at the Faculty of the Technology Management - HIT

Sofia Amador Nelke and Michael Winokur[✉]

Department of Technology Management, HIT - Holon Institute of Technology,
Holon, Israel
michaelw@hit.ac.il

Abstract. Introducing IoT concepts in an existing B.Sc. degree at the Department of Technology Management in HIT has proven to be challenging. This Work in Progress paper will describe the challenges, the progress and the expected results of this initiative.

1 Introduction

Holon Institute of Technology (HIT) offers a B.Sc program in Technology Management. This program prepares students for positions as industrial engineers, information system managers and data analysts with an emphasis in the technology management aspects faced by industrial and business organizations. Therefore, the content must be updated to cover ubiquitous technologies, e.g. Internet of things, embedded systems and cybernetics [3]. In addition, the positions that students hold when completing their degree require close interaction and cooperation with electrical and software engineers as well as the ability to manage these engineers. It is important to note that the students in the program have, generally, little or no background in electrical and software engineering, thus, they must receive the appropriate qualification during the program that will allow them to speak a common language with the other engineers.

As the department progresses to offering a B.Sc degree in Industrial Engineering and Technology Management, one of the first of its kind, the updated study programs include revised as well as new courses that put a strong emphasis on the technologies mentioned above. In this framework, the B.Sc program includes a track in information systems which offers an elective course, Introduction to Internet of Things (IoT), introduce recently. Moreover during the 2017–2018 academic year an experimental track was started at the B.Sc program on Autonomous Transportation Systems which includes the Intro to IoT course as mandatory. The course is described briefly in Sect. 2. Section 3 presents the main experience in terms of challenges, achievements and future plans of this Work in Progress which we can share with academics facing similar challenges.

R. Chamberlain et al. (Eds.): CyPhy 2018/WESE 2018, LNCS 11615, pp. 193–196, 2019.
https://doi.org/10.1007/978-3-030-23703-5_10

2   Introduction to Internet of Things (IoT) at B.Sc Degree

Prerequisites to the IoT course are: Introduction to Programming, Database Analysis and Design and Computer Integrated Manufacturing.

The course is relatively practical, consisting of theoretical topics interlaced with hands-on training. The theory is taught in frontal lectures and presentations which include the following topics:

1. Introduction to IoT - definitions; statistics about sensors and IoT devices; and examples of cutting edge IoT products and applications [2,3].
2. History of IoT - from machine-to-machine (M2M) system solution to IoT solutions [3,4].
3. Key enabling technologies - radio-frequency identification (RFID), communication technologies (cellular, WiFi, Bluetooth, ZigBee and Z-wave) and wireless sensor and actuator networks [1].
4. Service-oriented architecture (SOA) - a four-layer model (sensing, network, service and interface) used for the design of IoT systems [8].
5. Key applications in industry - health care services, food supply chain, safer mining, transportation and logistics, firefighting, etc. [8].
6. Sensors and actuators - introduction to different types of sensors, cameras and actuators; and explanation of how they designed and how they work.

For practical experience, during the course students produce project plans and product development based on the IoT architecture, using sensors, modules, cloud computing and software services to store and manage messages. The project is implemented on Raspberry Pi computers by coding in Python.

Topics covered during practical exercises include:

1. Open source operation systems - installation of the Linux operating system for Raspberry Pi (Raspbian) [6].
2. Cloud services - using Amazon Web Services for data storage (S3), sending notification (SNS) and sending emails (SES).
3. Consumption of information from public APIs using HTTP.
4. Camera - connecting a camera to the Raspberry Pi and recording photos and videos using python.
5. Sensors - explanation of the different pins of GPIO, connecting various types of sensors to Raspberry Pi and performing measurements using python.
6. Database - installation of a local database (SQLite) and using a cloud database (Amazon Relational Database Service).

The IoT course has already been taught twice and taken by 32 students in total, receiving positive reviews.

3   Preliminary Results

During the first two semesters of the IoT course we encountered and coped with difficulties. We dealt with some of them prior to the first semester, others prior to the second, while some issues remain to be handled. The following sections describe challenges, achievements and future plans.

3.1   Challenges

The following list presents the challenges and how they were addressed.

- **Lack of technological background** - As mentioned in Sect. 1 most students do not have knowledge and experience in electrical or mechanical engineering. It is the first time they work with and assemble hardware.
- **Programming language** - During the B.Sc program students learn Introduction to Programming in C# and Objected Oriented Programming in Java. The first instance of the course was taught in Java. The students found it difficult and complicated to program in a more verbose and strict language and spent most of the working time on the figuring out the correct syntax.
- **Not enough practical exercises** - One of the major criticisms that we received from students was that the course did not have enough practical exercises. One of the reasons for this was a shortage in sensors, motors and other electromechanical components.

3.2   Achievements

- **Working with Raspberry Pi** - In order to make the hardware more accessible to the students we used Raspberry Pis, a friendly single board computer that students can easily turn into IoT products [7]. Raspbian, a Linux distribution with a friendly user interface, can be installed on it. In addition, the Raspberry Pi web site provides detailed information and instructions for working with the micro computer.
- **Changing programming language** - In the second semester of the course we changed the programming language to Python. It is a dynamically typed language that's more programmer friendly and more suitable for students without a background in software engineering [5]. The results were outstanding, on the one hand students had to learn a new language, but on the other hand using Python made programming easier. Students were able to focus on the design of the application and not on programing issues.
- **The new equipment** - We ordered more hardware for the course in order to enrich the practical exercises. The new equipment consists of: large selection of sensors, motors, lights, buttons, etc. The new components will be delivered before the third semester of the course and will allow more diverse projects and more practical content.

3.3   Future Plans

- **IoT laboratory** - One of the main technological goals of the department is to establish an advanced IoT laboratory. It will contain the existing and newly ordered equipment. Moreover, we have plans to equip the lab in advanced components for building robots that will cooperate with IoT applications. This laboratory will catalyze advanced projects for educational and research purposes.

- **Updating curriculum** - As a part of upgrading the program to be most relevant, the course "Introduction to programming" will be modified to teach students Python; and a new course, "Advanced topics in programming", will be added to the program. These changes will provide students a better starting point for the course.
- **IoT laboratory for other courses** - the most long term vision for the laboratory to serve other courses as well. Students will use the equipment for small projects in the "Introduction to programming" course and for exercises in the "Advanced topics in programming" course. In addition, students will work in the lab on their degree's final project.

References

1. Atzori, L., Iera, A., Morabito, G.: The Internet of Things: a survey. Comput. Netw. **54**(15), 2787–2805 (2010)
2. Giusto, D., Iera, A., Morabito, G., Atzori, L.: The Internet of Things: 20th Tyrrhenian Workshop on Digital Communications. Springer, New York (2010). https://doi.org/10.1007/978-1-4419-1674-7
3. Gubbi, J., Buyya, R., Marusic, S., Palaniswami, M.: Internet of Things (IoT): a vision, architectural elements, and future directions. Future Gener. Comput. Syst. **29**(7), 1645–1660 (2013)
4. Holler, J., Tsiatsis, V., Mulligan, C., Karnouskos, S., Boyle, D.: From Machine-to-Machine to the Internet of Things: Introduction to a New Age of Intelligence. Academic Press, Cambridge (2014)
5. Monk, S.: Programming the Raspberry Pi: Getting Started with Python. Mcgraw-Hill, New York (2013)
6. Richardson, M., Wallace, S.: Getting Started with Raspberry Pi. O'Reilly Media Inc., Sebastopol (2012)
7. Upton, E., Halfacree, G.: Raspberry Pi User Guide. Wiley, Hoboken (2014)
8. Xu, L.D., He, W., Li, S.: Internet of Things in industries: a survey. IEEE Trans. Ind. Inf. **10**(4), 2233–2243 (2014)

Computers Interacting with the Physical World: A First-Year Course

Roger D. Chamberlain$^{(\boxtimes)}$, Ron K. Cytron, Doug Shook, and Bill Siever

Deparment of Computer Science and Engineering,
Washington University in St. Louis, St. Louis, MO, USA
{roger,cytron,dshook,bsiever}@wustl.edu

Abstract. Most introductory embedded systems offerings are upper-division courses. At Washington Univ. in St. Louis, embedded systems principles are introduced in a first-year course that is required for both computer scientists and computer engineers. This paper describes the motivation for the course, its content, the pedagogical techniques used, and lessons learned while developing and administering the course.

Keywords: First-year course · Cyber-physical systems

1 Introduction

In the spring of 2015, the Dept. of Computer Science and Engineering at Washington Univ. in St. Louis decided to alter its first-year course sequence for computer science and computer engineering majors. While the first course follows the CS1 curriculum from the ACM/IEEE [6], our second semester course had a focus on thread-based parallelism. The faculty decided that material should be moved to a later year and that a new course should focus on how computers interact with the physical world. The new course was offered concurrently with the previous course in the fall of 2015 and has been offered every semester since. It is required for all computer science and computer engineering majors, and is a technical elective to computer science minors and electrical engineering majors.

This paper describes that course: what we teach, how we teach it, and what we have learned in the process. The course content was motivated by the core concepts that are foundational to both computer science and computer engineering while simultaneously being critical to interactions with the physical world. This includes information representation (e.g., digital inputs and outputs represented at the bit level, analog input and output values as non-negative binary integers), timing (*when* something happens as a functional property), automata models (finite-state machines), etc.

The authors would like to acknowledge the generous support of the Larsen family, which has been instrumental in the development of this course.

© Springer Nature Switzerland AG 2019
R. Chamberlain et al. (Eds.): CyPhy 2018/WESE 2018, LNCS 11615, pp. 197–205, 2019.
https://doi.org/10.1007/978-3-030-23703-5_11

The course is lecture-free, but meets twice a week in the instructional laboratories. One meeting is devoted to studio, where students perform guided exercises through the material we expect them to master. The other session provides opportunities for assistance on assignments and is used for assessment purposes.

The students work on an Arduino Uno, which has an 8-bit microcontroller programmed in C/C++, and a traditional computer programmed in Java. There are two significant advantages to using the Arduino platform. First, it has a supportive maker/hobbyist community, which can motivate students. Second, its simplicity is conducive to learning computer architecture and machine/assembly language. While there are a plethora of texts available within the Arduino ecosystem, they primarily target the hobbyist community. Since our course is intended to focus on core concepts, we have authored a text [2] for use with the course, which has the obvious advantage of being well matched to the course goals.

The resulting course is suited to the common needs of both computer science and computer engineering students. In addition, we believe it is well positioned as an important course for any student who wishes to be well educated in cyber-physical systems, independent of major. The subject matter is central to the National Academies' report on cyber-physical systems (CPS) education [9]. Unlike many introductory embedded systems courses, which are upper-division offerings, this is intentionally designed to be a first-year course, accessible after only one semester of introductory computer science.

2   Intellectual Topics

The course provides both exposure to and mastery of a variety of concepts in embedded systems and CPS. Below we list the topics covered. An asterisk (*) indicates topics in which students are expected to gain significant mastery while non-marked items indicate concepts with lesser depth.

2.1   Information Representation

- Binary, hexadecimal, unsigned, and 2's complement representations*
- Non-integer numbers: fixed point and IEEE-754 floating point
- Character representations: ASCII* and Unicode
- Character strings, both as objects and as null-terminated C-style strings
- Bitwise operations*
- Real-world values as voltages and conversion (e.g., to a temperature)*

2.2   Automata

- Moore style finite-state machines*

2.3   Timing and Events

- Using delays in execution (or sleep) to control time-based behavior*
- Delta timing techniques for either a fixed period or fixed rate*
- Using time-division multiplexing of a shared signal line
- The basic structure of an event loop for event-driven programming*

2.4   Circuits Principles, Physical I/O, and User I/O

- Physical buttons and the concept of "bounce" on real digital inputs*
- Analog voltages and digitization of voltages (ADC)
- Pulse Width Modulation
- Ohm's Law and current constraints/current limiting*
- Challenges of noisy data (e.g., step detection in accelerometer data)*
- Pixel displays*

2.5   Communications

- Serial data exchanges*
- Non-blocking communication*
- Byte-ordering concerns when exchanging multi-byte entities*
- Basic protocols and the exchange of tagged records*

2.6   Architecture/Assembly Language

- Assembly language for integer arithmetic*
- Registers and register conventions*
- Function call/use protocols*
- Stack use conventions*
- C-style memory segmentation (stack, heap, and text segments)

3   Instructional Delivery

3.1   Active Learning

For the last decade, the department has had a strong commitment to active learning [11]. Evidence for the benefits of active learning is extensive [10], and while active learning is applied broadly, it is particularly compelling in science, math, and engineering design [3], including computer science [1], computer engineering [12], and cyber-physical systems [8].

While active learning is often associated with a *flipped* classroom, the active learning approach we use across the entire first year is *studio*-based [5]. Our studio sessions evolved from observation of our colleagues in Art and Architecture as they work with their students.

Collaboration is important for the following reasons. Studies [7] have shown that women are attracted in greater numbers to the study of computer science when they appreciate the extent to which it is practiced collaboratively. Because the field is largely collaborative, featuring collaboration in our early courses provides a more accurate impression of professional practice to all of our students.

Continual feedback during studio sessions is important to keep groups on track and to reinforce that the material is important to their studies. For our courses, the feedback and guidance is provided by teaching assistants (TA) and by faculty who roam between the groups. The TAs are close in age to the students in the course. Studies have shown that novices are more likely to predict the difficulty of a task for other novices than are experts [4]. Moreover, the TA is more likely to empathize with the difficulty of a task than is an expert.

Finally, the types of problems we pose in studio session are purposefully amenable to multiple solutions and approaches. Examples from the first semester course include designing a flag and anthem for a fictitious country and determining how to draw a Sierpinski triangle. Examples from this course include peak detection (counting steps in accelerometer data) and finite-state machine design for parsing incoming messages from another processor. Students know there is more than one way to solve any of these problems, which liberates them from finding the *right* way and empowers them to find their *own* way.

3.2   Student Assessment

The assessment of students includes studio participation, on-line quizzes, assignments, and three exams. For an individual module on a typical week, students are expected to watch the videos and do any required reading prior to the studio session. A pre-studio quiz (completed on-line) is used to incentivize this requirement. These quiz questions are designed to be straightforward to answer if they have done what was asked of them (e.g., repetition of facts, very simple analysis). Studio is not graded based on correct answers, but rather participation.

The assignment for each module is started on the following laboratory session (on Wednesday following a Monday studio) and is due during the laboratory session one week later. Students are provided with a rubric with the assignment instructions, so they know how their work will be graded. These rubrics often evaluate not just the functionality of a submission (does it work?) but also the approach that students use (did they choose an appropriate implementation?).

The second quiz is due Wednesday evening, the same day that the assignment is due. It is also on-line, and for this quiz the questions are similar in content, scope, and style as those that they are likely to experience on the exams.

4   Modules

The class starts a new module each non-exam week, completing it the following week. There are minor schedule adjustments around the exam, but students generally have one calendar week to complete each module's assignment. Also, the first laboratory meeting (labeled studio 0) is used to familiarize the students with various logistics, such as the development environment (both Eclipse and Arduino IDEs), the code repository, etc. The modules are described below.

Information Representation (Module A) – How information is represented in digital systems, including binary and hexadecimal conversions, integer number representations (including 2's complement), as well as ASCII and UTF text. Introduction to the finite-state machine abstraction, and how to implement a finite-state machine in software.

Table 1. Relationship between intellectual topics and modules.

Topic ⇩ Module ⇒	A	B	C	D,E	F	G	H,I,J
Information Representation (§2.1)	■	■	■	■		■	■
Automata (§2.2)	■	■		■		■	
Timing (§2.3)			■	■	■	■	
Circuits & I/O (§2.4)			■	■	■	■	■
Communications (§2.5)					■	■	
Architecture/Assembly Lang. (§2.6)							■

Microcontroller Platform (Module B) – How to physically implement electrical circuits, a brief introduction to electricity (a physics course is not a prerequisite) and voltage, digital inputs and outputs, and finite-state machine design.

Real-Time Computing (Module C) – Techniques for including time as a functional element in software. Starting with delay-based timing, students progress to delta timing (checking each loop to determine if the desired time has elapsed). This is combined with analog inputs (including the conversion of raw A/D input values into engineering units) and simple filtering (averaging).

Communications (Modules D, E) (2 weeks) – This pair of modules investigates the issues inherent in using a byte stream to communicate between two dissimilar computer systems (the Arduino using C and the desktop PC using Java). Students explore how to serialize multi-byte data types, design protocols that enable synchronization in the face of dropped bytes, and design finite-state machine recognizers to parse incoming messages.

Multiplexing (Module F) – Introduction to the concept of time-division multiplexing, asking the students to interface to and author the software to drive a 5 by 7 pixel LED display. Real-time computing concepts are reinforced, and students are introduced to the fundamental mechanisms involved in larger, more sophisticated, pixed-based displays (e.g., font design, time multiplexing).

Integrative Project (Module G) – Design and implementation of an integrative project that seeks to reinforce concepts that have been introduced earlier in the semester. A second analog sensor is made available (an accelerometer) for the project. Different projects have been used in different semesters, including the development of a pedometer and a predator-prey game (using the accelerometer to sense the tilt of the microcontroller).

Assembly Language (Modules H, I, J) (3 weeks) – This three week set of modules has an introduction to basic computer architecture and machine language, and then focuses on assembly language, using the simple, 8-bit instruction set. Week 1 covers data representation (especially multi-byte data) and data manipulation (e.g., understanding the need for a carry bit). Week 2 introduces techniques for implementing if-then-else logic and looping structures. Week 3 covers pointers and array access.

The relationship between intellectual topics and individual modules is shown in Table 1. The columns in the table represent modules, and the rows represent

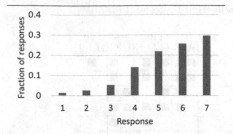

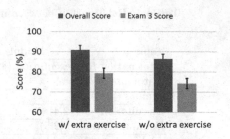

Fig. 1. Student ratings of statement, "The material was covered at a reasonable pace" (scoring: 1 - Strongly Disagree, 7 - Strongly Agree).

Fig. 2. Relationship between overall scores and exam 3 scores with and without the extra exercise. Bars indicate mean and whiskers std. err.

topics. There is some overlap between topic names and module labels; however, that typically implies that the specific topic is central to the module of the same name, not that it is the only topic present in the module.

In addition to the modules described above, there are a few modules that have been developed and used in previous semesters, but are not in current use.

Interrupts – Students explore how interrupts literally interrupt currently executing code. In addition, students see how interrupts improve responsiveness to events, like button presses (which can further exacerbate bouncing).

IP Networking – This module introduces students to topics in networking. IP protocols, including both TCP/IP and UDP/IP are covered, as well as domain name service and socket-based communications.

5   Lessons Learned [1]

5.1   Pacing of Material

As recently as the spring semester of 2017, the pacing of material was uneven and somewhat too fast. The following are quotes from end-of-semester student evaluations.

- "The pace was inconsistent."
- "It moved a little too fast in parts and wasn't always as in-depth as I would've liked."
- "We moved pretty quickly through material and I never felt like I had time to fully grasp concepts because the assignments took so much time."

In reaction to these comments, we've evolved the course into the organization that is described in Sect. 4. For example, the networking module was (at least temporarily) retired and the assembly language material was converted from a 2 week series into a 3 week series, without expanding the content.

---

[1] This Work Conducted Under Washington Univ. in St. Louis IRB ID #201807038.

The results of the pace ratings for spring 2018 are shown in Fig. 1 (using a 7-item Likert scale). The mean score of 5.47 (std. dev. of 1.41) is very close to the department's average of 5.66, and a substantial improvement from the mean score of 4.51 for the course in spring of 2017.

5.2 Analysis Problems

Based on commentary in the literature that posits the benefits of analysis problems in the context of design courses [13], we were concerned that the present course doesn't have sufficient analysis content (i.e., the bulk of studio questions and assignment questions are design questions rather than analysis questions).

To test this theory, we generated an additional set of analysis problems, designed to be helpful in preparing students for the third exam, and made them available to students one week prior to the exam. To provide an incentive for the students to attempt them, students were told that there would be a small amount of extra credit for those that did well.

We then compared scores for the two groups of students, those who did attempt the extra credit exercise and those who did not. The results of this comparison are shown in Fig. 2. There clearly is a correlation between overall course grade and whether or not a student attempted the extra exercise. Those who attempted the extra exercise scored over 4% higher overall (the scores presented exclude the extra credit provided from the exercise). This is statistically significant ($p = 0.02$, non-paired data). When we examine the scores on exam 3, however, the story is different. While the mean score differential is similar (at 5% in this case), the variability in scores is wide enough that this result is not statistically significant ($p = 0.11$, non-paired data), so we cannot rule out the null hypothesis that the difference in the means is due to chance.

Our current opinion is that the correlation seen in the overall scores is likely due to the fact that better students (more likely to achieve a higher score prior to the availability of an optional exercise) are also more likely than their peers to take advantage of an optional exercise, especially when it provides extra credit. Going forward, we are still interested in whether or not additional analysis problems can help students learn the material better, and will likely pursue it by altering the mix of analysis vs. design problems within the studio exercises.

5.3 Logistics

The removal of a live lecture session in favor of on-line videos has been a challenge for some students. Since videos are static content, there is an extra layer of effort that students must take if they do not understand the presented concepts or need additional explanation. Interactions with professors are also fewer and farther between as students are spread out across multiple computer labs instead of meeting as a single, large group.

In the fall of 2017, we introduced a recitation section to address these issues. The recitation sections would occur after the weekly studio, but before the weekly assignment was due, so students could ask questions about topics they had seen in the on-line videos and studio. The effect of these recitation sessions was somewhat mixed, as shown by comments on student evaluations:

- "I only attended a handful of the recitation, specifically when I was confused on a topic, and every time I came my questions were answered and it was very helpful."
- "Kind of a waste of time."

A common complaint is that recitation sessions were short and unstructured. While they were intended to be loosely structured and student-driven by design, a more structured approach with pre-prepared review questions and practice problems may prove to be more beneficial for students.

6 Conclusions

We have described a first-year course that provides foundational material common to both computer science and computer engineering majors. We believe it is helping students discover an interest in computer engineering despite limited prior exposure to the field. Moreover, we believe it provides an introduction to the pervasiveness and breadth of computing early in the curriculum.

References

1. Ahmad, K., Gestwicki, P.: Studio-based learning and App Inventor for Android in an introductory CS course for non-majors. In: Proceeding of 44th ACM Technical Symposium on Computer Science Education, pp. 287–292 (2013)
2. Chamberlain, R.D., Cytron, R.K.: Computing in the Physical World. Pre-release edn. (2017). http://www.ccrc.wustl.edu/~roger/cse132/cc_v0_06.pdf
3. Freeman, S., Eddy, S.L., McDonough, M., Smith, M.K., Okoroafor, N., Jordt, H., Wenderoth, M.P.: Active learning increases student performance in science, engineering, and mathematics. Proc. Nat. Acad. Sci. 111(23), 8410–8415 (2014)
4. Hinds, P.J.: The curse of expertise: the effects of expertise and debiasing methods on predictions of novice performance. J. Exp. Psychol. Appl. 5(2), 205–221 (1999)
5. Hundhausen, C.D., Narayanan, N.H., Crosby, M.E.: Exploring studio-based instructional models for computing education. In: Proceeding of 39th ACM Technical Symposium on Computer Science Education, pp. 392–396 (2008)
6. Joint Task Force on Computing Curricula, Association for Computing Machinery (ACM) and IEEE Computer Society: Computer Science Curricula: Curriculum Guidelines for Undergraduate Degree Programs in Computer Science. ACM, New York (2013)
7. Krause, J., Polycarpou, I., Hellman, K.: Exploring formal learning groups and their impact on recruitment of women in undergraduate CS. In: Proceeding of 43rd ACM Symposium on Computer Science Education, pp. 179–184 (2012)
8. Marwedel, P., Engel, M.: Flipped classroom teaching for a cyber-physical system course - an adequate presence-based learning approach in the internet age. In: Proceeding of 10th European Workshop on Microelectronics Education (EWME), pp. 11–15, May 2014

9. National Academies of Sciences, Engineering, and Medicine: A 21st Century Cyber-Physical Systems Education. The National Academies Press, Washington, DC (2016)
10. Prince, M.: Does active learning work? A review of the research. J. Eng. Edu. **93**(3), 223–231 (2004)
11. Sowell, R., Chen, Y., Buhler, J., Goldman, S.A., Grimm, C., Goldman, K.J.: Experiences with active learning in CS3. J Comput. Sci. Coll. **25**(5), 173–179 (2010)
12. Striegel, A., Rover, D.T.: Problem-based learning in an introductory computer engineering course. In: Proceeding of 32nd IEEE Frontiers in Education Conference, vol. 2, pp. F1G-7–F1G-12 (2002)
13. Wood, K.L., Jensen, D., Bezdek, J., Otto, K.N.: Reverse engineering and redesign: courses to incrementally and systematically teach design. J. Eng. Educ. **90**(3), 363–374 (2001)

CPS/IoT Ecosystem: A Platform
for Research and Education

Haris Isakovic[1(✉)], Denise Ratasich[1], Christian Hirsch[1], Michael Platzer[1],
Bernhard Wally[1], Thomas Rausch[1], Dejan Nickovic[2], Willibald Krenn[2],
Gerti Kappel[1], Schahram Dustdar[1], and Radu Grosu[1]

[1] Technische Universität Wien, Vienna, Austria
{haris.isakovic,denise.ratasich,christian.hirsch,michael.platzer,
bernhard.wally,thomas.rausch,gerti.kappel,schahram.dustdar,
radu.grosu}@tuwien.ac.at
[2] Austrian Institute of Technology, Seibersdorf, Austria
{dejan.nickovic,willibald.krenn}@ait.ac.at

Abstract. The CPS/IoT Ecosystem project aims to build an IoT infrastructure that will be used as a platform for research and education in multiple disciplines related to CPS and IoT. The main objective is to provide a real-world infrastructure, and allow students and researchers explore its capabilities on actual use cases.

Keywords: Internet-of-Things · Infrastructure ·
Cyber-Physical System

1 Introduction

We are experiencing a major paradigm shift in terms of computing systems. The ability to collect big data, use it to model physical environments with astonishing precision and use it to improve existing systems is a principal factor behind the upcoming revolution. We are using Cyber-Physical Systems (CPS) to observe and manipulate our physical environment, and the Internet-of-Things (IoT) to transfer and transform this raw data into profitable information. CPS/IoT Ecosystem is a project that materializes this idea. It embodies an infrastructure for IoT integrated together with a set of use cases that represent CPS. It is a joint project of three research institutions Technische Universität Wien (TU Wien), Austrian Institute of Technology (AIT), and Institute for Science and Technology (IST). It serves as a research platform for a variety of related disciplines and as an educational tool for bringing concepts of IoT and CPS closer to the students in a "hands-on" type of an approach.

The preliminary forecasts state that IoT it will continue to grow rapidly in the next ten years. Multiple studies predict a number of new IoT devices to reach 75–100 billion until 2025 [20]. The global network of IoT devices will include both public and private IoT domains, with the ability to share and monetize not only results but also the usage of the infrastructure itself [8,15]. We will highlight just few important challenges:

© Springer Nature Switzerland AG 2019
R. Chamberlain et al. (Eds.): CyPhy 2018/WESE 2018, LNCS 11615, pp. 206–213, 2019.
https://doi.org/10.1007/978-3-030-23703-5_12

- **Development.** Each scope of operation ion CPS and IoT (e.g., cloud, fog/edge, sensor, network) is traditionally observed as a separate discipline. The development methods and tools for each scope have been created accordingly and they are not necessarily mutually compatible. To build an IoT application the tools for development, testing, and deployment need to be fully inter-operable.
- **Management.** The holistic idea of IoT is to have billions of heterogeneous devices serving millions of different applications connected to Internet. Running these systems requires configuration, deployment, software updates and maintenance etc. Managing these tasks on a system this magnitude is a major challenge and requires enormous amount of effort.
- **Security.** In the world where "every single thing" is connected to the Internet, security represents crucial requirement. Standardized approach to security and related topics, i.e., privacy and trust must be is a major challenge in IoT. Example from data breaches and recent changes in EU regulation regarding handling private data [26] highlights just how important is security in IoT. In the future data will influence policies and indirectly lives of people. Making sure that the data is valid and secure is extremely important.
- **Power Consumption.** Over 75 billion new devices in just under ten years will create a massive overhead on the existing power infrastructure. The current production of electrical energy in the European Union on a yearly basis is around 3000 TWh [6]. An average IoT device like the Raspberry Pi 3 consumes up to 5 Wh of electrical energy. If we pessimistically project it onto new IoT devices we get 3240 TWh on a yearly basis just for these devices.

The project will focus on implementing hardware structure of devices with custom build cloud system, fog/edge nodes, and COTS and custom built sensor and actuator devices that will form an infrastructure. It explores development frameworks, tools and mechanisms that will ensure standardized design and help establish functional system between hardware, software, and applications. A major aspect of the project is its educational value in terms of bringing state-of-the-art technology directly into curriculum. A new IoT infrastructure providing means for realistic implementations and applications, it enables students to experience complexity, real-time, security and dependability issues on real-world examples. Beside using the infrastructure in courses, the infrastructure will become central topic for numerous bachelor and master theses.

In this chapter we introduced the motivation behind the project and its core concepts. In Sect. 2 we provide short overview of the related projects. Section 3 describes methodology for the project execution and its most essential components. Two use cases implemented in the project are described in Sect. 4. The final chapter concludes the paper and provides future directions for the project.

2   Related Work

IoT represents a super set of multiple disciplines i.e., machine learning, artificial intelligence, real-time systems, embedded systems, high performance computing, web and mobile technologies, networking, enterprise organization, civil engineering and a number of others. Vermessan et al. define IoT as *"a concept and a paradigm that considers pervasive presence in the environment of a variety of things/objects that through wireless and wired connections and unique addressing schemes are able to interact with each other and cooperate with other things/objects to create new applications/services and reach common goals"* [28]. In this section we will give a short overview of the relevant research topics with respect to the CPS/IoT Ecosystem project and related research projects within the scope of EU research community.

The heterogeneity of IoT is one of its most prominent features however on the development and run-time level it is often primary source of **interoperability** issues. This is why the interoperability is one of the most researched topics in IoT. A significant number of projects in are working to enable or increase interoperability between existing and new IoT platforms and devices [5,14,18].

Second major topic in the scope of IoT research and development is **security**. It is arguably the most difficult challenge in IoT. It is a rather complex topic, as it branches in a numerous subtopics, each pf which is highly complex and demanding on its own. Thus a large variety of projects and research initiatives on the variations of security and security related topics (e.g., encryption, trust, privacy, block chain, user, data and ip protection) [4,13,19,23].

The IoT represents a large heterogeneous system with a enormous variety of applications. Providing generic rules and guidelines allows us to create systems with standardized system properties. However, systems also need to be tailored to each individual application and its requirements. According to Gabriel in [12] *"a system that can be customized, specialized, or extended to provide more specific, more appropriate, or slightly different capabilities"* is called **framework**. A framework allows us to use it for different purposes without having a need to write the code each time from the beginning. Multiple research initiatives are exploring different frameworks for IoT, with different specialization abilities (e.g., security, safety, service-oriented design, social aspect, education and others) [7,10,19,22,23,25].

Providing generic rules and guidelines allows us to create systems with standardized system properties. However, systems need to be tailored to specific application requirements. According to Gabriel in [12] *"a system that can be customized, specialized, or extended to provide more specific, more appropriate, or slightly different capabilities"* is called **framework**. It allows us to use it for different purposes without having a need to write the code each time from the beginning. Building such systems is one of the most explored questions in IoT. Multiple research initiatives are exploring different IoT frameworks with different specialization abilities (e.g., security, safety, service-oriented design, social aspect, education and others) [7,10,19,22,23,25].

The applications are strongest driver behind IoT revolution. IoT applications are normally spearheaded by commercial subjects and the number of different ways IoT is improving existing systems changes every day. The research aspects with respect to IoT applications focuses on model and framework design, big data, social and economical implications, security and privacy issues, and cooperation with other fields of science (e.g., biology, medicine, mechanical engineering, geo-engineering, etc.) [1,2,9,18].

3 CPS/IoT Ecosystem Methodology

CPS/IoT Ecosystem is conceived as a heterogeneous structure of hardware devices, and corresponding software components distributed over tree intertwined scopes of operation: cloud, fog/edge, and sensor/actuator nodes. The cloud provides high performance computation and large capacity storage. The fog, also referred as edge, level indicates a network of devices with real-time communication capabilities, and mid-range computational and storage capabilities. The sensor/actuator level serves as a direct interface with physical environment. They posses capabilities of collecting and transforming physical signals using sensors and manipulating the environment via diverse actuators. The CPS/IoT Ecosystem infrastructure is a geographically distributed system. Parts of the infrastructure will be located on multiple sites on a wider area of Vienna, Austria.

CPS/IoT Ecosystem Cloud. The cloud system is a general purpose high-performance computing platform located at a server center of TU Wien. It provides services that facilitate handling of big data (e.g., storage, analysis, aggregation). It is an essential part of the infrastructure. In CPS/IoT Ecosystem we are implementing a custom built cloud server. Its purpose is to serve the applications, but also to be used as a research subject. It will be deployed in two parts: (a) a general purpose computing platform, and (b) specialized computing platform for calculation intensive tasks.

CPS/IoT Ecosystem Fog/Edge. Ability to react fast and ensure quality of service (QoS) on a factory floor level or similar plane of execution is implemented in the fog/edge level. It represents a network of computing nodes which are both capable of handling certain significant of data and still ensure service dependability. The fog/edge devices can be in direct connection to the sensor/actuator nodes or as an intermediate gateways for the ultra low energy/performance devices.

CPS/IoT Ecosystem Sensor Device. The sensor/actuator nodes are direct interfaces with a physical environment. These devices are limited in computational performance, size and power consumption. They can be deployed individually or in swarms as explained in Sect. 4.

CPS/IoT Ecosystem Information Model. As mentioned above management, development, and security are three major challenges in IoT. Part of the solution for these challenges is a functional IoT information model for the CPS/IoT infrastructure. It will allows us to describe the system from multiple perspectives: hardware platform, services, application, management and communication. The acquired models can be used as templates for application design, code generation, development and operations (DevOps), testing and validation.

COTS vs. Custom Built Hardware. CPS/IoT Ecosystems generally comprises a substantial amount of sensor nodes. Buying a lot of sensor hardware can quickly consume an important amount of a project's budget, since commercially available ready to use hardware is usually expensive. Therefore designing and building custom hardware can be an attractive alternative. Designing custom hardware also has the advantage of increased flexibility, since one is not limited by the choice of existing components. The hardware design can be tailored to specific requirements as described in Sect. 4.

Technology in CPS/IoT Ecosystem. The objective of the CPS/IoT Ecosystem project is to build a technology agnostic IoT infrastructure. Often the IoT is connected to a single framework, communication protocol or cloud environment. This project will provide general purpose cloud environment based on OpenStack [24]. It uses variety of open source and research community frameworks to build middle-ware and application software [10,11,17,27]. In CPS/IoT Ecosystem we are not limited to a single communication protocol, typical IoT communication standards described in [3,16,21] will provide a basis for networking and communication standards.

4   Use Cases

4.1   Smart Parking

Smart Parking application provides status information of public or private parking places in a city or garage. Each parking spot is equipped with a sensor or group of sensors capable of detecting objects (cars or similar) on a surface of the parking spot. Data of each sensor is then transmitted to a central application software located on a remote server via Internet connection. The information is further delivered to end user over Web or mobile application. The Smart Parking application is build on the principle of CPS/IoT Ecosystem. The cloud environment serves as mass storage device and a service provider to external users. It collects all parking information from the fog all fog nodes and provides them to external applications (e.g., web site). The edge/fog nodes serve as sensor data aggregation and filtering nodes. The data collected from the sensors is transformed in the application useful information. The parking spot is a virtual concept and can be formed on arbitrary surface with a single or multiple heterogeneous sensors. Figure 1 provides an architectural overview of the Smart Parking application. The middleware backbone of the Smart Parking application is a service-oriented Arrowhead IoT Framework [10]. The Smart Parking application services are distributed over local clouds both on cloud and edge/fog level of operation. Senor nodes are connected via Bluetooth Low Energy (BLE) protocol. Future work on this use case considers adding multiple additional services (e.g., payment, allocation and reservation of spaces), also adding support for multiple sensor types and building vehicle-2-infrastructure interface for autonomous parking. Another feature is the implementation of sensor node simulator which is able to project sensors on the scale of the city and provide simulated data to the

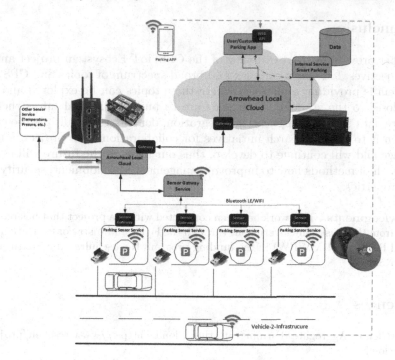

Fig. 1. Smart parking architecture overview

rest of the infrastructure. This allows us to test scaleability and manageability of the application without deploying hardware devices.

4.2 Smart Vineyards

IoT can help to overcome arising problems in the agricultural sector. For example, the increasing labor shortage do to the depopulation of rural areas. This is possible because such infrastructures help farmers to work more efficiently. Examples are disease prediction systems, that warm farmers of arising diseases in certain areas. Farmers can use this information to bring out pesticides only when it is necessary and also only where it is necessary. This reduces the workload of farmers, the costs for pesticides and the negative impact on the environment.

We are building such an infrastructure for vineyards in cooperation with the Vienna University of Natural Resources and Life Sciences (BOKU Wien) as part of the CPS/IoT Ecosystem project. The aim is to bring out several hundreds of swarm nodes that measure the environment. This information is transmitted to the cloud via fog nodes. Later, the information is processed by means of big-data analysis and machine-learning algorithms to learn correlations between diseases and environmental influences to create new and improve existing diseases prediction models.

5   Conclusion

The paper provides a short overview of the CPS/IoT Ecosystem project and its main objectives. IoT has a complex and broad spectrum of topics and CPS/IoT Ecosystem is providing a platform where these topics can be explored and also bring closer to the students. Our goals are to build a physical infrastructure, to ensure data flow and application integration, demonstrate multiple use cases, and open it to other research initiatives for collaboration. The project is in its first stage and will continue to develop, thus our focus in the future will change on research of methods how to improve management, development, security and other properties.

Acknowledgments. This work has been conducted within a project that has received funding from the Austrian Government through the Federal Ministry of Education, Science and Research (BMWFW) in the funding program Hochschulraum-Strukturmittel 2016 (HRSM).

References

1. AfarCloud: Aggregate Farming in the Cloud. https://www.ecsel.eu/projects/afarcloud
2. AGILE: Aircraft 3rd generation MDO for innovative collaboration of hetergeneous teams of experts. https://www.agile-project.eu
3. Al-Sarawi, S., Anbar, M., Alieyan, K., Alzubaidi, M.: Internet of Things (IoT) communication protocols: review. In: 2017 8th International Conference on Information Technology (ICIT), pp. 685–690, May 2017. https://doi.org/10.1109/ICITECH.2017.8079928
4. ARMOUR: Large scale experiment of IoT security and trust. https://www.armour-project.eu/
5. BIGIoT: Bridging the Interoperability Gap of the Internet of Things. http://big-iot.eu
6. BP: BP statistical review of world energy, June 2017. https://www.bp.com/content/dam/bp/en/corporate/pdf/energy-economics/statistical-review-2017/bp-statistical-review-of-world-energy-2017-full-report.pdf
7. Brain-IoT: A model-based framework for dependable sensing and actuation in intelligent decentralized IoT systems. http://www.brain-iot.eu
8. Chen, S., Xu, H., Liu, D., Hu, B., Wang, H.: A vision of IoT: applications, challenges, and opportunities with China perspective. IEEE Internet Things J. $1(4)$, 349–359 (2014). https://doi.org/10.1109/JIOT.2014.2337336
9. ClouT: Cloud of things for empowering the citizen clout in smart cities. http://clout-project.eu/
10. Delsing, J.: IoT Automation: Arrowhead Framework. CRC Press, Boca Raton (2017). https://books.google.at/books?id=6mMlDgAAQBAJ
11. FU Berlin: RIOT - The Friendly Operating System for the Internet of Things. http://riot-os.org. Accessed 18 July 2018
12. Gabriel, R.P.: Patterns of Software: Tales from the Software Community. Oxford University Press Inc., New York (1996)

13. GhostIoT: Safe-Guarding Home IoT Environments with Personalised Real-Time Risk Control. https://www.ghost-iot.eu
14. InterIoT: Interoperability of heterogeneus IoT platforms. https://vicinity2020.eu
15. Kyriazis, D., Varvarigou, T., White, D., Rossi, A., Cooper, J.: Sustainable smart city iot applications: heat and electricity management & eco-conscious cruise control for public transportation. In: 2013 IEEE 14th International Symposium on "A World of Wireless, Mobile and Multimedia Networks" (WoWMoM), pp. 1–5, June 2013. https://doi.org/10.1109/WoWMoM.2013.6583500
16. Ngu, A.H., Gutierrez, M., Metsis, V., Nepal, S., Sheng, Q.Z.: IoT middleware: a survey on issues and enabling technologies. IEEE Internet Things J. 4(1), 1–20 (2017). https://doi.org/10.1109/JIOT.2016.2615180
17. Open Source Robotic Foundation Inc.: Robot Operating System (ROS). http://www.ros.org/. Accessed 06 July 2018
18. Productive4.0: Electronics and ICT as enabler for digital industry and optimized supply chain management covering the entire product lifecycle. https://productive40.eu
19. RERUM: REliable, Resilient and secUre IoT for sMart city applications. https://ict-rerum.eu/
20. Rose, K., Eldridge, S., Chapin, L.: The Internet of Things: An Overview, February 2015. https://www.internetsociety.org/wp-content/uploads/2017/08/ISOC-IoT-Overview-20151221-en.pdf
21. Schachinger, D., Kastner, W.: Semantic interface for machine-to-machine communication in building automation. In: 2017 IEEE 13th International Workshop on Factory Communication Systems (WFCS), pp. 1–9, May 2017. https://doi.org/10.1109/WFCS.2017.7991956
22. Semiotics: Secure Multi-protocol Integration Bridge for the IoT. https://www.semiotics-project.eu
23. SerIoT: Secure and Safe Internet of Thing. https://seriot-project.eu/
24. Shrivastwa, A., Sarat, S., Jackson, K., Bunch, C., Sigler, E., Campbell, T.: OpenStack: Building a Cloud Environment. Packt Publishing, Birmingham (2016)
25. SOCIOTAL: Creating a socially aware citizen-centric Internet of Things. http://sociotal.eu/
26. The European Parliament: Regulation (EU) 2016/679 of the European Parliament and of the Council on the protection of natural persons with regard to the processing of personal data and on the free movement of such data, and repealing directive 95/46/EC (general data protection regulation). https://eur-lex.europa.eu/legal-content/EN/TXT/PDF/?uri=CELEX:32016R0679&from=DE
27. Thingsboard: Thinsboard IoT Platform. https://thingsboard.io/
28. Vermesan, O.: Internet of Things: Converging Technologies for Smart Environments and Integrated Ecosystems. River Publishers, Aalborg (2013)

MicroITS: A Scaled-Down ITS Platform

Judicaël Marchand[1,2], Gaël Puissochet[1,2], Thomas Lithén[2],
and Walid Taha[2(✉)]

[1] École polytechnique de l'Université de Nantes, Nantes, France
{judicael.marchand,gael.puissochet}@etu.univ-nantes.fr
[2] Halmstad University, Halmstad, Sweden
{tomas.lithen,walid.taha}@hh.se

Abstract. Intelligent Transportation Systems (ITS) are an excellent
illustration of the types of challenges that future technologists must
address. In previous work we presented a course designed to engage
students with theoretical aspects of embedded and cyber-physical systems. In this paper we present MicroITS, a platform addressing applied
aspects. We articulate the design goals that we believe are needed to
achieve engagement in an educational setting, and describe the platform
and its baseline functionality. We briefly describe example projects that
can be realized using MicroITS. Our hope is that this report will encourage the development of a community of educators and students interested
in the use and the continued development of the platform.

1 Introduction

The Intelligent Transportation Systems (ITS) sector is highly representative of
the future needs for engineering and computing workforce. The ITS sector poses
technical challenges at a variety of levels, and often requires interdisciplinary
expertise to address. Educating this future workforce requires engaging them
with both theoretical and applied aspects in embedded and cyber-physical systems. Over the last several years, a novel course on Cyber-Physical Systems was
developed at Halmstad University. This course has had as primary focus the aim
of engaging students with more theoretical aspects, including the early stages of
model-based design. In this work, we present a platform that we have developed
with the aim of addressing the more applied aspects of that course. The design
goals for the platform, called MicroITS, are as follows:

Ease of Use: We would like to allow the user (whether she is a student or
researcher) from a wide variety of backgrounds to easily become engaged with
the platform and to easily experiment with a wide variety of aspects of embedded
and cyber-physical systems. This requirement includes ease of acquisition (both
in terms of logistics and cost), configuration, programming, operation, and modification. It also includes robustness of the design. A system that requires special
expertises to operate or often fails would interfere with the learning process.

R. Chamberlain et al. (Eds.): CyPhy 2018/WESE 2018, LNCS 11615, pp. 214–221, 2019.
https://doi.org/10.1007/978-3-030-23703-5_13

Large Design Space: The unique feature of cyber-physical systems is the communicating/interacting combination of computing and physical components. The value of this combination comes from the vast space of possibility for solutions and innovations. Having a rich set of possible types of hardware, software, sensors, physical components, and communication components is important to allow the user to begin to grasp the full potential of cyber-physical systems. This includes allowing the user to explore kinematics, dynamics, embedded computing, communication, sensing (including vision), control, and cooperation.

Compatibility with Model-Based Design: A key benefit of model-based design is that it can integrate both the theoretical and applied views of a design. For the user to see this, however, there should be comprehensible models of the platform used to illustrate the method. This means that the components used should be open source or described in enough detail that they can be easily modeled.

Flexibility and Extensibility: The system should be easy to reconfigure to represent a wide variety of problems and test cases. It should also be easy to introduce additional components/agents into the system without additional programming. The performance of the system may change or degrade (w.r.t. certain user-defined metrics) but the operation of extending the system should be simple.

Support for Systematic Investigation: The system should facilitate the collection of data for offline analysis.

Collectively, these goals are expected to facilitate the use of this platform for education, starting from informal exploration and extending to systematic research.

1.1 Contributions and Organization of the Rest of This Paper

The main contributions of this paper are to articulate the design goals above and to report on a realization of a scaled-down platform aimed at addressing them. The design features a small (10 cm wide by 10 cm tall, depicted in image to the right) robot that comes with basic line-following and collision-avoidance functionality and costs around $200 in materials.

The rest of the paper is organized as follows. We begin by describing the MicroITS platform in terms of both hardware and software (Sect. 2). Next, we present a baseline example that comes with the platform and test runs that represent the baseline performance of the system (Sect. 3). Finally, we briefly describe a basic set of project suggestions that illustrate the intended use of the platform (Sect. 4).

More details about the hardware and the software can be found in a technical report that is available online [6].

1.2　Related Work

Prior work exists on scaled-down models of vehicular and other cyber-physical systems. In what follows, we discuss key differences with some concrete representative examples from different types of scaled-down platforms.

Longoria and Al-Sharif [5] provide a detailed analysis of a scaled-down model of a single vehicle, with a focus on using a scaled-down model for testing anti-locking brakes. Similarly, Verma et al. [8] develop a scaled-down model with a focus on power-train fidelity. In contrast, our work uses a scaled-down vehicle with significantly simplified mechanics. This choice reflects our focus on enabling experimentation that involves multiple aspects of design (communication, control, sensing, etc.) rather than a particular mechanical feature in the context of an otherwise largely established physical design.

He et al. [3] develop a sophisticated scaled-down physical road environment with associated vehicles, with the primary focus of evaluating macro-level traffic characteristics. The focus of this work is on the vehicles, with the goal of facilitating experimentation (by students and researcher) with the vehicles and their autonomous-driving functions.

Ozbilgin et al. [7] develop a scaled-down platform based on iRobot systems LIDAR. The components of MicroITS are significantly more modestly priced. For example, the costs of the complete MicroITS robots are closer to $200, whereas the base iRobot is closer to $400. Similarly, their platform uses a localization package that has a precision of about 1 cm, whereas the solution selected in our work has a nominal precision of 10 cm. These choices are consistent with our goal of maintaining a reasonable cost for the components.

Bhattarai et al. [1] develop a scaled-down smart-grid environment for investigating power-delivery for smart vehicles. The work is similar to our proposal in that packet behavior is considered. The concern about communications makes this framework one of the closest to ours, with the main difference being that ours involves mobile rather than static components. This provides significantly more opportunities for evaluating the performance characteristics of communication systems. At the same time, it creates a dual need for localization, namely, in dynamic control and for recording the state to enable later analysis of the collected data.

Finally, drone platforms, such as that of Krajník et al. [4] are similar in that they use vision and generally need to have redundant sensors (in their case, to sustain flight under realistic conditions). There are also drone platforms with peer-to-peer communication. The main distinguishing feature of our platform in this respect is the ease of operation, robustness, and dynamic stability. The latter implies that, within a confined environment, there is low risk of damage to the system if control fails or human supervision is discontinued. With the exception of these characteristics, quadcopters are themselves very attractive platforms for a wide range of issues that can be of benefit to the ITS domain, including vision (see for example Engle et al. [2]) and SLAM.

2 The MicroITS Platform

In this section we describe the hardware and the software of the MicroITS platform.

2.1 Hardware

The figure on the right gives an overview of the main physical components of the MicroITS system. The details for the components are as follows:

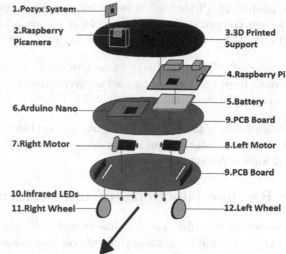

1.Pozyx System
2.Raspberry Picamera
3.3D Printed Support
4.Raspberry Pi
5.Battery
6.Arduino Nano
9.PCB Board
7.Right Motor
8.Left Motor
9.PCB Board
10.Infrared LEDs
11.Right Wheel
12.Left Wheel

Prozyx (1): The Pozyx positioning system consists of an ultrasonic receiver ("antenna") for each robot and four beacons that should be stationed around the track on which the robots will operate.

Camera (2): The PiCamera is a camera designed for the Raspberry Pi.

Raspberry Pi (4): The Raspberry Pi is running Linux and is connected to a board that has WiFi, four USB ports, an Ethernet port, and a video port. It runs the high-level functions such image processing, navigation, and logging.

Battery (5): The battery is the mobile power source for this robot.

Arduino Nano (6): The Arduino performs low-level control of the robot motor. The version of this Arduino is called Nano.

Motors (7&8): The robot has a DC motor on each side. A gearbox is also used to get more mechanical torque and to step-down the speed.

Infrared LEDs (10): There are infrared LEDs on the underside the robot to sense markers such as a track.

Wheels (11&12): A wheel connects each motor to the floor. The wheels are also instrumented with position encoders.

2.2 Software

We now turn to the software running on the two microcontrollers in MicroITS. Here we briefly describe the three main types of codes needed for the platform to operate. More details can be found in the technical report [6].

Arduino: The Arduino is programmed in C++. The code performs the low-level control tasks. When running this code, this processor receives commands from the Raspberry Pi through a serial communication connection, processes them, and then responds with, for example, a command to the motors. It also reads and gives the value of the wheel position encoders to the Raspberry Pi.

Raspberry Pi: The Raspberry Pi controls and processes most data traffic. It gets the data from the camera to see the environment to decide the command it has to send to the Arduino.

Configuration of the Network: The connection between the robots and any laptop being used to control them is peer-to-peer, so as to enable operation without the need for a separate access point.

3   Baseline Functionality and Performance

This section describes the baseline functionality implemented on the platform, and reports some basic measurements on how these baseline functions perform.

3.1   Baseline Functionality

Baseline functionality consists of positioning, manual remote control, line following, and obstacle detection.

Positioning System: We assume that the robot will operate in the context of a test area that has other robots, lanes, and obstacles.

The Pozyx system allows us to know the current position of the robot with a 10 cm accuracy. The system uses four fixed anchor modules, and one tag module for each tracked object. The pozyx system relies on a novel wireless radio technology called ultra-wideband (UWB). The tag is put on a robot and the anchors on four points around the test area. The image on the right depicts our test area. The square shape inside the test area is the track that will be used for the performance tests we report on in this paper. The red circles show the position of the four Pozyx beacons for this test. In this paper, we will report raw measurements without post-processing.

Manual Remote Control: We provide a Java program to allow the user to remotely control the speed and the direction of the robot via a graphical interface on a laptop. In this interface, the arrow keys control the robot in a way similar to controlling a car in a video game.

Line Following: We provide a basic line-following function that allows the robot to autonomously track a path marked by a black line on the track. To do this, we use vision processing with the PiCamera. This code is written in Python, and uses OpenCV (the Open Source Computer Vision Library) for image processing.

Obstacle Detection: We also provide a basic obstacle-detection function. This also uses the video image, and is based on the overall area covered by the obstacle in the image. This function assumes that the track is mostly white and that obstacles result in a non-white colour with intensity above a preset threshold. As an obstacle is detected, the system slows down and eventually stops when the obstacle is "near" (visually large) enough.

3.2   Baseline Performance

We report on the performance of the baseline MicroITS functions to provide a reference point for projects and future developments of the platform. The results are from two different experiments, one relating to positioning, and the other relating to wireless communication. We see these as two fundamental issues for such a platform.

Positioning, Remote Control, and Line Following: The measurements we present here show the position of the robot on a square track marked with black lines (electric tape). In the three tests that we use, the robot logs only the position. The tests are as follows:

A. Manual Physical Displacement: The robot is taken by hand all around the track.
B. Remote Control: The robot is controlled manually using a laptop.
C. Autonomous Line Following: The robot runs the line-following function.

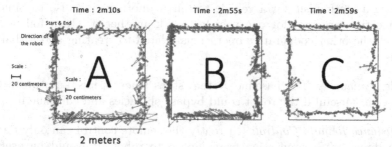

The times shown are total travel times. We interpret deviations from track as indicating primarily the noise in the position measurement, which appears in practice to be possibly as large as 20 cm rather than the nominal 10 cm. It is possible that this is due to the particular configuration used in this experiment. We assume that offsets are due to the use of the average position for centering even though the speed varies around the track. It will be interesting to explore how this can also be improved.

Signal Strength with Distance: The measurements we present here show the strength of the wireless signal (in a peer-to-peer connection) between two robots as the distance between the two robots varies. These measurements give an idea of the type of challenges that communications introduces to the design of cyber-physical systems. To collect the data we simply have one robot move closer to the other robot. We measure both signal strength and the position of the robots, and calculate an estimate of the distance between them.

The results are shown on the graph to the right. The value plotted is $-1/\sqrt{10^{\frac{s}{10}}}$ where s is the raw dBm signal from the 802.11 modem. This value should be linearly related to the distance. It is clear that even if it is linear, the variability in individual measurements is significant.

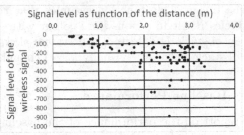

It would be very interesting in future work to select a suitable rate and variability to model this kind of behavior. An additional interesting aspect of this data is that the variability is not purely in one dimension but in two.

4 Project Concepts

We offer the following examples of projects using MicroITS:

Managing Intersections: The baseline system cannot, among other things, handle intersections. Supporting intersections both in terms of managing intersecting lines and also dealing with traffic at intersections would enhance the system.

Vehicle Following: This is the basic operation for forming a platoon. It requires developing a mechanism for a vehicle to follow another, and also to build the communication protocol for one vehicle to ask another if it can follow it, as well as all the other cooperative operations related to creating and disbanding platoons.

Obstacle Avoidance: The baseline system stops when it meets an obstacle. It would be very useful if the robot could bypass obstacles and continue its trip.

Long-Distance Remote Control: Currently the remote control can only be done through direct WiFi connection from laptop to robot. It would be useful to extend this system over the Internet. This leads to possible delays and lost connections.

Improved Positioning: The current precision for position is quite low (plus or minus 20 cm). It should be possible to improve this dramatically using a wide range of additional information available in the system.

Communication Modeling: An interesting question to investigate is the relation between signal-to-noise ratio and bit error rate (see for example [9]).

Faster Driving: For the baseline design, a modest speed was sufficient. How fast can we make the vehicle without resulting in collisions, large steering errors, or other undesirable behavior?

Power Efficiency: Power consumption is affected by many factors, including speed, path, and control algorithm. How can we improve efficiency?

5 Conclusion

In this paper we have presented MicroITS, a scaled-down platform designed to facilitate exploration and experimentation with embedded and cyber-physical systems in a context inspired by Intelligent Transportation Systems (ITS). The platform is designed to meet several goals that we believe will help make it an effective and practical platform in the educational setting. The baseline functionality provides sufficient behavior for non-trivial data collection. Some amount of programming is still needed for data logging. In the future, we hope to support simple platooning and to simplify data logging. We hope that this report will encourage the development of a community of developers of MicroITS.

Acknowledgements. The base hardware platform was developed by Tomas Lithen and Tommy Salomonsson, both of whom provided significant input during this work. We benefited greatly from discussions with Wagner Ourique de Morais, Johan Thunberg, Cheng Zhang, Yingfu Zheng, Wojciech Mostowski, Per-Olof Karlsson, and Tony Larsson during the work. This effort is funded by the KK AstaMoCA project, the ELLIOT network, an NSF CPS Project, and two ERASMUS Mundus scholarships awarded to Gal and Judicial.

References

1. Bhattarai, B.P., Lvesque, M., Maier, M., Bak-Jensen, B., Pillai, J.R.: Optimizing electric vehicle coordination over a heterogeneous mesh network in a scaled-down smart grid testbed. IEEE Trans. Smart Grid **6**(2), 784–794 (2015)
2. Engel, J., Sturm, J., Cremers, D.: Camera-based navigation of a low-cost quadrocopter. In: 2012 IEEE/RSJ International Conference on Intelligent Robots and Systems (IROS), pp. 2815–2821. IEEE (2012)
3. He, W., et al.: A scaled-down traffic system based on autonomous vehicles: a new experimental system for ITS research. In: 2012 15th International IEEE Conference on Intelligent Transportation Systems (ITSC), pp. 13–18. IEEE (2012)
4. Krajník, T., Vonásek, V., Fišer, D., Faigl, J.: AR-drone as a platform for robotic research and education. In: Obdržálek, D., Gottscheber, A. (eds.) EUROBOT 2011. CCIS, vol. 161, pp. 172–186. Springer, Heidelberg (2011). https://doi.org/10.1007/978-3-642-21975-7_16
5. Longoria, R.G., Al-Sharif, A., Patil, C.B.: Scaled vehicle system dynamics and control: a case study in anti-lock braking. Int. J. Veh. Auton. Syst. **2**(1–2), 18–39 (2004)
6. Marchand, J., Puissochet, G., Lithn, T., Taha, T.: MicroITS: a scaled-down ITS platform. Technical report (2018). http://bit.ly/MicroITS-TR
7. Ozbilgin, G., Kurt, A., Ozguner, U.: Using scaled down testing to improve full scale intelligent transportation. In: 2014 IEEE Intelligent Vehicles Symposium Proceedings, pp. 655–660. IEEE (2014)
8. Verma, R., Del Vecchio, D., Fathy, H.K.: Development of a scaled vehicle with longitudinal dynamics of an HMMWV for an ITS testbed. IEEE/ASME Trans. Mechatron. **13**(1), 46–57 (2008)
9. Zhang, J., Marsic, I.: Link quality and signal-to-noise ratio in 802.11 WLAN with fading: a time-series analysis. In: VTC Fall, pp. 1–5 (2006)

Further Experiences Teaching an FPGA-Based Embedded Systems Class

Stephen A. Edwards(✉)(iD)

Columbia University, New York City, NY, USA
sedwards@cs.columbia.edu
http://www.cs.columbia.edu/~sedwards

Abstract. I describe thirteen years of teaching an embedded systems class at Columbia University that spans three "board eras." Students now develop Linux systems with custom FPGA-based peripherals.

The soaring complexity of these systems has enabled more ambitious projects at the expense of making it impossible for students to learn "everything" about what they are developing. As such, should students be learning similar skills or specializing in hardware or software?

Keywords: Embedded systems · Undergraduate education · Graduate education · FPGAs · Linux · Device drivers · VHDL · System Verilog

1 Introduction

In 2004, I started teaching an embedded systems project course with hardware implemented on FPGAs. I reported my initial experiences at WESE in 2005 [2]; in this paper I summarize how my course has evolved since then.

The class has always centered around students implementing a self-designed project on a supplied FPGA board; as such, the choice of board has been both a key driver and limiter of the class. This paper discusses my experiences with the class chronologically, which I think of as consisting as three "eras," one for each FPGA board.

The basic outline of the class has always consisted of a sequence of canned lab assignments designed to familiarize the students with the board and its development tools followed by work in teams on the project. This division has worked well, although it means the projects themselves are often quite rushed given that the students only effectively work on them for half the semester. Given the complexity of the boards and the development tools, however, there is probably no alternative short of extending the class across two semesters.

We started with a Xilinx Spartan IIE board that quickly showed it limitations brought on by too few pins for many peripherals, switched to an Altera Cyclone II-based board that eliminated the pin limitations to expose the next

© Springer Nature Switzerland AG 2019
R. Chamberlain et al. (Eds.): CyPhy 2018/WESE 2018, LNCS 11615, pp. 222–230, 2019.
https://doi.org/10.1007/978-3-030-23703-5_14

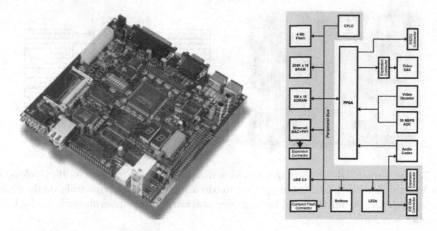

Fig. 1. The XESS XSB-300E Board and its block diagram [5]. The limited number of pins on the Spartan IIE FPGA demanded a bus-based architecture that made using multiple peripherals challenging.

problem: insufficient software support for complex peripherals, then switched to an Altera Cyclone V with on-chip ARM processors to enable the use of Linux to ameliorate the software challenges and replace them with sheer complexity. Below, I discuss details of these three eras.

2   2003–2006: The XESS XSB-300E Era

We used a Xilinx Spartan IIE (XC2S300E) board from XESS Corporation for the first four years of the class [2]. While well-equipped with peripherals, including video input and output, Ethernet, USB 2.0, a serial port, SRAM, DRAM, Flash, and an audio CODEC, these peripherals were connected to a shared bus (i.e., each peripheral's data lines were connected to the same FPGA pins; see Fig. 1), which made using multiple peripherals difficult since students would have to develop their own bus arbiter. The board designers likely did this because of the paucity of pins (only 208, including power) on the QFP package, but it constrained the designs students could implement.

During this era, students did six lab assignments, hardware-only, software-only, and hardware/software interfacing, before moving on to projects that had to incorporate both custom hardware and software. This structure has remained to this day, but I have changed the details. During this era, students built video games with custom video-generation hardware (generally without a frame-buffer, given the limited on-chip memory and difficulty of using the large off-chip SDRAM), audio projects, and networking projects.

Most project teams encountered similar challenges when designing custom hardware blocks. Limited on-chip memory forced them to either become parsimonious with their storage of data or utilize off-chip memory. Using the 512 K

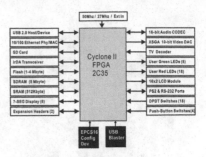

Fig. 2. The Terasic DE2 Board and its block diagram [1]. Ample pins on its Cyclone II FPGA enabled a star-based topology that made using external peripherals vastly easier than with the XSB, but the need for complex software for peripherals such as the USB controller was limiting.

of off-chip SRAM was straightforward but often still insufficient; the 16 MB of SDRAM was much larger but difficult to use because if its complex protocols, timing constraints, and refresh requirements. Moreover, using either of these memories from hardware meant either creating an OPB bus master and vying for control of the bus, or simply dominating the off-chip bus and foregoing the use of any other bussed peripherals. Most groups took the latter route.

3   2007–2013: The Terasic DE2 Era

After four years of grappling with the shared bus topology of the XSB board, in 2007 we made a big switch and adopted the DE2, an Altera Cyclone II-based development board developed by Terasic Technologies in 2005 (Fig. 2). Ample pins (672 total; 475 for I/O) allowed the DE2 designers to connect the peripherals on the DE2 in a star configuration, making it far easier to use multiple peripherals from VHDL compared to the bus-based XSB board. Moreover, the array of peripherals on the DE2 was similar to that on the XSB, so the knowledge of which projects would work transferred over easily.

The switch from Xilinx to Altera ecosystems was annoying but largely lateral: Xilinx had XST, the Microblaze processor, the OPB, and Platform Generator; Altera had Quartus, the Nios II processor, the Avalon bus, and SOPC Builder.

3.1   Lab Assignemnts

For the DE2 era, we streamlined the initial lab assignments down to three:

1. *A pure hardware problem:* an old-style computer front panel that allows the user to examine and modify the the contents of on-chip memory locations. The students found it challenging to turn the level-sensitive signals from the pushbuttons into events (i.e., single-cycle pulses).

2. *A pure software problem:* a network chat client that receives, displays, and
   sends broadcast UDP packets interpreted as text. We supplied custom hardware consisting of a Nios II processor with a VGA character display, a PS/2
   keyboard receiver, and an interface to the Ethernet controller along with
   skeletal software that exercised each of these.
3. *A mixed hardware/software problem*: a custom video hardware peripheral that
   displays a ball on the screen and moves the ball under the control of a C
   program running on a Nios II. The students could also implement a sound
   synthesizer or an image convolver, but virtually all chose the ball.

3.2 Projects

Many projects of the DE2 era featured video. The on-chip memory of the FPGA
was generally too small for a framebuffer, but some groups used the off-chip
SRAM, which allowed a byte per pixel at VGA resolutions (640 × 480).

One group did a digital picture frame that displayed JPEG files read from
an SD card with a FAT filesystem. They used the SRAM for a 15-bit-per-pixel
color framebuffer, the SDRAM as Nios II memory, and communicated with the
SD card through a "bit banged" SPI interface.

Another group did a Pac-man clone with custom video hardware for tile
backgrounds, sprite foregrounds and interfaced classical NES controllers to the
FPGA. At the last minute, they switched the sprites to a "Pac-Edwards" theme.

Another group's project read AES encrypted (uncompressed) monochrome
video from a raw-formatted SD card for display. Their resolution and frame rate
were modest, but they implemented the AES decoding algorithm in hardware.

A real-time hardware ray tracer was one of the few projects that actually
consumed most of programmable logic of the DE2's Cyclone II (others routinely
exhausted on-chip memory). They had to restrict their rendered models to just
six rectangles to achieve the performance they wanted, but were able to achieve
color and reflections at 60 frames per second by running 20 ray units in parallel.

3.3 Challenges

The use of communication peripherals was the big challenge with the DE2. While
the students could develop code to send UDP packets through the Davicom
DM9000A Ethernet controller, it was not realistic for them to code a TCP/IP
stack. The Philips ISP1362 USB controller was even worse. Furthermore, networking or USB controller software is not something that is easily coded as a C
library; most implementations rely on the facilities of a multitasking operating
system. So the use of an existing library was not an option.

Running Linux on the DE2 was theoretically possible, but very difficult.
Linux normally relies on hardware virtual memory support to deliver multitasking with memory protection, but the μClinux project has developed kernels
designed to run on processors without MMUs. David Lariviere and I experimented with the use of μClinux on the DE2 in 2008 [3], but we were never able
to get this working well enough for students to use it routinely. The option of

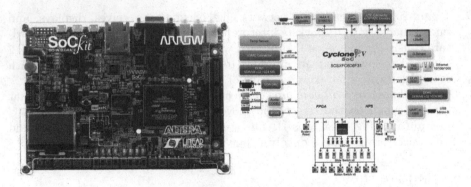

Fig. 3. The Terasic SoCKit Board [4] brought dual hard ARM9 cores via a Cyclone V FPGA, enabling the use of Linux software and its device drivers. The main failing of these boards has been the fragile micro-USB connectors

an MMU was later added to Altera's Nios II processor, making a full Linux port possible, but we never experimented with getting this to work.

The DE2 board ultimately grew obsolete. In 2012, we managed to order additional DE2s to accommodate our growing enrollments and replace broken boards, but this was the last gasp for them. Operating a lab with multiple, incompatible boards was not realistic for the students, so it was time to move on. Terasic and Altera had started moving on long before: Terasic released the similar, but slightly incompatible DE2-70 board (with a 2C70 Cyclone II FPGA) in 2009, and in 2012, the much more incompatible DE2-115 (with a Cyclone IV EP4CE115 FPGA). Altera discontinued software support for the Cyclone II family of chips after Quartus 13.0sp1 (June 2013).

4   2014–2016: The Terasic SoCKit Era

In 2014, we switched to Terasic's SoCKit board, one of the first to incorporate Altera's System-on-chip Cyclone V FPGA (a 5CSXFC6D6F31), which integrated dual ARM9 Cortex cores with standard peripherals (collectively, the "HPS" or Hard Processor System) with a traditional programmable FPGA fabric (Fig. 3). The HPS portion of the chip was capable of directly running a stock Linux distribution (i.e., without any custom FPGA hardware) and exposed an Avalon bus to the FPGA fabric that could be used to build peripherals.

While not flawless, the Linux distribution for the SoCKit board was a breath of fresh air compared to software that could run on the DE2. Networking, USB, and the package manager just worked, enabling students to easily make use of USB peripherals, modern network services, and the like. It was no longer necessary for students to pour over the hundreds of registers in the Ethernet chip to write software to received a single packet.

We switched to the System Verilog hardware description language. We had chosen VHDL in 2003 because another instructor was using it, but by 2014 that class was gone and had been replaced with other classes that were using System Verilog. The synthesizable subset of System Verilog is more succinct and less error-prone than the equivalent VHDL, so we are happy with the switch.

4.1 Device Drivers

The move to the SoCKit board with Linux made it harder to access custom peripherals from software. We had been running "bare metal" C code on the DE2, allowing custom hardware peripherals to be accessed directly, e.g., by casting integer literals to `volatile` pointers. While this can be done in the Linux world (e.g., by running programs as root and using `mmap()` to map the peripheral memory into userspace), device drivers are the preferred mechanism.

I now spend a lecture on Linux device drivers. I begin with the structure of modern operating systems (userspace processes are isolated from hardware by the kernel and device drivers), then move on to the Unix device driver model (everything is a file; devices have major and minor numbers; the distinction between block and character devices), the Linux kernel module system, the catch-all `ioctl()` function, the device tree system (.*dtb* files and the in-memory database of peripheral memory layout), and all the various functions for managing resources. Most of the code in students' device drivers is a mix of boilerplate (e.g., modules must have both *init()* and *exit()* functions that are called when the module is loaded and unloaded) and error-handling (when a request for a resource fails, release all the resources that were acquired earlier and terminate).

4.2 Booting Linux

The SoCKit has a dizzying array of options (selected by a difficult-to-explain mix of jumpers and absurdly tiny DIP switches) for booting Linux and configuring its FPGA. One easy way is to boot from an SD card that carries a bootloader (uboot), a Linux kernel image, a bitstream file for the FPGA, and the Linux root filesystem. We considered this for the lab, but because we do not have the room or budget to assign each team its own board and workstation, teams have to share workstations and boards, meaning they would have to manage one SD card per team, which seemed problematic (e.g., "I thought you had the card," or "Fred has the card but couldn't make it to lab this time so we can't work").

Instead, we configured our boards to be "diskless workstations" that booted and ran off a fileserver. Each board was configured to boot from a small onboard flash chip containing a modified uboot image that would use DHCP to configure its network interface, then use PXE to download both a Linux kernel image and an FPGA bitstream. The Linux kernel would then boot and mount its root filesystem via NFS from the same server. The result was that each team could have one or more board configurations (kernel, root filesystem, and FPGA bitstream) and access them from any board. When first booted, the bootloader would download a list of available PXE images, display them on the serial console, and then allow the user to select one (i.e., the team's image) to boot.

This "diskless" configuration ultimately worked, but was challenging to set up. DHCP, PXE, and NFS servers all had to be configured to work in concert; the uboot source and boot script had to be modified because the existing PXE mechanism did not know about FPGA bitstreams; a custom bootloader had to be flashed to each board by booting yet another version of uboot and running the appropriate flashing commands; NFS had to be set up not only to serve the root filesystems to the boards but the root filesystems, kernel images, and FPGA bitstream files to the workstations so students could modify them as needed. Security was incomplete. While the fileserver and network for the boards were local to our lab and fairly well-protected from the public Internet (the fileserver functioned as a firewall between the boards and our campus network), there is little to stop one team of students from seeing or corrupting another team's files.

4.3 Lab Assignments

For the SoCKit era, we continued to start the class with three lab assignments adapted from the DE2 era. We supplied a starting point for each lab: a code skeleton that implemented a rudimentary version of the lab for students to modify.

1. *Hardware: An old-style computer front panel.* Unlike the DE2, the SoCKit has no seven-segment LEDs, so I provided a VGA LED emulator that displayed eight seven-segment digits on a VGA monitor. This component exposed a signal for each segment of each digit, making it easy to use.
2. *Software: A text chat client.* I supplied the students with a VGA framebuffer that they accessed after calling mmap(). We switched to USB keyboards accessed through *libusb* because the SoCKit did not have the DE2's PS/2 port. The students used the standard socket API to connect to a simple chat server I implemented in Python. They used pthreads to listen to the keyboard in one thread and handle incoming network communication on another.
3. A *mixed hardware/software system: The bouncing ball.* Students had to write System Verilog for a VGA peripheral that would display a raster with a ball whose position was controlled by registers written from an ARM processor through an Avalon bus. They also had to write a device driver that would ferry coordinates from userspace to those registers, update the .dtb (Device Tree Blob) file that characterized the memory map visible to the processors to include the VGA peripheral, and finally write a C program that bounced the ball around.

4.4 Projects

In the SoCKit era, projects grew more elaborate and utilized fancier peripherals.
Accelerators grew more common in this era. One group implemented an accelerator that could compute "inverse kinematics," i.e., angles for robot arm joints to reach a desired position in space for the end effector. Another group implemented a cryptographic accelerator for RSA able to perform modular multiplication and exponentiation.

One team implement a 3D pottery game in which a player manipulated a virtual pot on a turntable. The novelty here was a custom graphics controller that would display a whole pot as a series of overlapping ellipses.

The SoCKit's standard hardware and software made it possible to integrate fancier peripherals. One group used a Leap Motion controller that, like Microsoft's Kinect, uses multiple cameras to capture a 3D model of object in space, such as your hands. They used the output of this controller to simulate the operation of a digital piano, displaying the image of a piano and your fingers on the screen and synthesizing sound through the audio CODEC on the SoCKit.

Another group used the SoCKit as a controller for an autonomous vehicle built from a LEGO kit. They interfaced the SoCKit to the various LEGO motors and sensors, ultimately enabling it to park itself in a space while avoiding the curb and nearby vehicles. While this group ultimately succeeded, they managed to destroy a SoCKit board by connecting the 3.3 V I/O of the SoCKit to 5 V devices.

4.5 Challenges

Complexity has been the challenge of the SoCKit era. In addition to digital hardware design an low-level C programming, students now need to understand Linux, the boot process, device drivers, and a variety of high-level APIs (sockets, libusb, etc.). While the projects have become more modern, the amount of knowledge needed to implement a project has also grown substantially.

The fragile micro USB connectors on the SoCKit boards break easily in a public student lab. Despite adding a Terasic-supplied metal bracket and securing the USB cables to the board with nylon twist-ties, students still found a way to routinely break off these connectors, rendering the US$250 boards irreparable.

5   Conclusions and Next Steps

After 2016, I took a two-year hiatus from teaching Embedded Systems because the department needed me to teach another course, but I will resume it again in the spring of 2019. I plan to switch to another SoCKit-like board, likely Terasic's DE10-Standard or DE1-SoC, but I have not made a final decision as I write this. These boards have addressed the physical failings of the SoCKit board while providing an almost identical development platform.

I am constantly faced with wondering how much to provide to the students versus how much to ask them to develop themselves. The trend is to supply more, isolating the students from implementation details to allow them to assemble more complex projects. But at what point does this stop being embedded systems with its emphasis on domain-specific peripherals and real-world data and simply turns into another class on software development for desktop machines?

Another big question is the extent to which students should be allowed to specialize in what they work on and thus learn about in the class. Practically, students typically split their teams into software and hardware portions and only learn more about what they already prefer. This is somehow realistic from a professional standpoint, but is it good pedagogy?

References

1. Altera, San Jose, California: DE2 Development and Education Board User Manual, version 1.4 (2006)
2. Edwards, S.A.: Experiences teaching an FPGA-based embedded systems class. In: Proceedings of the Workshop on Embedded Systems Education (WESE), Jersey City, NJ, pp. 52–58, September 2005
3. Lariviere, D., Edwards, S.A.: uClinux on the Altera DE2. Technical report CUCS-055-08, Columbia University, Department of Computer Science, New York, NY, USA, December 2008
4. Terasic Technologies, Hsinchu City, Taiwan: SoCKit User Manual (2013)
5. XESS Corporation, Franklinton, North Carolina: XSB Board V1.0 Manual, August 2003

Author Index

Andalam, Sidharta 28
Antoni, Sven-Thomas 170

Bujorianu, Manuela L. 134

Chamberlain, Roger D. 197
Cytron, Ron K. 197

Denil, Joachim 71
Dustdar, Schahram 206

Easwaran, Arvind 28
Edwards, Stephen A. 222

Fribourg, Laurent 154

Ghassemi, Fatemeh 3
Grosu, Radu 206

Hirsch, Christian 206

Isakovic, Haris 206

Jahandideh, Iman 3

Kappel, Gerti 206
Krenn, Willibald 206

Larsen, Kim Guldstrand 113
Le Coënt, Adrien 113, 154
Lehmann, Sascha 170
Lithén, Thomas 214

Marchand, Judicaël 214
Mikučionis, Marius 113
Mitsch, Stefan 91
Moradi, Mehrdad 71
Müller, Andreas 91

Naderlinger, Andreas 51
Nelke, Sofia Amador 193
Nickovic, Dejan 206

Park, Heejong 28
Platzer, André 91
Platzer, Michael 206
Puissochet, Gaël 214

Ratasich, Denise 206
Rausch, Thomas 206

Schlaefer, Alexander 170
Schupp, Sibylle 170
Schwinger, Wieland 91
Shook, Doug 197
Siever, Bill 197
Sirjani, Marjan 3

Taankvist, Jakob Haahr 113
Taha, Walid 214

Van Acker, Bert 71
Vanherpen, Ken 71

Wally, Bernhard 206
Winokur, Michael 193

Printed in the United States
By Bookmasters

Printed in the United States
By Bookmasters